Discrimination Law

Edited by Malcolm Sargeant

PEARSON
Longman

Harlow, England • London • New York • Boston • San Francisco • Toronto
Sydney • Tokyo • Singapore • Hong Kong • Seoul • Taipei • New Delhi
Cape Town • Madrid • Mexico City • Amsterdam • Munich • Paris • Milan

Pearson Education Limited
Edinburgh Gate
Harlow
Essex CM20 2JE
England

and Associated Companies throughout the world

Visit us on the World Wide Web at:
www.pearsoned.co.uk

First published 2004

ISBN 0 5828 2289 0

British Library Cataloguing-in-Publication Data
A catalogue record for this book is available from the British Library

10 9 8 7 6 5 4 3 2 1
08 07 06 05 04

Typeset in 10/12pt New Baskerville by 35
Printed in Great Britain by Henry Ling Ltd.,
at the Dorset Press, Dorchester, Dorset.

The publisher's policy is to use paper manufactured from sustainable forests.

Contents

26.99

Discrimination Law

We work with leading authors to develop the
strongest educational materials in law, bringing cutting-edge
thinking and best learning practice to a global market.

Under a range of well-known imprints, including
Longman, we craft high quality print and
electronic publications which help readers to understand
and apply their content, whether studying or at work.

To find out more about the complete range of our
publishing, please visit us on the World Wide Web at:
www.pearsoned.co.uk

Preface

This book is intended for students and for those who are coming to the serious study of discrimination law for the first time. It is considered to be a much needed book because it covers all aspects of discrimination, including those most recently legislated upon, such as sexual orientation, religion or belief, and age. Each chapter attempts to explain the law relating to a particular area of discrimination and raises issues for further thought and study.

The contributing authors are all either law academics or legal practitioners and, if the book is read from cover to cover, it will be seen that the authors' individual styles shine through. One of the strengths of a book such as this is its ability to draw upon the expertise of a large number of contributors, each having an individual approach to explaining and discussing the issues.

There is a large amount of information to be found elsewhere, especially on relevant websites such as those of the Disability Rights Commission (*www.drc-gb.org.uk*), the Equal Opportunities Commission (*www.eoc.org.uk*) and the Commission for Racial Equality (*www.cre.gov.uk*), as well as the UK Government (*www.dti.gov.uk*). Some further reading is suggested in the various chapters.

Malcolm Sargeant

The Contributors

The Editor

Malcolm Sargeant BA PhD is a Reader in Employment Law at Middlesex University Business School, where he is also a member of the Centre for Legal Research. He is the author of *Employment Law* (Longman), co-author of *Essentials of Employment Law* (CIPD) and editor of *The Law at Work* (Spiro Press) and *Employment Law Statutes* (Sweet & Maxwell).

The Authors

Richard Benny BA, LLB MA, LLM is a Senior Lecturer in Law at the University of Surrey. He teaches employment law and the law of tort on the undergraduate LLB programmes and medical law & ethics on a postgraduate degree programme. He has written in the areas of employment law and discrimination law. He is also in part-time practice as a solicitor.

Jeremy Cooper is Professor of Law at Middlesex University where he heads the Disability Law and Policy Research Unit. He is also a part-time Mental Health Review Tribunal President. He has written and taught widely in the field of social services, mental health, and disability law. In 2000 he was appointed the UK member of the European Commission Network of National Experts on Combating Discrimination on Grounds of Disability.

Penny English PhD is Senior Lecturer in Law at Middlesex University where she teaches EU law as well as public international law and land law. Her research interests focus on the legal regulation of the cultural heritage, particularly the issues of ownership of archaeological sites and material and access to ancient monuments.

David Lewis LLB MA (Industrial Relations), MCIPD is Professor of Employment Law and Programme Leader for the LLM in Employment Law at Middlesex University. He is the editor of and main contributor to *Whistleblowing at Work* (Athlone Press) and is joint author of *Essentials of Employment Law* (CIPD). He is also an ACAS arbitrator.

Susan Mayne is a senior employment lawyer at CMS Cameron McKenna. She is co-editor of *Employment Law in Europe* (Butterworths) and has contributed chapters on redundancy, family-friendly rights and employment tribunals to *Tolleys Employment Law* and *Tolleys Policies and Procedures* looseleaf. Susan deals with all aspects of employment law, both contentious and non-contentious.

Sam Middlemiss is a senior lecturer in law at the Robert Gordon University. He teaches and provides consultancy and training in employment law and has had numerous articles published in UK and international journals (primarily on employment law, but also on criminal law and the law of delict). He is also an ACAS arbitrator.

Erica Neustadt LLM qualified as a solicitor in 1990. She has worked both as a litigator and an employment lawyer, currently as a professional support lawyer for Field Fisher Waterhouse. She has lectured for some years at the College of Law and has written on the subject of maternity and parental rights.

John Spencer MA (Oxon) BSc LLM, Barrister is Chief Reporter at the Incorporated Council of Law Reporting. He is Honorary Visiting Lecturer at Middlesex University and has published in the areas of human rights, public law and employment law.

Maureen Spencer MA (Oxon) LLM, PhD, is Principal Lecturer in Law at Middlesex University Business School where she teaches public law, human rights law and evidence. She researches and publishes in the fields of human rights, evidence and legal history.

Abbreviations

AML	Additional Maternity Leave
AMRA 1988	Access to Medical Reports Act 1988
CA	Court of Appeal
CEDAW	Convention on the Elimination of All Forms of Discrimination against Women
CERD	Committee on the Elimination of All Forms of Racial Discrimination
CHR	Committee on Human Rights
CML	Compulsory Maternity Leave
CRE	Commission for Racial Equality
CSW	Commission on the Status of Women
Ct Sess	Court of Session
DDA 1995	Disability Discrimination Act 1995
DRC	Disability Rights Commission
DTI	Department of Trade and Industry
DWP	Department for Work and Pensions
EAT	Employment Appeal Tribunal
EC	European Community
ECHR	European Court of Human Rights
ECJ	European Court of Justice
ECOSOC	Economic and Social Council of United Nations
EERB	Employment Equality (Religion or Belief) Regulations 2003
EOC	Equal Opportunities Commission
EPA 1970	Equal Pay Act 1970
ERA 1996	Employment Rights Act 1996
ESC	European Social Charter
ET	Employment Tribunal
ETA 1996	Employment Tribunals Act 1996
EU	European Union

FETO 1998	Fair Employment and Treatment (Northern Ireland) Order 1998
F/HEI	Further/Higher Education Institutions
GMF	Genuine material factor
GOQ	Genuine Occupational Qualification
HRA 1998	Human Rights Act 1998
HRC	Human Rights Committee (of United Nations)
ICCPR	International Covenant on Civil and Political Rights
ICESCR	International Convention on Economic, Social and Cultural Rights
ICMA	Institute of Certified Management Accountants
ICR	Industrial Cases Reports
ILO	International Labour Organisation
IRLR	Industrial Relations Law Reports
JES	Job Evaluation Study
LEA	Local Education Authorities
MPLR 1999	Maternity and Parental Leave etc Regulations 1999
NIA 1998	Northern Ireland Act 1998
OML	Ordinary Maternity Leave
QB	Queen's Bench Division
RNID	Royal National Institute for the Deaf
RRA 1976	Race Relations Act 1976
SDA 1975	Sex Discrimination Act 1975
SENDA 2001	Special Educational Needs and Disability Act 2001
SMP	Statutory Maternity Pay
TUC	Trades Union Congress
TULRCA 1992	Trade Union and Labour Relations (Consolidation) Act 1992

Table of Cases

United Kingdom

Court of Justice of The European Communities

Chronological List of Cases

Alphabetical list of all European and other Cases

Table of Statutes

Table of Statutory Instruments

Table of Treaties and Conventions

List of International Treaties and Conventions

List of European Union Material Treaties

Regulations

Directives

Other

Chapter 1

The context

Malcolm Sargeant

Introduction

The 2001 census calculated that the population of the United Kingdom was 58.8 million people. This was an increase of 17% or 8.6 million people when compared to 1951. The causes of this growth are really interesting for students of discrimination law. The majority of the increase has been due to the number of births exceeding the number of deaths, especially during the 1950s and the 1960s when the population increased by 5.6 million. After this period, birth rates declined and the population remained static, although it began to grow again during the 1980s and 1990s, growing by another 2.4 million. In this period the natural cause of births exceeding deaths was the main factor, but since the late 1990s migration has been the main cause of growth.

There have also been important changes in the make up of family households: the proportion of households containing a married couple has dropped to 45%, compared to some 64% only 20 years earlier (in 1981). In contrast, single person households have increased to 30.3% (almost 7.4 million) of the total and almost one in ten households are single parent.

The result of these changes has been an ageing population together with an increasingly diverse family and ethnic make up. The areas of discrimination related to this diverse population which are considered in this book include discrimination on the grounds of gender, race, disability, religion or belief, and age (as well as discrimination in related fields which the State has considered important enough to legislate on).

The purpose of this chapter is to put the work of the subsequent chapters into a contextual perspective, in relation to the population of the United Kingdom.

Sex discrimination

Of the population of 58.8 million, 30.2 million are female. Despite the long existence of the Equal Pay Act 1970 and the Sex Discrimination Act 1975, women still suffer from discrimination on the basis of their gender. In the year 2001/02, for example, there were 10,092 sex discrimination claims presented to employment tribunals (i.e. just under 9% of all claims made to employment tribunals in that year).

A leading case illustrating issues related to sex discrimination is *James v Eastleigh Borough Council*:[1] Mr and Mrs Jones were both aged 61 years. The local authority had decided that residents of pensionable age should be allowed free access to the municipal swimming pool. At the time, the pensionable age for men was 65 years and for women it was 60 years. As a result Mrs Jones was allowed free entry, but Mr Jones had to pay the full price. He obviously took exception to this and challenged the council's policy by proposing that it amounted to sex discrimination. Clearly, the council had not intended to discriminate on the grounds of sex but was simply following a policy of giving extra help to those of pensionable age and beyond.

Intention and motivation were, however, irrelevant. The less favourable treatment would not have occurred but for Mr Jones' sex, and the use of a criterion such as retirement age was in itself discriminatory on the grounds of sex. As a result, the council was found liable for direct discrimination.

Women are more likely to be working part time, especially those with dependent children. Some 43% of all women workers are part time, compared to only 9% of male workers who work on a part-time basis. The overwhelming reason for women working part time is the need to look after families (see Table 1.1).

Women's employment is likely to be concentrated in certain occupations: e.g. some 90% of nurses are female; around 64% of teaching professionals are female (ranging from 38% in universities to 86% in primary and nursery schools), as are about 79% of personnel and industrial relations officers. In contrast, only 6% of engineers and technologists, 21% of computer analysts and programmers and 13% of architects and town planners are female.[2]

There are attempts to concentrate on getting the work–family life balance right, with measures designed to protect female employees and to give them further rights, such as regulations protecting part-time workers from discrimination and regulations giving the parent of a child under the age of six years the right to ask for more flexible hours (see Chapter 7).

[1] [1990] IRLR 288.
[2] Information from Equal Opportunities Commission website, reporting a survey on pay disparities in the professions.

Table 1.1 Part-time employees: by reason for working part-time
(Spring 2002)[3]

Reason for working part-time	Women (000s)	Percentage of all female employees	Men (000s)	Percentage of all male employees	Women as percentage of women + men
Student or at school	602	12	499	44	55
Ill or disabled	67	1	44	4	60
Could not find FT job	319	6	189	17	63
Did not want FT job, because:					
– no need to work FT	536	11	158	14	77
– family or domestic reasons	2 679	54	55	5	98
– other reasons	802	16	181	16	82
All part-time	5 005	100	1 125	100	82

In general, women are paid less than men. Women working full-time in Great Britain earned 81% of the average full-time earnings of men in 2002, resulting in a pay differential of some 19%. Women who worked part-time earned only 59% of the average hourly earnings of men who worked full-time, giving a pay differential of 41%. This latter gap has changed little since 1975. There is a large pay gap between married women and married men, with a pay differential of 27.3%; and a much smaller gap between full-time single women and full-time single men. This rather suggests that there is greater discrimination against married women (see Table 1.2).[4]

Table 1.2 Average hourly earnings of employees: by marital status (GB, 2002)

Marital status	Women		Men		Pay gap (%)	
	FT	All	FT	All	FT	All
Married/cohabiting	9.45	8.45	11.74	11.62	19.50	27.30
Single	8.44	7.36	8.78	8.15	–	9.70
Separated/divorced/ widowed	9.28	8.24	10.83	10.60	14.30	22.30

[3] Information from Equal Opportunities Commission website using findings from the Labour Force Survey.
[4] Information from Equal Opportunities Commission 'Women and Men in Great Britain: Pay and Income'; using information from the Labour Force Survey, Spring 2002.

Sex discrimination is not just about discrimination against women in comparison to men. Other issues relate to discrimination against men in comparison to women and also the protection of transsexuals. Discrimination on the basis of a person's sexual orientation is also included (see Chapter 4).

Race discrimination

The ethnic diversity of the British population is shown in the 2001 census. If one looks first at the place of birth of the population, the census reveals the following:

Table 1.3 Place of birth of the United Kingdom population

Born in the United Kingdom	–	53 883 986
Born elsewhere in the EU	–	1 306 731
Born outside the EU	–	3 598 477

Some 87.4% of people living in England gave their place of birth as England, although the proportion varied enormously in different parts of the country. In London, for example, 72.9% were born in the United Kingdom. In contrast, the North East of England had 97.1% born in the United Kingdom. This was a drop overall as compared to 1991, when 89% of those living in England were English born, and, perhaps, represents the increase in migration in the 1990s.

When one looks at ethnic origins, some 87% of the population of England and some 96% of the population of the United Kingdom gave their ethnic origin as white British. Again there is enormous diversity between different areas. People who were of white Irish origin make up 1.2% of the population of England and Wales, but in the London Borough of Brent they make up 6.9% of the population. Some 2% of the English and Welsh population were of Indian origin, but in Leicester it was 25.7%. Finally, in England and Wales, some 1.1% described themselves as Black Caribbean, 0.9% as Black African and a further 0.2% from other Black groups. In some London Boroughs, such as Lewisham and Lambeth, Black Caribbean form more than 10% of the population, as do Black Africans in Boroughs such as Southwark and Hackney.

The Race Relations Act 1976 made discrimination on racial grounds unlawful. Discrimination on racial grounds means discrimination on the grounds of colour, race, nationality, or ethnic or national origins (Race Relations Act 1976, s 3(1) – see Chapter 4). However, discrimination on racial grounds continues. The employment rate for the ethnic minority population, for example, is much less than that for the white population (Table 1.4).

Table 1.4 Economic activity and employment rate by ethnic group
(Spring 2002)[5]

Ethnic group	All aged 16+ (000s)	Economic activity rate (%)	Employment rate (%)	Unemployment rate (%)
White	44 184	80	76	5
All ethnic Minorities	3 148	65	58	11
Mixed	220	72	61	15
Asian or Asian British	1 605	63	57	9
Black or Black British	859	70	61	11
Chinese	154	62	60	*
Other ethnic groups	309	61	53	12

* No meaningful figures are available.

Within these figures, there are further differences between ethnic groups. The economic activity rate for those of Indian ethnic origin was 71%, but for those of Pakistani origin it was 54%, and, for those of Bangladeshi origin, only 47%. Similarly, the unemployment rate was 6% for Indians, 12% for Pakistanis and 24% for Bangladeshis.

The difficulty of defining what is meant by discrimination on racial grounds was shown in the case of *Mandla v Dowell Lee*.[6] This concerned a father and son who were Sikhs. The father took his son to an interview for a place at an independent school in Birmingham. At the interview the father explained that he wished to bring up his son as an orthodox Sikh, which included the wearing of a turban. The headmaster told them that the wearing of turbans could not be allowed because it would be against the school rule about the wearing of the approved school uniform. The Commission for Racial Equality took up the case and complained that the school had discriminated against the boy on racial grounds. Much of the case in the House of Lords concerned consideration of what constituted an ethnic group. The Court put forward a number of characteristics which have been followed in many cases since: the group should have a long shared history, a cultural tradition of its own, either a common geographical origin or descent from a small number of common ancestors, a common language, a common literature, a common religion, and be a minority or an oppressed or dominant group within a larger community. The Court accepted that Sikhs did have these characteristics and therefore there had been discrimination on racial grounds against the boy.

[5] Information from the Labour Force Survey; see (2002) 112 *Equal Opportunities Review* 23.
[6] [1983] IRLR 209.

Discrimination on grounds of religion or belief

Religious discrimination can be closely linked to racial discrimination, but was not expressly made unlawful until 2003. A good example was the case of *Ahmad v ILEA*,[7] which concerned a Muslim school teacher who required a short time off on Friday afternoons to attend prayers at a nearby Mosque. He resigned and claimed unfair dismissal when his employers refused him paid time off. They had offered him a part-time position working 4.5 days per week. The United Kingdom had not at the time incorporated the European Convention on Human Rights into national law, but, as Lord Denning stated in this case, 'we will do our best to see that our decisions are in conformity with it'. In this case it still meant rejecting the claim as its acceptance would give the Muslim community 'preferential treatment'. The court held that Article 9(2) of the Convention did not give an employee the right to absent him- or herself from work in breach of the contract of employment. Lord Scarman dissented, stating that the issue began, but did not end, with the law of contract. The judgment would mean that any Muslim, who took their religious duties seriously, could never be employed on a full-time contract as a teacher. This is an old case and one must doubt whether the same decision would be reached today, even without the new Regulations (see Chapter 8). It does, however, illustrate how it is possible to penalise someone for carrying out the activities and ritual connected to their religious beliefs.

The 2001 census did ask a question about religion. It was a voluntary question and over 4 million people did not answer it. Of those that did, their professed religious loyalty was as shown in Table 1.5.

Table 1.5 Religious affiliations (2001 census)

Christian	42 079 417
Muslim	1 591 126
Hindu	558 810
Sikh	336 149
Jewish	266 740
Buddhist	151 816
Other	178 837
No religion/religion not stated	13 626 299

Again there are wide geographical differences. The highest proportion of Christians in England was in the North-East with 80.1%; in London this figure fell to 58%. In the Borough of Tower Hamlets, 36% gave their religion as Muslim, as well as 24% of the population of the London Borough of Newham. The London Borough of Harrow had 19.6% who

[7] [1977] ICR 490.

stated that they were Hindu; and in Barnet the figure for the Jewish population was 14.8%.

On a lighter note, at the time of the census there was a campaign to persuade people to answer the religious question with 'Jedi Knight'. As a result some 370,000 people (0.7% of the population) declared their religion as Jedi Knight![8]

Disability discrimination

Some 19% of people of working age in the United Kingdom have a long-term disability: there are approximately 6.8 million disabled people, 3.6 million of whom are men and 3.2 million women. In a Labour Force Survey,[9] the most common problems amongst those surveyed were as follows:

- musculo/skeletal problems relating to arms, legs, neck, back, hands and feet: 36%
- chest or breathing problems: 13%
- heart, blood pressure and circulatory: 11%
- mental illness: 8%.

The 2001 census revealed that 10,855,835 people had a limiting long-term illness and some 5,490,865 stated that their general health was 'not good'. It also revealed that there were 2,464,717 people who were permanently sick or disabled thus making them 'economically inactive' in terms of the general workforce.

People with disabilities face barriers in many aspects of their life (see Chapter 6), including the employment field. In a study by the Department for Work and Pensions (DWP) of attitudes towards, and experiences of, disabled people[10] the disparities in employment status amongst those of working age is shown (see Table 1.6). A broad definition of disability was used in line with the Disability Discrimination Act 1995 (DDA 1995).

The Disability Rights Commission Helpline took more than 5,000 calls in 2001–02 from disabled people about employment; these led to hundreds of cases where disabled people were helped to secure their rights. The DWP study asked disabled people about the discrimination they had faced (see Table 1.7).

---

[8] This will only mean something to those who have watched the *Star Wars* movies.
[9] This is a reflection of the Labour Force Survey, Summer 2000. See (2001) 98 *Equal Opportunities Review* 28: a broad definition of disability in line with the Disability Discrimination Act 1995 is used.
[10] *Disabled for life? Attitudes towards, and experiences of, disability in Britain*; see (2002) 110 *Equal Opportunities Review* 19.

Table 1.6   Employment status (extracts from DWP study)

Status	DDA disabled (%)	Non-disabled (%)
Working in a job as paid employee	33	66
Working in a paid job as self-employed	6	10
Unemployed and actively seeking work	3	2
Full-time student or pupil	3	8
Not working because long-term sick or disabled	32	1

Table 1.7   Discrimination suffered by disabled people in the labour market

Form of discrimination	All (%)
When applying for a job, it was assumed I would not be able to do the job as well as a person with no disability	25
Some other form of discrimination	21
Treated differently by colleagues because of disability	16
Dismissed because of health problems/disability	16
Not allowed reasonable time off for treatment/medical conditions	15
Job interview focused on health problem	14
Employer would not/did not take steps to provide equipment/support for needs resulting from disability	13
Denied opportunities for promotion because of disability	13
Demoted/given less of a challenging role because of disability	12
Not allowed to work flexible hours to cope with disability	12
Not allowed to take sick leave disability required	11

An example of how discriminatory practices can affect people with disabilities was shown in *British Sugar plc v Kirker*.[11] An individual selected for redundancy claimed that he had been discriminated against because of a visual impairment, suffered since birth. The employers had carried out an assessment exercise in order to select those to be dismissed; this had consisted of marking employees against a set of factors. The complainant claimed that the marks attributed to him were the result of a subjective view arising out of the disability. The employee had scored 0 for promotion potential and 0 out of 10 for performance and competence. The Employment Appeal Tribunal observed that such marks would indicate that the employee did not always achieve the required standard of performance and required close supervision. Yet the employee had never been criticised for poor performance and did not have any supervision. There was no need to consider the scores of other employees as the DDA

---

[11] [1998] IRLR 624.

1995 did not require comparisons. It was clear that this individual had been under-marked by reason of his disability.

Age discrimination

The population of the United Kingdom is growing and ageing. The 2001 census revealed the age breakdown shown in Table 1.8.

Table 1.8 Population of the United Kingdom by age

All ages	58.8 million
Under 16	11.9 million
Men 16–64, women 16–59	36.1 million
Men 65+, women 60+	10.8 million

For the first time there are now more people over the age of 60 years than there are children under 16 years. The change in the age population is noticeable when compared to the 1951 census. During this 50-year period the proportion of the population aged under 16 years has fallen from 24% to 20%. At the same time, the proportion aged 60 years and over has increased from 16% to 21%.[12]

The average age of the population in the United Kingdom as a whole is increasing, as is the average age of the economically active population. Over the 25-year period between 1996 and 2021 the proportion of people over the age of 44 years will increase from 38% to 46%; the 45 to 59 age group will increase by almost one-quarter; the 60 to 74 age group will increase by over one-third; and the 75 years and over group will increase by 28%. In contrast, the 16 to 29 years age group will fall by 5.7%.[13] This process is a Europe-wide one, although the speed of the process is variable.[14] The number of people in the European Union aged between 50 and 64 years is projected to increase by 6.5 million during the next ten years.[15]

Discrimination on the grounds of age is not unlawful in the United Kingdom, provided that it does not amount to discrimination on other grounds such as sex. In *Secretary of State v Rutherford (No 2)*,[16] for example, a man aged 67 years was told that he was to be dismissed on the grounds

[12] These statistics come from the 2001 census and are to be found, like the comparisons used here, on the Office for National Statistics website at www.statistics.gov.uk.
[13] The immediate source was 'Tackling age bias: code or law?' (1998) 80 *Equal Opportunities Review* 32, although the ultimate source was ONS Monitor 10.3.98.
[14] See *Ageing and the Labour Market: Policies and initiatives within the European Union.* Report of a European conference at the University of Twente, Netherlands (Eurolink Age, 1998).
[15] These and other statistics are available from European Commission Office for Official Publications, Demographic Report (Luxembourg, 1997).
[16] [2003] IRLR 858.

Table 1.9 Age at which someone was too old to employ

Age	Percentage of respondents
40 years	12
50 years	25
55 years	43
60 years	60

of redundancy. Sections 109 and 156 of the Employment Rights Act 1996 provided that any person over the age of 65 years was not entitled to make a claim for unfair dismissal and was not entitled to any redundancy payments. As a higher proportion of males worked beyond retirement age than women, the legislation, according to the employment tribunal, was indirectly discriminatory against men. The EAT reversed this judgment, but it illustrates the relationship between age and sex discrimination.

The age at which someone is too young or too old to employ is something that is likely to be the result of a subjective judgment by an employer. In one survey of 500 companies employing more than 500 employees, the employers were asked to consider their most common job and estimate at what age, on average, they would consider someone as being 'too old' to employ.[17] The result is in Table 1.9.

Discrimination on the grounds of age takes place against younger people as well as older ones (see Chapter 9). The Age Discrimination in Employment regulations taking effect in October 2006 will make discrimination on the grounds of age in employment unlawful. There are also many other areas where older people are liable to be discriminated against – for example, in the provision of health care.

Stereotyping

It is suggested that the word 'stereotype' was first used in the eighteenth century to describe a printing process whose purpose was to duplicate pages of type.[18] The usage of the word later developed from the idea of producing further images from a stereotype into reproducing 'a standardised image or conception of a type of person'.[19] The problem with producing this 'standard image', or stereotyping, is that individuals are treated as members of a group, rather than being treated as individuals. It is the group to whom we attribute generalised characteristics, which clearly cannot possibly be the characteristics of every individual within that group.

[17] P Taylor and A Walker 'The ageing workforce: employers' attitudes towards older people' (1994) 8(4) *Work, Employment and Society* 569.
[18] Taken from *Stereotyping* (1995), a monograph prepared by Robert Jelking and Emanuelle Sajous, Public Services Commission of Canada.
[19] This definition comes from *The Collins Dictionary and Thesaurus* (1988).

One simple assumption, for example, might be that men are stronger than women. The result of this is that only men might be considered for physically demanding jobs, which, in turn, may be the higher paid jobs in a certain industry. The outcome is that women are discriminated against in the selection process and as a result earn less than men. The assumption is patently false: not all men are stronger than all women; some women will be stronger than many men, and so on. The discrimination comes from the stereotyping of women in the first place. It is the allocation of a generalised characteristic to an identifiable group.

In two attitude surveys carried out by the Commission for Racial Equality (CRE),[20] some stereotypes of certain ethnic groups were identified. The negative stereotypes of African Caribbeans held amongst white people included the following:

- 'they have a chip on their shoulder'
- 'they have an attitude problem/they are rude'
- 'they are aggressive'
- 'they use drugs'.

Negative stereotypes of South Asians were also held amongst white people, including the following:

- 'they overclaim benefits'
- 'they have too many children'
- 'they have backward religious practices, e.g. halal meat slaughter and call to prayer'
- 'they have dirty shops'.

These statements reflect the prejudice that African Caribbeans and South Asians are likely to face. The younger Muslims in the focus groups were also very aware of the stereotypes of Islam that prevailed in British society.

What was clear from the CRE study was that these prejudices often broke down on an individual level, when individuals from different ethnic groups interacted with individuals from the white community, which perhaps further shows how wrong generalised stereotyping is.

The underlying assumption in this book is that 'unjustified' discrimination, often resulting from the use of stereotyping, is wrong. This book considers the laws which seek to contribute to the ending of this discrimination.

> The purpose of anti-discrimination laws is to prevent the violation of human dignity and freedom through the imposition of disadvantage, stereotyping, or political or social prejudice.[21]

---

[20] *Stereotyping and Racism* (1998).
[21] Ontario Human Rights Commission.

Chapter 2

The European Union and discrimination law

Penny English

Introduction

The EU dimension of discrimination law has particular characteristics. In some respects it is more limited than domestic law as it reflects the specific objectives of the European Community rather than being part of a comprehensive social policy. In addition, it applies only to situations which fall within the scope of European Community law. Its role has evolved from being secondary to the achievement of the original, primarily economic, goal of creating a single European market to becoming one which is closely linked to citizenship and respect for individual fundamental rights.

The original purposes of the Community

The European Community was called, until the Treaty of European Union (which came into force in 1993), the European Economic Community. This title is significant: it indicates that the Community was originally concerned with *economic* matters. It therefore comes as no surprise that matters of more social and political concern do not take centre stage in the early years. Plans for European integration in the period immediately following the Second World War led to the creation of the European Coal and Steel Community, founded by France, Germany, Italy and Benelux in 1951. It established a system of pooled control over, as the name suggests, the coal and steel industries of the participating states. Ambitious hopes for political integration in Europe did not bear fruit, but there was sufficient will amongst the Member States to move further towards economic integration. The result was the establishment of two more Communities – the European Atomic Energy Community and the European Economic Community – by the Treaty of Rome in 1957.

This background to the formation of the European Community is important since it establishes the context within which co-operation between the Member States was to take place. Initially, this was primarily focused on economic aspects, as set out in the Treaty in its preamble and Article 2. Article 2 states the aim of the Community as follows:

> by establishing a common market and progressively approximating the economic policies of Member States, to promote throughout the Community a harmonious development of economic activities, a continuous and balanced expansion, an increase in stability, an accelerated raising of the standard of living and closer relations between the States belonging to it.

The key objective therefore was to establish a common market, later defined in the Single European Act in 1986 as an area where there would be free movement of the four factors of production: goods, persons, services and capital. Although there was some mention of social issues, these were subsidiary to the goal of market integration.

Nevertheless, it is impossible to isolate economic and social matters from one another. Subsequent revisions of the founding treaties (the Single European Act in 1986, the Treaty on European Union (the Treaty of Maastricht) in 1992, the Treaty of Amsterdam in 1997 and the Treaty of Nice in 2001) have progressively included additional areas of policy within their scope, including social policy. The nature of Community intervention in social matters has always been somewhat ambiguous, existing both as a necessary part of the overall economic goal and as a source of rights for individuals.

Discrimination on grounds of nationality was prohibited by EC law from the start, whereas discrimination on grounds of sex has had a progressive development from a limited Treaty base. The founding Treaty did establish the basic principle of equal pay for men and women but it was not until the 1970s that secondary legislation[1] included the broader concept of equal treatment in the workplace. The Treaty of Amsterdam, which came into force in 1999, expanded the scope of the Community to legislate against discrimination. Article 13 EC now gives the Community the power to legislate to combat discrimination based on sex, racial or ethnic origin, age or disability. It also elevates equality between men and women to one of the tasks of the Community (in Article 2 EC). This principle should be integrated into all the Community's actions:

> In all the activities referred to in this Article, the Community shall aim to eliminate inequalities, and to promote equality, between men and women.
>
> (Article 3 EC)

What is Community non-discrimination law seeking to achieve?

It is fundamental to the fulfilment of the purposes of the European Community, especially the goal of creating a single economic market, that the

---

[1] Directive 76/207 EEC.

barriers between the nation states of Europe should be removed. This can only become a reality if discrimination on grounds of nationality is eliminated at the level of both the nation and the individual. It is therefore not surprising that this principle was enshrined in the Treaty from the start. The need for the inclusion of legislation to prevent discrimination on grounds of sex is less obvious. Article 141 (ex Article 119)[2] provides that men and women should receive equal pay. Although included from the establishment of the European Community, the principle was not intended as the beginning of a broad social agenda; it was motivated largely by economic concerns expressed by the French Government when the Community was founded. France had feared that it would be put at an economic disadvantage within the common market as a result of the protection of equal pay for equal work enshrined in French national law. As a consequence of this law, France had a small differential between the pay of men and women compared with other Member States and this would potentially have meant that its production costs could be undercut by Member States where women were paid substantially lower wages than men.

The origins of Community discrimination law were therefore intended more to achieve the economic aim of ensuring the efficient functioning of the internal market than to ensure fundamental social rights. Nevertheless, the European Court of Justice (ECJ) was active in the recognition that there is also a human rights dimension to the equal treatment of men and women.

The Court expressed this inherent duality in the judgment in the *Defrenne*[3] case:

> Article 119 [now Article 141] pursues a double aim . . . to avoid a situation in which undertakings established in states which have actually implemented the principle of equal pay suffer a competitive disadvantage in intra-Community competition as compared with undertakings established in states which have not yet eliminated discrimination against women workers as regards pay. Second, this provision forms part of the social objectives of the Community, which is not merely an economic union, but is at the same time intended, by common action, to ensure social progress and seek the constant improvement of living and working conditions of their peoples . . .

Community non-discrimination policy in the present still reflects these two different goals: first, to ensure the functioning of the internal market; and, secondly, a more ambitious and wider goal of creating an inclusive society. Bell[4] describes this in terms of two different models: the market integration model and the social citizenship model. The market integration model justifies intervention in social matters only insofar as it

---

[2] The Treaty of Amsterdam, somewhat confusingly, renumbered the Treaty Articles. The number in brackets is the Article number which applied before this date.
[3] Case 43/75 *Defrenne v Sabena* [1976] ECR 455 at 472.
[4] M Bell *Anti-Discrimination Law and the European Union* (Oxford University Press, 2002).

is necessary to prevent unfair competition which will distort the functioning of the internal market. The social citizenship model, in contrast, sees a wider role for the Community in which the guaranteeing of fundamental social rights, including the right of equality, is central. A strengthened perception of rights becomes the basis for building a sense of shared European identity attached to citizenship.

The activism of the European Court of Justice

In a number of respects, the European Court of Justice has been active in developing the scope of EC law. Although the original founding of the European Economic Community did not include reference to fundamental rights, the ECJ soon began to develop the concept of general principles of law: a set of principles which underlie the whole Community legal order. Amongst these general principles has been a developing body of fundamental rights.[5] The principle of equality has been identified by the ECJ as one of the general principles it will uphold. As it stated in *Defrenne*:[6]

> . . . respect for fundamental personal rights is one of the general principles of Community law, the observance of which it has a duty to ensure. There can be no doubt that the elimination of discrimination based on sex forms part of those fundamental human rights.

The growing importance of the protection of fundamental rights in comparison to the original economic aim was emphasised in the more recent case of *Schröder*:[7]

> . . . it must be concluded that the economic aim pursued by Article 119 [now Article 141] of the Treaty, namely the elimination of distortions of competition between undertakings established in different Member States, is secondary to the social aim pursued by the same provision, which constitutes the expression of a fundamental human right.

The ECJ has always been active in ensuring the *effectiveness* of EC law. A key principle of EC law which was developed by the Court is that of direct effect. Under this principle, provisions of the Treaty which are sufficiently clear, unambiguous and unconditional can be relied on directly by individuals in their national courts, in the same way as they would be able to rely on provisions of their national law.[8] Enforcing individual rights through the courts is only the first stage. The individual also needs to

---

[5] More recently, the Charter of Fundamental Rights has brought together the rights in one document. This does not have legal effect, as it was 'solemnly proclaimed' at the Nice Summit in 2000, giving it political rather than legal status. The future status of the Charter is as yet uncertain.

[6] Case 149/77 *Gabrielle Defrenne v Sabena* [1978] ECR 1365 at 1378.

[7] Case C-50/96 *Deutsche Telekom v Schröder* [2000] ECR I-743 at 794.

[8] Case 26/62 *Van Gend en Loos v Nederlandse Administratie der Belastingen* [1963] ECR 1.

have access to effective remedies, and this is also an area where the ECJ has been active.[9]

Discrimination on grounds of nationality

The effective functioning of the internal market requires that workers (as one of the factors of production alongside goods, services and capital) should be able to move freely in order to find work. Such persons are likely to find this difficult if they face discrimination on grounds of nationality. The Treaty therefore provides in Article 12 EC (ex Article 6) that:

> Within the scope of application of this Treaty, and without prejudice to any special provisions contained therein, any discrimination on grounds of nationality shall be prohibited.

The ECJ has made it clear that the requirement of non-discrimination also extends beyond the actions of the state. In *Walrave and Koch*,[10] the issue was whether measures taken by a body other than the state would be covered by Article 12 (ex Article 6). In this case, the discriminatory rules laid down by a sporting body concerning professional cycling were challenged. Medium-distance cycling events employed pacemakers riding motorcycles and the rules stated that the cyclist and the pacemaker had to have the same nationality, which clearly constituted discrimination on grounds of nationality. The Court said that the actions by a sporting body such as this would be covered. Furthermore, the prohibition is applicable to discriminatory actions by private persons as well as organisations.[11]

Within the scope of application of the Treaty

It needs to be remembered that Article 12 applies only 'within the scope of the application' of the Treaty. From its inception, the Treaty provided for the free movement of the economically active, i.e. workers (Articles 39–42 (ex Articles 48–51)) and the self-employed (Articles 43–55 (ex Articles 52–66)). Exercising this right by moving to another country in the European Union in order to work brings such migrant workers within the scope of the Treaty, and thus they are able to rely on EC law to protect them from discrimination on grounds of nationality. Later, secondary legislation extended the rights of free movement to the 'economically

---

[9] See, e.g., Case 14/83 *Von Colson v Land Nordrhein-Westfalen* [1984] ECR 1891, discussed below.
[10] Case 36/74 *Walrave and Koch v Association Union Cycliste Internationale* [1974] ECR 1405.
[11] Case C-281/98 *Angonese v Cassa di Riparmio di Bolzano SpA* [2000] ECR I-4139.

inactive', i.e. retired persons, students and those of independent means,[12] subject to limitations (including the possession of adequate resources to support themselves), thus bringing their situation also within the scope of EC law.

Article 18 (ex Article 8a), part of the citizenship provisions introduced by the Treaty of Maastricht, states:

> Every citizen of the Union shall have the right to move and reside freely within the territory of the Member States, subject to the limitations and conditions laid down in this Treaty and by the measures adopted to give it effect.

This initially seemed to have a purely symbolic role since, rather than conferring new substantive rights, it merely restated existing rights. However, the concept of citizenship has been utilised by the ECJ to extend the scope of application of the Treaty further and so as to extend the range of situations in which the non-discrimination provision will apply.

The first case where the citizenship rights were used in this way by the ECJ was that of *Maria Martinez Sala*.[13] A Spanish national had been living in Germany for a number of years and, although for some years she had had a residence permit and had undertaken work, at the time in question she did not have a current residence permit. When she applied for a child-rearing benefit, she was refused on the grounds that she did not have German nationality, residence entitlement or a residence permit. She argued that this was discriminatory. The German Government responded that, even if this was a case of discrimination on grounds of nationality, she did not come within the scope of the Treaty. The ECJ disagreed. She was lawfully resident in Germany as she had previously been authorised to live there, even though she did not have a current permit. As a national of a Member State lawfully residing in Germany, she came within the scope of the Treaty provisions on citizenship and could therefore rely on the non-discrimination provision in Article 6 (now Article 12 EC).

The ECJ developed this further in the case of *Grzelczyk*.[14] A student with French nationality was studying in Belgium. He had worked part-time during the first three years of his course, but in his final year applied instead for a non-contributory minimum subsistence allowance (the *minimex*). This was withdrawn on the grounds that he was not a Belgian national. As the Court pointed out, a Belgian student in his position would have been entitled to the allowance. The ECJ was able to use his citizenship of the European Union as the basis for the application of Article 12

---

[12] Directive 90/364 (General right of free movement), Directive 90/365 (Right of free movement for retired persons), Directive 93/96 (Right of free movement for students).
[13] Case C-85/96 *Maria Martinez Sala v Freistaat Bayern* [1998] ECR 1–2691.
[14] Case C-184/99 *Rudy Grzelczyk v Centre Public d'Aide Sociale d'Ottignes-Louvain-la-Neuve (CPAS)* [2001] ECR 1–6193.

EC. As he was a citizen of the European Union, and was lawfully resident in another Member State (as a student), he came within the scope of EC law and so was entitled to be treated in the same way as nationals.

The Court reached a similar conclusion in *D'Hoop*.[15] In this case, a Belgian woman who had completed her secondary education in France had returned to Belgium to study at university. After finishing her degree she applied for a 'tide-over allowance', an allowance paid in Belgium to young unemployed people who are looking for their first job. She was turned down because her secondary education had not been in Belgium. The ECJ relied on its previous case law and said that she should not be treated less favourably because she had exercised her right of free movement within the Community.[16] The active use of citizenship by the ECJ has ensured that it has more than a purely symbolic function. As the Court said in *Grzelczyk*, EU citizenship is destined to be the factor 'enabling those who find themselves in the same situation to enjoy the same treatment in law irrespective of their nationality'.[17]

The nature of rights to non-discrimination

A consistent theme in the European Court of Justice's judgments is to seek to remove obstacles to the free movement of persons. This involves ensuring that the principle of non-discrimination on grounds of nationality is observed, since anything that puts an individual at a disadvantage in comparison with nationals of the host state is a disincentive to the exercise of those rights. Article 12 (ex Article 6) EC applies to both direct and indirect discrimination. An example of direct discrimination is the provision in the French Maritime Code which required that a set percentage of the crews of French ships must hold French nationality.[18] Indirect discrimination is illustrated by the case of *O'Flynn*.[19] An Irish migrant worker in the United Kingdom applied for a funeral grant to bury his son in Ireland. His grant application was refused because UK law only allowed this to be payable for funerals taking place in the United Kingdom. The ECJ held that this was indirect discrimination because it was intrinsically likely to affect migrant workers more than it did nationals; it was not necessary to establish that it did in fact affect a substantially higher proportion of migrant workers.

There may be objective justifications which will allow certain types of indirect discrimination. An obvious one is a language requirement: Article 3(1) of Regulation 1612/68 specifically permits 'conditions relating to linguistic knowledge required by reason of the nature of the post to

---

[15] Case C-224/98 *Marie-Natalie D'Hoop v Office National d'Emploi* [2000] ECR I-6191.
[16] Referring to Case C-370/90 *R v Immigration Appeal Tribunal and Singh ex parte Secretary of State for the Home Department* [1992] ECR I-4265.
[17] [2001] ECR I-6193 at 6194.
[18] Case 167/73 *Commission v French Republic* [1974] ECR 359.
[19] Case C-237/94 *O'Flynn v Adjudication Officer* [1996] ECR I-2617.

be filled'.[20] There is a fine dividing line between measures which are indirectly discriminatory and those which hinder the exercise of free movement without discrimination (so-called 'equal burden' rules). The ECJ has gone beyond the prohibition of discriminatory measures and included any other measures which may hinder the exercise of free movement. In the *Bosman* case,[21] the UEFA/FIFA rules governing the transfer of football players between clubs were held to be contrary to the provisions on free movement, even although they were not discriminatory:

> Provisions which preclude or deter a national of a Member State from leaving his country of origin in order to exercise his right to freedom of movement therefore constitute an obstacle to that freedom even if they apply without regard to the nationality of the workers concerned.[22]

The importance of ensuring that workers who choose to work in another Member State are not hindered in their exercise of this right is reinforced by specific reference to non-discrimination in Article 39 (ex Article 48) EC. It makes it clear that the principle of non-discrimination applies:

> Such freedom of movement shall entail the abolition of any discrimination based on nationality between workers of the Member States as regards employment, remuneration and other conditions of work and employment.
>
> (Article 39(2) EC)

Regulation 1612/68 provides more concrete detail of the non-discrimination provisions in the context of workers. Article 1 of the Regulation reinforces that nationals of every Member State should be free to take up employment in another Member State on the same basis and under the same conditions as its own nationals. Articles 3–6 of Regulation 1612/68 provide more examples, including stating that there should be no discrimination in such matters as employment contracts, recruitment or advertising (with the exception of linguistic requirements which are genuinely necessary).

However, it is not enough for the removal of practices which discriminate on grounds of nationality to apply just to the employment context itself. An important provision is Article 7 of Regulation 1612/68, which provides that there should be equal access to social and tax advantages for nationals and non-nationals. The application of this Article has been the subject of considerable litigation.

The initial approach of the ECJ was restrictive. In *Michel S*,[23] an Italian national had worked in Belgium until his death. His son, who was disabled, was unable to receive benefits available under Belgian laws which

---

[20] Case 379/87 *Groener v Minister for Education* [1989] ECR 3967.
[21] Case C-415/93 *Union Royal Belge des Sociétés de Football Association ASBL v Bosman* [1995] ECR I-4921.
[22] Ibid at 5069.
[23] Case 76/72, *Michel S v Fonds National de Reclassement Handicapés* [1973] ECR 457.

were designed to enable people with disabilities to enter work. The ECJ held that 'social and tax advantages' needed to be directly connected with employment; this benefit for his son was not sufficiently connected with employment. However, this approach was later broadened. In *Cristini v SNCF*,[24] the right to concessionary rail fares for large families was refused to the Italian widow (living in France) of an Italian man who had been working in France, on the grounds of her nationality. The Court held that Article 7 of the Regulation went beyond rights directly connected with employment and included 'all social and tax advantages, whether or not attached to the contract of employment'. She was able to receive the reduced fares designed for large families. The case of *Inzirillo*[25] emphasises further that discrimination against family members of the worker is also covered: this case concerned a disability benefit paid to an adult dependent son. The Court held that this was a social advantage to the worker, even though the direct benefit was to his son.

The ECJ clarified the position in *Even*,[26] taking a broad definition of what constitutes a 'social advantage' and relating this aspect of non-discrimination to the encouragement of the free movement of workers within the Community:

> the advantages which this regulation extends to workers who are nationals of other Member States are all those which, whether or not linked to a contract of employment, are generally granted to national workers primarily because of their objective status as workers or by virtue of the mere fact of their residence on the national territory and the extension of which to workers who are nationals of other member states therefore seems suitable to facilitate their mobility within the Community.[27]

The children of workers are entitled not to be discriminated against in respect to access to education. In the case of *Michel S* (above), the benefit in question was not payable as a social advantage. Nevertheless, he was able to receive the benefit under Article 12 of Regulation 1612/68, which states that the children of workers should have equal access to the state's general educational, apprenticeship and vocational training courses. *Casagrande*[28] extended this further, beyond just equal access to courses: it held that the principle would also include a grant for secondary school education in Germany, since this would be a part of the requirement that workers' children should be enabled to receive education 'under the best possible conditions'.

The position concerning the children of workers is clear. The provision of education on an equal basis for university students is less clear;

---

[24] Case 32/75 *Fiorini (née Cristini) v Société Nationale des Chemins de Fer Français* [1975] ECR 1085.
[25] Case 63/76 *Inzirillo v Caisse d'Allocations Familiales* [1976] ECR 2057.
[26] Case 207/78 *Ministère Public v Even and ONPTS* [1979] ECR 2019.
[27] Ibid at 2034.
[28] Case 9/74 *Casagrande v Landeshauptstadt München* [1974] ECR 773.

there is not the same direct link to encouraging the freedom of movement for workers. Education, in the broad sense, lies outside the scope of EC law and is a matter for the Member States. However, since education also involves vocational training, it can fall within the ambit of EC law. Workers have the right under Regulation 1612/68, Article 7(3) to access to training in vocational schools and retraining centres under the same conditions as national workers. In *Forchieri v Belgium*,[29] the Italian spouse of a worker in Belgium was entitled to attend vocational and training courses without having to pay the enrolment fee, which was not charged to Belgian nationals. This was because Article 128 (now Article 150 EC) brings vocational training within the scope of application of the Treaty, so it is a context within which there should be no discrimination on grounds of nationality.

A wider range of educational experience can be enjoyed without discrimination on grounds of nationality by students. In *Gravier v City of Liège*,[30] Mlle Gravier (who had French nationality) enrolled for a course in strip-cartoon art at the University of Liège in Belgium. She was charged the *minerval*, a fee not charged to Belgian nationals. She claimed that this was discrimination on grounds of nationality. The ECJ agreed that this could be discriminatory, but it needed to be established that her situation fell within the scope of the Treaty. The Court repeated that vocational training is a part of the scope of Community activities linked to the right of free movement:

> Access to vocational training is in particular likely to promote free movement of persons throughout the Community by enabling them to obtain a qualification in the Member State where they intend to work and by enabling them to complete their training and develop their particular talents in the Member State whose vocational training programmes include the special subject desired.

The ECJ then took a broad view of what constitutes 'vocational training': it held that any education which was preparation for a profession, trade or employment could be described as 'vocational training', even if it included an element of general education. Her university course therefore fell within the scope of EC law, so she could not be charged different fees from a Belgian national. The court expanded this point in *Blaizot v University of Liège*[31] when it held that university courses would generally constitute vocational education (the course in question here was veterinary medicine). The only type of course that would not be covered would be one which had the purpose of improving general knowledge without any element of preparation for a future occupation.

---

[29] Case 152/82 *Forcheri v Belgium* [1983] ECR 2323.
[30] Case 293/83 *Gravier v City of Liège* [1985] ECR 593.
[31] Case 24/86 *Blaizot v University of Liège* [1988] ECR 379.

The ECJ was less generous when considering the issue of funding for attending such courses. Obviously, the reality of equal access to educational courses includes not simply equal access to the courses themselves but also equal access to financial support. The Court's approach was to draw a distinction between the two: although discriminatory enrolment and tuition fees would be covered, maintenance grants would be restricted to persons who had been working in another state and where there was a link between the employment and the subsequent studies. It would not apply to someone who was undertaking study in another country.[32] However, *Grzelczyk*,[33] discussed above, has broadened the scope of maintenance support for students.

Public service exception

There are certain categories of job where states are permitted to discriminate against workers from other states by reserving those posts for their own nationals. Article 39(4) EC (ex Article 48(4)) excepts the free movement provisions in the case of employment in the public service. The Treaty did not specify what was meant by the 'public service'. The ECJ clarified the meaning of this provision in *Commission v Belgium*.[34] Jobs with Belgian local authorities and public undertakings were open only to Belgian nationals, whatever the nature of the work. The Court took a restrictive approach, stating that there needed to be 'the existence of a special relationship of allegiance to the State and reciprocity of rights and duties which form the foundation of the bond of nationality'.

The self-employed

It is not just workers who benefit from the right not to be discriminated against on grounds of nationality. This applies also to the self-employed (in Community terminology, those who are exercising the right of establishment or who are providing services). In general, the rules applicable to the self-employed are similar to those applying to workers. These rights also apply to those who are in receipt of services as well as those who are providing them. In *Cowan*,[35] a British tourist who was mugged while visiting Paris was refused compensation under the criminal compensation scheme in France. However, it was held that, as the recipient of services, he came within the scope of EC law. He therefore could not be treated in a way that discriminated against him on the grounds that he was not a national of France.

---

[32] See Case 197/86 *Brown v Secretary of State for Scotland* [1988] ECR 3205.
[33] [2001] ECR I-6193.
[34] Case 149/79 *Commission v Belgium* [1980] ECR 3881.
[35] Case 186/87 *Cowan v Le Trésor Public* [1989] ECR 195.

Indirect discrimination can be a particular problem for the self-employed. For example, a state may fail to recognise qualifications obtained in another Member State. Failure to have one's qualifications accepted clearly amounts to a major obstacle to the free movement of professionals. As the ECJ stated in *Vlassopoulou*:[36]

> It must be stated in this regard that, even if applied without any discrimination on the basis of nationality, national requirements concerning qualifications may have the effect of hindering nationals of the other Member States in the exercise of their right of establishment guaranteed to them.

This case concerned a Greek national who had qualified as a lawyer in Greece, and subsequently worked in Germany. Her application for admission to the German Bar was refused on the grounds that she did not have German qualifications. The case law of the Court, culminating in *Vlassopoulou*, has made it clear that in such cases the national authorities must take account of qualifications obtained in another state. In *Heylens*,[37] a case which concerned a football trainer who had Belgian qualifications and was working in France, but who was refused recognition of this qualification by the French Ministry of Sport, the ECJ held that the authorities must:

> assure themselves on an objective basis, that the foreign diploma certifies that the holder has knowledge and qualifications which are, if not identical, at least equivalent to those certified by the national diploma.[38]

As well as the principles developed by the ECJ, there is also legislation which covers the recognition of qualifications. In the early years of the European Community, there was an attempt to harmonise qualifications, i.e. to produce directives which covered an agreed minimum standard of training for specific sectors of professional activity. These covered a number of health-related professions, such as doctors. Later, the approach changed to one of 'mutual recognition', i.e. basing recognition of qualifications on mutual trust. In principle this means that a Member State cannot refuse to allow nationals of another Member State to exercise their profession, if they hold the qualifications to practise in their home state. This system has gradually been expanded from (at first) covering higher education qualifications of three years' duration (Directive 89/48), later supplemented by Directive 92/51, covering qualifications of at least one year's duration. (These were amended in 2001 by Directive 2001/19 EC.)

Another area where the self-employed may encounter indirect discrimination is in connection with the rules of conduct of a profession, e.g.

---

[36] Case 340/89 *Vlassopoulou v Ministerium für Justiz, Bundes un Europaangelegenheiten Baden-Württemberg* [1991] ECR 2357 at 2383.
[37] Case 222/86 *UNECTEF v Heylens* [1987] ECR 4097.
[38] Ibid at 4116.

where there is a residence requirement. In *Van Binsbergen*,[39] a Dutch national was acting as legal adviser in proceedings before a Dutch social security court. When he moved to Belgium he was told he could no longer represent his client at the court because a Dutch law stated that only persons established in the country could act as legal advisers. The ECJ held that this was indirect discrimination on grounds of nationality: the Treaty does not permit discrimination 'against the person providing the service by reason of his nationality or the fact that he is established in a Member State other than that in which the service is to be provided'.

Indirectly discriminatory provisions that hinder free movement can be justified in certain situations. The ECJ set out these conditions in *Gebhard*.[40] National measures which are liable to hinder free movement must fulfil four conditions in order to be allowed: they have to be applied in a non-discriminatory manner; they must be justified by imperative requirements in the general interest; they have to be appropriate to the attainment of their goals; and they must not go beyond what is necessary for the achievement of those goals.

Official authority exception

Article 45 (ex Article 55) EC provides for an 'official authority' exception, which allows certain activities to be reserved to nationals of the Member State. This is very similar in scope to the public service exception for workers. It was defined in *Reyners v Belgium*[41] as:

> that which arises from the sovereignty and majesty of the State; for him who exercises it, it implies the power of enjoying the prerogatives outside the general law, privileges of official power and powers of coercion over citizens.

The case concerned a question of whether the profession of *avocat* should be excluded from the requirement not to discriminate on grounds of nationality. The ECJ held that: 'The most typical activities of the profession of *avocat*, in particular, such as consultation and legal assistance and also representation and the defence of parties in court, even when the intervention or assistance of the *avocat* is compulsory or is a legal monopoly, cannot be considered as connected with the exercise of official authority.' The Court has taken a similar approach in subsequent cases and has therefore been vigilant to ensure that the extent to which exceptions are employed does not go beyond the purpose for which they were intended.

---

[39] Case 33/74 *Van Binsbergen v Bestuur van de Bedrijfsvereniging voor de Metaalnijverheid* [1974] ECR 1299.
[40] Case C-55/94 *Gebhard v Consiglio dell'Ordine degli Avvocati e Procuratori de Milano* [1995] ECR I-4165.
[41] Case 2/74 *Reyners v Belgium* [1974] ECR 631 at 664.

Discrimination on grounds of sex

This is an area where there has been considerable expansion in EC intervention. Initially concerned only with employment-related discrimination, there is a now a commitment to mainstreaming gender equality throughout the Community's activities. The ECJ has repeatedly stated that the general principle of equal treatment between men and women is fundamental to the Community legal order.[42] There is now a considerable body of legislation in this area:

- Article 141 (ex Article 119) of the EC Treaty lays down the principle of equal pay for equal work for men and women.
- Directive 75/117 implements the equal pay principle in more specific terms to include equal pay for work of equal value.
- Directive 76/207 (revised by Directive 2002/73) provides for equal treatment for men and women in the context of employment.
- Directive 79/7 applies the equal treatment principle to matters of social security.
- Directive 86/378 extends the equal treatment principle to occupational pension schemes.
- Directive 86/613 provides for equal treatment in self-employment.
- Directive 92/85 covers pregnancy and maternity.
- Directive 97/81 concerns part-time workers.

Equal pay

The principle of equal pay for men and women engaged in equal work was included in the original Treaty in Article 119 EEC. This has, since the Treaty of Amsterdam, been strengthened and expanded in Article 141 EC. The case of *Defrenne v Sabena* (below) demonstrates the activism of the ECJ in making this provision an effective source of rights. The Court established that provisions of the Treaty, where they are sufficiently clear and precise, can be relied upon in the national courts by individuals both against the state and, as in this case, against a private employer. Without this activism on the part of the ECJ in deciding that Article 119 did have direct effect, the provision would have been unlikely to have been so important.

Gabrielle Defrenne was involved in a series of cases against her employer, the Belgian airline Sabena.[43] She worked as a member of the cabin crew, and women working in that capacity were treated differently from their male colleagues on a number of counts: they were subject to

---

[42] Case C-13/94 *P v S and Cornwall County Council* [1996] ECR I-2143.
[43] Case 80/70 *Defrenne v Belgium (Defrenne I)* [1971] ECR 445, Case 43/75 *Defrenne v Sabena (Defrenne II)* [1976] ECR 455, Case 149/77 *Defrenne v Sabena (Defrenne III)* [1978] ECR 1365.

discriminatory retirement ages, as women were required to retire at the age of 40 whereas men could continue until normal retirement age; women were paid less, and on retirement received a smaller state pension. In the first case, taken against the Belgian state in challenging the differential level of state pension, the ECJ held that state pensions were not covered by the requirement for equal pay in Article 119: 'A retirement pension established within the framework of a social security scheme laid down by legislation does not constitute consideration which the worker receives indirectly in respect of his employment from his employer...' Since state social security schemes fall outside the Treaty article, the discrimination was lawful.

However, on the issue of equal pay she was successful. The case not only confirmed that she had been unlawfully discriminated against, but (because Article 119 gave rise to horizontal direct effect) also that she was able successfully to enforce her right to equal pay through the courts.

The meaning of equal work

Defrenne dealt with the straightforward situation of people doing the same work. She was doing the same job, at the same time, for the same company as the male employees who were paid more. The ECJ has been faced with more complex situations where the comparison is not straightforward. In *Jenkins v Kingsgate*[44] the Court accepted that work of equal value, not only identical work, was a basis for claim under Article 119. In *Macarthys*,[45] a woman was paid less than the man she replaced. He had been paid £60 a week, whereas she earned £50 a week. The Court held that to establish that there was discrimination in rates of pay, there needed to be an actual, not hypothetical comparator. Comparison had to be with employees of different sex working within the same establishment or service. However, they need not be contemporaneous.

There are situations where equal work will not always be paid at equal rates. In *Weiner Gebeitskrankenkasse*[46] it was held that the 'same work' comparison did not apply where graduate psychologists working as psychotherapists did the same as medical doctors. The psychologists were mostly women and the doctors were mostly men. However, higher pay was justified by the higher training and qualifications of the doctors.

Directive 75/117 added detail to the bare bones of the Treaty Article, ensuring that equal pay applied not only to equal work but also work of equal value. Article 141 now makes explicit reference to work of equal value, but this was not the case with the old Article 119. This has to be determined on objective criteria.[47]

---

[44] Case 96/80 *Jenkins v Kingsgate (Clothing Productions) Ltd* [1981] ECR 911.
[45] Case 129/79 *Macarthys Ltd v Smith* [1980] ECR 1275.
[46] Case C-309/97 *Angestelltenbetriebsrat der Weiner Gebeitskrankenkasse* [1999] ECR I-2865.
[47] Case 237/85 *Rummler v Dato-Druck* [1986] ECR 2101.

The meaning of pay

In general, the ECJ has taken a wide interpretation in deciding what constitutes 'pay', not least because the Court has tried to eliminate the possibility of employers attempting to undermine the equal pay provisions by making payments which, although technically not 'pay', have the same effect. Garland[48] was the first case to discuss non-pay benefits or 'perks': in this instance reduced rail fares for the worker and his family. When female workers retired, the families lost the concessions, whereas male workers' families did not. This was considered to be pay. Botel[49] provided a definition for pay as 'all consideration, whether in cash or in kind, whether immediate or future, provided that the worker receives it, albeit indirectly, in respect of his employment, by virtue of legislation or on a voluntary basis'. Rinner-Kuhn[50] concerned sick pay: a part-time cleaner challenged German legislation which allowed employers to exclude from sick pay schemes anyone who worked for less than 10 hours a week. This was also covered by Article 119.

Are pensions pay?

The issue of deciding whether pensions should be considered as pay has caused some problems. As discussed above, Defrenne made it clear that state pensions fell outside the meaning of 'pay'. Bilka Kaufhaus[51] concerned a private pension scheme. A claim by a female part-time worker challenged the employer's occupational pension scheme; this was non-contributory, financed by the employer. Part-timers were only entitled to become part of it if they had worked for the firm for at least 15 out of a total of 20 years; this limit did not apply to full-time workers. Ms Weber claimed it was indirectly discriminatory as most of the part-time workers were women. The ECJ held that, as it was financed solely by the employer as a supplement to existing social security schemes, the benefit constituted consideration paid by the employer to the employee in respect of his employment; it was therefore pay. A distinction was set up therefore between pensions as pay (arising from contract) and as social security (arising from legislation).

The important case in this area is Barber,[52] involving a claim by a male employee relating to an opted-out non-contributory pension scheme which operated as a substitute for the statutory social security scheme and also under a statutory redundancy payment scheme. Mr Barber was made redundant at the age of 52. The terms of his contract provided that, in the event of redundancy, a male employee was entitled to an immediate

---

[48] Case 12/81 Garland v British Rail [1982] ECR 359.
[49] Case C-360/90 Arbeiterwohlfahrt der Stadt Berlin v Botel [1992] ECR I-3589.
[50] Case 171/88 Rinner-Kühn v FWW Spezial-Gebäudereinigung GmbH [1989] ECR 2743.
[51] Case 170/84 Bilka Kaufhaus GmbH v Weber von Hartz [1986] ECR 1607.
[52] Case C-262/88 Barber v Guardian Royal Exchange Assurance Group [1990] ECR I-1889.

pension at the age of 55, and a woman at the age of 50. He therefore argued that he had been discriminated against on grounds of his sex. The UK government argued that contracted-out pensions, which replace the state pension rather than supplement it, did not come under Article 119 (now Article 141). The ECJ disagreed, stating that 'the fact that a benefit is in the nature of pay cannot be called into question where the worker is entitled to receive the benefit in question from his employer by reason of the existence of the employment relationship'.

Barber set out the distinguishing characteristics of a pension scheme which is pay rather than social security. It must be wholly financed by the employer or by the employer and the worker without any contribution coming from the state. Belonging to such schemes derives from the employment relationship with a particular employer. Even if such contracted-out schemes are based on statute, this cannot preclude the application of the equal pay provisions. They may grant employees greater benefits than the statutory scheme, therefore their economic function is similar to the top-up schemes such as in the *Bilka* case.

This clarified that the only schemes outside Article 141 are those which are general statutory schemes provided as a matter of social policy and funded from the public purse. This ruling would obviously have had a profound impact on the funding of such schemes which had been established on the basis that the payments to men and women would begin at different ages. The ECJ therefore held that it would not apply retrospectively. A Protocol was subsequently added to the Treaty of Maastricht to confirm this:

> For the purposes of Article 119, . . . benefits under occupational social
> security schemes shall not be considered as remuneration if and insofar as
> they are attributable to periods of employment prior to May 1990, except
> in the case of workers . . . who have before that date initiated legal
> proceedings . . .

Coloroll and *Neath*,[53] two pensions cases decided after *Barber*, retreat a little from the progressive broadening of the concept of pay. As there is a difference in life expectancy between men and women, the amount of money in the pension funds needs to take account of this, so employer contributions to the funds were higher for female employees. The Court held that contributions by employees had to be the same for men and women, but in schemes like these the employers' contributions varied over time and were adjusted to take account of the pensions that would have to be paid. Although the final pensions payable to men and women were not discriminatory, the use of sex-based actuarial factors to calculate the level of employers' contributions to the funds meant that, in the case of redundancy, women received larger payments than men.

---

[53] Case C-152/91 *Neath v Hugh Steeper* [1993] ECR I-6935 and Case C-200/91 *Coloroll Pension Trustees Ltd v James Richard Russell* [1994] ECR I-4389.

In *Roberts*,[54] different bridging pensions which were paid to employees who were forced to retire early because of ill health did not infringe Article 119 (now Article 141). The object of the pension, which was funded by the employer *ex gratia*, was to cover the difference between the occupational pension which was paid at once on early retirement and the overall sum the employee would receive on reaching state retirement age. Up to the age of 60 it was the same for men and women. At 60, women were entitled to a state pension, therefore the bridging pension was reduced. The ECJ held that this was sexually neutral and did not infringe Article 119 (now Article 141).

A case currently before the ECJ[55] concerns the position under current UK law with regard to the marriage of transsexuals and the consequences this has for the payment of pensions. KB worked for the National Health Service for 20 years, during which time she made contributions to the pension fund, which included provision for a surviving spouse's pension. Her partner is a female-to-male transsexual, and the position under current UK law is that they cannot marry. As the equal pay provisions define pay as including pensions, KB considered that her position was in breach of the Treaty. The Advocate General[56] concluded that, although Member States are free to lay down the requirements for marriage, a state cannot impose a condition contrary to fundamental rights. He concluded that Article 141 therefore precludes national rules which, by not recognising the right to marry, deny transsexuals the right to a widower's pension. This decision has to be seen in the context of the European Court of Human Rights decision of July 2002 in *Goodwin v United Kingdom*,[57] which held that the prohibition of marriage for transsexuals is contrary to the European Convention on Human Rights.

Justifying indirect discrimination

Cases have made it clear that indirect discrimination is included within the scope of equal pay. In *Jenkins v Kingsgate*,[58] part-time workers (of whom only one was male) were paid 10% less than full-time workers, all of whom were male. The question the ECJ was asked to consider was whether such a situation would be covered by Article 119 (now Article 141). The Court set out guidelines for determining this:[59]

> the fact that part-time work is paid at an hourly rate lower than pay for full-time work does not amount per se to discrimination prohibited by

---

[54] Case C-132/92 *Roberts v Birds Eye Walls Ltd* [1993] ECR I-5579.
[55] Case C-117/01 *KB v National Health Service Pensions Agency and the Secretary of State for Health* [2003] Pens LR 163; Celex No 601C0117.
[56] The Advocate General's Opinion is delivered before the ECJ considers the case; it is not binding on the Court.
[57] No 28957/95 (2002) EHRR 18.
[58] Case 96/80 *Jenkins v Kingsgate (Clothing Productions) Ltd* [1981] ECR 911.
[59] Ibid at 952.

Article 119, provided that the hourly rates are applied to workers belonging to either category without distinction based on sex.

Differences may be justified:

in so far as the difference in pay . . . is attributable to factors which are objectively justified and are in no way related to any discrimination based on sex . . . Such may be the case, in particular, when by giving hourly rates of pay which are lower for part-time work than those for full-time work the employer is endeavouring, on economic grounds which may be objectively justified, to encourage full-time work irrespective of the sex of the worker.

However,

if it is established that a considerably smaller percentage of women than men perform the minimum number of weekly working hours required in order to be able to claim the full hourly rate of pay, the inequality in pay will be contrary to Article 119 of the Treaty where, regard being had to the difficulties encountered by women in arranging to work that minimum number of hours per week, the pay policy of the undertaking in question cannot be explained by factors other than discrimination based on sex.

Thus, although making it clear that such indirect discrimination will be covered by Article 119 (now Article 141), the notion of objective justification is less clear. This will be a matter for the national court or tribunal to determine on the facts of each case.

A similar situation was seen in the case of *Bilka* (discussed above): part-time workers could only claim pension rights if they had been employed for 15 years out of 20. No such requirement was placed on full-time workers. The ECJ found that this was discrimination in favour of full-time workers. If the full-time workers were predominantly men then, following *Jenkins*, the only defence would be where there are 'objectively justified factors unrelated to any discrimination on grounds of sex'. The presence or absence of intention to discriminate is not a factor. If the national court found that the measures chosen by *Bilka* corresponded to a 'real need on the part of the undertaking' and that they are 'appropriate with a view to achieving the objectives pursued, and are necessary to that end, the fact that the measures affect a far greater number of women than men is not sufficient to show that they constitute an infringement of article 119'.[60] Justification for differences in pay therefore needs to satisfy three tests: there must be a real need, they must be necessary, and they must be appropriate. The latter two requirements are a reflection of the general principle of proportionality.[61]

---

[60] [1986] ECR 1607 at 1630–1631.
[61] The same principles were repeated by the court in Case 171/88 *Rinner-Kühn v FWW Spezial-Gebäudereinigung GmbH* [1989] ECR 2743.

Burden of proof

Where indirect discrimination is at issue, it can be difficult to prove that differences in pay are in fact the result of discrimination. The problem is illustrated by the case of *Danfoss*:[62] jobs were classified into grades and the basic pay for each grade was the same for men and women. Individual supplements were added for mobility, training and seniority. Although basic pay was the same, it was shown that the average pay for the men in two of the grades was higher than that of the women in the same grades. The ECJ found that the system lacked transparency and in such a case the burden of proof is reversed. It is then up to the employer to show that the differences are not the consequence of discrimination. Directive 97/80 on the burden of proof in sex discrimination cases now provides that the burden of proof is on the respondent to show that there has been no breach of the principle of equal treatment, if the alleged discrimination can be presumed from the facts of the case.

Equal treatment

Equal pay is only a first step towards the elimination of discrimination between women and men in the context of employment. Equality in rates of pay alone is clearly not enough to ensure that women and men are able to enjoy the same rights and conditions at work as each other.

Directive 76/207 provides a broader base for the elimination of discriminatory treatment by providing for equal treatment in the context of employment. Article 1 of the Directive states that its purpose is to 'put into effect the principle of equal treatment for men and women as regards access to employment, including promotion, and to vocational training and as regards working conditions'. Article 2 defines what is meant by equal treatment: 'there shall be no discrimination whatsoever on grounds of sex either directly or indirectly by reference in particular to marital or family status'.

Certain exceptions are permitted. Article 2(2) allows Member States to exclude activities which 'by reason of their nature or the context in which they are carried out, the sex of the worker constitutes a determining factor'. Article 2(3) permits provisions concerning the protection of women, particularly as regards pregnancy and maternity. Article 2(4) provides that positive discrimination measures can be put in place 'to promote equal opportunity for men and women, in particular by removing existing inequalities which affect women's opportunities'.

---

[62] Case 109/88 *Handels- og Kontorfunktionaerernes Forbund i Danmark v Dansk Arbejdsgiverforening (for Danfoss)* [1989] ECR 3199.

What is meant by 'on grounds of sex'?

Clearly this includes treating men and women differently, but the ECJ has also considered broader questions of whether this includes discrimination on grounds of transsexuality or sexual orientation. In *P v S*[63] the question was whether dismissal on grounds of transsexuality amounts to discrimination on grounds of sex. This case provides an example of the way the ECJ takes a broad approach to the interpretation of EC legislation. The number of people undergoing gender reassignment is small so the decision, in itself, would affect only a relatively limited number of people.

P was employed by Cornwall County Council from 1991 to 1993. She was dismissed after she had informed her employer of her intention to undergo gender reassignment and had begun to dress and behave as a woman but before she had undergone surgery. She brought an action against her employer on the grounds that her dismissal was unlawful sex discrimination. The Employment Tribunal in Truro found that the reason why she was dismissed was her intention to undergo gender reassignment and referred two questions to the European Court of Justice under the preliminary reference procedure, seeking to clarify the meaning of 'on grounds of sex' in the Equal Treatment Directive.

The United Kingdom argued that the Directive prohibits discrimination based on differing treatment because of being female or because of being male and does not cover transsexuality. The Advocate General took a very broad approach to the meaning of 'on grounds of sex' and said that this meant discrimination based on anything connected with sex. Gender reassignment is clearly related to sex, therefore discrimination on grounds that an employee is undergoing gender reassignment would be discrimination on grounds of sex. The ECJ agreed that this situation was covered by the Equal Treatment Directive, but used a different line of reasoning to come to this conclusion, by comparing the pre-operative male with the post-operative female and finding that they would be treated differently. Generally, sex equality law requires that there is a comparison made between persons of different sexes and arguments tend to centre on the question of finding the right comparator. Here, the Advocate General had taken a broad approach, saying that the argument that a female to male transsexual would be treated in the same way as a male to female transsexual was a 'quibbling formalistic interpretation and a betrayal of the true essence of that fundamental and inalienable value which is equality'. The ECJ, however, took the more cautious route of using a comparator to establish that discrimination had taken place.

At the time, it was thought that the decision in *P v S* might lead the way to an extension of the Equal Treatment Directive to include discrimination based on sexual orientation. However, in the case of *Grant*,[64] the ECJ made it clear that the Equal Treatment Directive did not apply. Lisa

[63] Case C-13/94 *P v S and Cornwall County Council* [1996] ECR I-2143.
[64] Case C-249/96 *Grant v South-West Trains* [1998] I-621.

Grant had appealed to an industrial[65] tribunal after her employer, SW Trains, refused to allow her same-sex partner a free travel pass. Such passes were available to married partners or common law spouses of the opposite sex, where a meaningful relationship had existed for at least two years. She claimed that this was discrimination on grounds of sex. The Court disagreed, drawing a distinction between the sex of the person and his or her sexual orientation. It was confirmed in *D & Sweden*[66] that the Directive does not apply to discrimination on grounds of sexual orientation. A Swedish national working for the European Community had a same-sex partner. The partnership was registered under Swedish law, which entitled them to the same legal effects as marriage (with certain exceptions). He applied for a household allowance paid to married EC employees. The ECJ upheld the refusal, taking a traditionalist view of marriage as being between persons of the opposite sex.

Pregnancy

As seen above, Directive 76/207 allows, under Article 2(3), for provisions to be adopted by Member States which concern 'the protection of women, particularly as concerns pregnancy and maternity'. Directive 92/85 (the Pregnancy Directive) goes even further by imposing a positive requirement of a minimum standard of protection for women who are pregnant, breastfeeding, or who have recently given birth.

However, is it possible to discriminate against a woman on the grounds that she is pregnant? As we have seen above, there is generally a need for there to be someone to compare the claimant with, in order to show that there has been unequal treatment. As pregnancy is an exclusively female condition, the search for a comparator is problematic. The legal position was unclear until the case of *Dekker*.[67] A woman had applied for a job as an instructor and at the time she was three months pregnant. Although she was the most suitable candidate she did not get the job because her employer would not have been able to obtain reimbursement from the state for the maternity benefits payable to her, and would therefore have been unable to afford a replacement for her during her absence. The ECJ was clear as to whether this amounted to discrimination on grounds of sex: only women can be refused employment because they are pregnant, therefore this is direct discrimination on the grounds of sex and cannot be justified. There is no need to try to find a man in a comparable situation with whom she can be compared.

When dismissal is on the grounds of pregnancy-related illness, the position is more nuanced. In *Hertz*,[68] the employee was absent from work

[65] Industrial tribunals were predecessors of employment tribunals.
[66] Cases C-122 & 125/99P *D & Sweden v Council* [2001] ECR I-4319.
[67] Case 177/88 *Dekker v Stichting Vormingscentrum Voor Jong Volwassen* [1990] ECR I-3941.
[68] Case 179/88 *Handels- og Kontorfunktionaerernes Forbund i Danmark v Dansk Arbejdsgiverforening (Hertz)* [1990] ECR I-3979.

on maternity leave. The pregnancy was complicated and she was ill for the period of her maternity leave. The illness continued beyond the maternity leave period and so she was still unable to return to work. After a further period of absence she was dismissed. Her employer argued that it was normal practice to sack employees who were so often ill. The ECJ held that, although pregnancy-related discrimination was direct discrimination, the Directive did not apply to dismissal due to illness-related absence outside the period of maternity leave. Its reasoning was that, in the case of an illness manifesting itself after the maternity leave period, there is no reason to distinguish illness attributable to pregnancy from any other illness. Men and women can become ill and if a sick man would have been dismissed then she had not suffered any discrimination.

Webb v EMO[69] concerned the question of fixed-term or indeterminate contracts. Webb was employed to cover the period of maternity leave of another employee. At the interview it was indicated that she might be kept on after the period of maternity leave and she was given an open-ended contract. Within two weeks of starting she found that she too was pregnant and, in consequence, was dismissed. The ECJ held that the dismissal of a woman who had been recruited for an indefinite period could not be justified on the grounds of her inability, on a purely temporary basis, to fulfil a fundamental condition of her employment contract. More recently the Court has made it clear[70] that dismissal on account of pregnancy amounts to direct discrimination on grounds of sex whether the contract was for a fixed or indeterminate period.

Directive 92/85 (the Pregnancy Directive) now provides for a minimum standard of protection for pregnant workers, workers who have just given birth and workers who are breastfeeding. It requires states to provide a period of maternity leave and protects against dismissal during such leave. The basis for this legislation is as a concern with ensuring health and safety at work, rather than preventing discrimination.

Derogations from Directive 76/207

Certain exceptions to the principle of equal treatment are allowed. Such exceptions have to be periodically reassessed in the light of social developments.

Article 2(2): occupational activities for which the sex of the worker is a determining factor

Activities may be justifiably reserved for persons of a particular sex. In *Johnston*,[71] a female member of the Royal Ulster Constabulary challenged

---

[69] Case C-32/93 *Webb v EMO Cargo (UK) Ltd* [1994] ECR I-3567.
[70] Cases C-438/99 *Jiménez Melgar v Ayuntamiento de Los Barrios* [2001] ECR I-6915 and C-109/00 *Tele Danmark A/S v HK* [2001] ECR I-6993.
[71] Case 222/84 *Johnston v Chief Constable of the RUC* [1986] ECR I-1651.

the decision not to renew her contract. The force had a policy not to employ any women as full-time members of the reserve as women were not trained in the use of firearms. The ECJ held that the exemption might apply to some activities carried out by police officers but not to police activities in general. It held that carrying firearms might increase the risk of assassination, but did not hear any evidence to support the implication that women could not be trained to use firearms safely and effectively.

In a case now pending before the ECJ, the Commission has lodged a case against Austria[72] which concerns restrictions in Austrian law concerning women working underground in mines and their employment as divers. The Commission claims that this infringes Directive 76/207, on the grounds that, although activities in underground mining are physically and mentally extremely demanding, they are not activities which can be carried out only by men. The dangers do not justify the different treatment.

Equal treatment in the armed forces

Two cases illustrate a context at the margins of the Community sphere of action: the organisation of the armed forces.[73] This is a sensitive political topic, intimately associated with one of the central concerns of national sovereignty: that of the ability of the state to defend its territory. The organisation of national armed forces lies outside the scope of EC law, but does that mean that EC law cannot come to the aid of persons who feel that they have been discriminated against on grounds of their gender by the armed forces?

In *Sirdar*,[74] the policy of interoperability in the Royal Marines was at issue. This policy means that all members of the Royal Marines, without exception, have to carry out a full range of duties including front-line commando duty. Angela Sirdar had been working as a chef in the British Army for 11 years when she was made redundant. She, along with a number of others, was invited to apply for transfer to the Royal Marines, subject to passing a selection board and completing training. When the Royal Marines realised that she was a woman they said that the invitation to apply for a transfer had been given in error. She later took a case to the employment tribunal on the grounds of sex discrimination. The tribunal made a reference to the ECJ, asking whether matters regarding employment in the armed services fall within the scope of the Treaty, and, if so, whether excluding women could be justified. The British government argued that the organisation of the armed forces falls outside EC law entirely.

[72] Case C-203/03 *Commission v Austria* [2003] OJ C158.
[73] See P Koutrakos 'Community law and equal treatment in the armed forces' (2000) 25 ELRev 433–442.
[74] Case C-273/97 *Angela Maria Sirdar v The Army Board and the Secretary of State for Defence* [1999] 3 CMLR 559 [2000] IRLR 47.

The ECJ's response was that:

> decisions taken by Member States in regard to access to employment, vocational training and working conditions in the armed forces for the purpose of ensuring combat effectiveness do not fall altogether outside the scope of Community law.

Exceptions from EC law would need to be shown to be exceptional and clearly defined cases. So, despite the organisation of the armed forces being a matter for the national governments, it does not fall entirely outside Community influence. Was this such a situation? The Court went on to reach the conclusion that the total exclusion of women could be justified on the basis of the interoperability rule. The Royal Marines is a small unit which fulfils a specific role, requiring that all members are able to undertake front-line duty as commandos.

The ECJ reached a different conclusion in another case which, although also concerning the armed forces, has slightly different facts. *Tania Kreil*[75] had trained in electronics. She applied to enlist as a volunteer in the German Army, hoping to use her skills in electronic weapons maintenance. She was turned down as a result of a German law which said that women may only enlist in the army as volunteers in the medical and music sections. The Court applied the same principles as the case of Angela Sirdar, repeating that it is for the Member States to decide on the organisation of the armed forces, but that this is not entirely excluded from Community law. It went on to say that it was not justifiable to exclude women from virtually all posts. Another case reinforcing the point that the organisation of the armed forces is a matter for the Member States is the recent case of *Dory*.[76] Here the question of compulsory military service, which applied to men only, was considered. Dory claimed that this was discriminatory as there was no objective justification for it to apply to men only. Although the ECJ repeated that measures concerning the organisation of the armed forces did not fall entirely outside the scope of Community law, Community law was not applicable in this case.

Article 2(3): provisions concerning the protection of women

The ECJ has restricted the application of this derogation to the protection of a woman's biological condition during and after pregnancy and the protection of the relationship between mother and child immediately following birth. In the case of *Johnston* (above), the Court did not accept the attempt to justify the discriminatory treatment of women on the grounds of the demand from the public that women be given greater protection against the dangers of policing in Northern Ireland. It was not covered by the exception in Article 2(3) of the Directive. An argument

---

[75] Case C-285/98 *Tania Kreil v Bundesrepublik Deutschland* [2000] ECR I-69.
[76] Case C-186/01 *Alexander Dory v Federal Republic of Germany* [2003] 2 CMLR 26.

that the Directive went beyond the protection of women before and after childbirth, and that its purpose was to care for the child on a long-term basis, has also failed. In *Hoffmann*,[77] a father claimed six months' paternity leave; he argued that either parent should be able to care for the child. The ECJ responded that the Directive was not designed to settle questions concerning the organisation of the family, or alter the division of responsibility between parents.

Habermann-Beltermann[78] considered the question of whether it was compatible with the Directive for a woman who had chosen to work at night to be dismissed when she became pregnant, as the consequence of national legislation which prevented pregnant women doing night work. The ECJ said that the national legislation was compatible with Directive 76/207 (Art 2(3)). However, it noted that this was an open-ended contract, therefore to terminate the contract on those grounds would be contrary to the objective of protecting such persons and would deprive the Directive of its effectiveness. It therefore specifically limited its ruling to the case of a woman working without a fixed-term contract.

Article 2(4): positive discrimination

Directive 76/207 states that it is 'without prejudice to measures which promote equal opportunity for men and women, in particular by removing existing inequalities which affect women's opportunities.' This provision makes it possible to begin to address structural inequalities in the workplace. The provisions in the Equal Treatment Directive discussed above are all based on the idea of individual claimants who have been treated in a discriminatory way when compared to a person of the other sex, and providing redress in such cases. For women, the choice of a male comparator is not always appropriate: it is most useful only to women who are able to follow the male pattern of work–life balance. Much more pervasive and difficult to tackle is the problem of ensuring substantive rather than formal equality. Positive discrimination measures which favour under-represented sections of society aim to tackle this by redressing group inequalities. In attempting to achieve this aim, such measures may then run the risk of discriminating against members of the over-represented section of society, since the resulting more favourable treatment of one sex is itself direct discrimination.

In the first case to consider this problem, the ECJ applied a narrow construction which did little to address structural inequalities. *Kalanke*[79] concerned a regional law in Bremen which provided that, if there were two equally well-qualified applicants for a post, then priority should go to an equally qualified woman if women were under-represented. Ms Glissman

---

[77] Case 184/83 *Hoffmann v Barmer Ersatzkasse* [1984] ECR 3047.
[78] Case C-421/92 *Habermann-Beltermann v Arbeiderwohlfahrt, Bezirksverband* [1994] ECR I-1657.
[79] Case C-450/93 *Kalanke v Freie und Hansestadt Bremen* [1995] ECR I-3051.

was promoted to section manager in the parks department, in preference to the equally well-qualified candidate, Mr Kalanke. He then claimed that this amounted to discrimination on grounds of sex. The Court said that measures, such as this one, which give women absolute and unconditional priority go beyond equal opportunities. The measure therefore went beyond the limits of the exception in Article 2(4) of the Directive.

The decision was criticised for its reliance on a formal notion of equality. The ECJ addressed this in *Marschall:*[80] Mr Marschall was a teacher who applied for promotion. However, an equally qualified woman also applied, and the state law, as in *Kalanke*, gave priority to equally qualified women (in terms of suitability, competence and professional perform-ance) where they were under-represented. However, in this case the state law had added a phrase which was sufficient to set it apart: it included the qualification that this would not apply if reasons specific to an indi-vidual candidate tilted the balance in his favour. The Advocate General had felt that it was the same position as *Kalanke*. The Court disagreed because the saving clause meant that it was not unconditional priority. The Court accepted that the mere fact that a man and a woman are equally qualified does not mean that they have the same chances:

> male candidates tend to be promoted in preference to female candidates particularly because of prejudices and stereotypes concerning the role and capacities of women in working life.

A provision which gives priority to women will be acceptable as long as there is an objective assessment which takes account of all criteria specific to the individual candidates which will override the priority accorded to female candidates where these criteria tilt the balance in favour of the male candidate. Barnard has described this decision as a 'delicate compromise'.[81]

This approach was repeated in *Abrahamsson v Fogelqvist*,[82] which con-cerned the appointment of a professor at a university in Sweden. National legislation provided that a candidate for a public post who belongs to the under-represented sex (and who possesses sufficient qualifications for the post) should be chosen in preference to a candidate of the opposite sex who would otherwise be selected. The ECJ held that, as this amounted to automatic preference for the under-represented sex, it was not permit-ted under Article 2(4) of the Directive because it was automatically oper-ating without an objective assessment of the individual candidates. Such a selection system was held to be disproportionate to the aim it sought to achieve. This was confirmed again in *Badeck*.[83]

---

[80] Case C-409/95 *Helmut Marschall v Land Nordrhein-Westfalen* [1997] ECR I-6363.
[81] C Barnard 'The principle of equality in the Community context: *Grant, Kalanke* and *Marschall:* four uneasy bedfellows' (1998) 57(2) *Cambridge Law Journal* 352.
[82] Case C-407/98 *Abrahamsson v Fogelqvist* [2000] ECR I-5539.
[83] Case C-158/97 *Badeck's Application* [2000] ECR I-1875.

Under the Treaty of Amsterdam, Article 141(4) EC (the amended Article 119) now incorporates the principle of positive discrimination:

> With a view to ensuring full equality in practice between men and women in working life, the principle of equal treatment shall not prevent any member State from maintaining or adopting measures providing for specific advantages in order to make it easier for the under-represented sex to pursue a vocational activity or to prevent or compensate for disadvantages in professional careers.

Adequate remedies

The European Court of Justice has developed the mechanisms of direct effect, indirect effect and state liability to ensure that individuals' rights under EC law have real effect. The Court has similarly been concerned with effectiveness when considering remedies. Although the nature of remedies is a matter for the national governments, the ECJ has set out a number of principles which need to be applied to their award. In essence, these are to ensure that the remedies for breaches of EC law are adequate and effective. In the case of *Von Colson*,[84] the question of remedies for a breach of the Equal Treatment Directive was at issue. Two women applied for jobs as social workers, but they were unsuccessful; the successful applicants were both men. The women claimed that they had been discriminated against contrary to Directive 207/76. Although the national court agreed, under German law they would only have travel expenses reimbursed. However, Article 6 of the Directive required that there should be adequate means of redress for breaches of the principle of equal treatment. The Article was not sufficiently clear and precise for the women to rely on direct effect, but national courts are required to interpret national law in the light of the wording and purpose of the Directive in order to ensure that the remedy available is an effective one. Member States are free to choose what type of remedy to apply, but:

> if a Member State chooses to penalize breaches of that prohibition by the award of compensation, then in order to ensure that it is effective and that it has a deterrent effect, that compensation must in any event be adequate in relation to the damage sustained and must therefore amount to more than purely nominal compensation such as, for example, the reimbursement only of the expenses incurred in connection with the application.

The same theme of ensuring the effectiveness of the equal treatment provisions is seen in *Coote*.[85] In this case a woman had made a claim of sex discrimination against her employer, alleging that she had been dismissed on grounds of pregnancy. The claim was settled and her employment with the company ended by mutual agreement. She was subsequently

---

[84] Case 14/83 *Von Colson v Land Nordrhein-Westfalen* [1984] ECR 1891.
[85] Case C-185/97 *Coote v Granada Hospitality* [1998] ECR I-5199.

unable to find another job and claimed that this was a result of victimisation by her former employer, who had refused to supply her with a reference. The ECJ held that the Directive would be deprived of its effectiveness if an employer were to be able to retaliate in such a fashion. It pointed out that:

> Fear of such measures, where no legal remedy is available against them, might deter workers who considered themselves the victims of discrimination from pursuing their claims by judicial process, and would consequently be liable seriously to jeopardize implementation of the aim pursued by the Directive.

Revised Equal Treatment Directive

Directive 76/207 has now been amended by Directive 2002/73 EC, which must be transposed into national law by October 2005. Based on Article 141(3), this incorporates principles developed in the case law which has been developed by the European Court of Justice and also takes into account the similar legislation which has been adopted under Article 13 EC (see below). It includes definitions of direct and indirect discrimination and sexual harassment; it also makes provision for the establishment of equality bodies and for there to be equality plans at company level. The legal protection for victims of discrimination is reinforced, notably by the possibility of action being taken by not only the victim of discrimination but also, with his or her approval, 'associations, organizations or other entities' which have a legitimate interest.

Equal treatment in matters of social security

This is covered by Directive 79/7 on statutory social security and Directive 86/378 (as amended by Directive 96/97) on occupational social security, which implement the principle of equal treatment in this field.

The purpose of Directive 79/7 is 'the progressive implementation . . . of the principle of equal treatment for men and women in the field of social security'. It therefore anticipates that this will be a process over a period of time during which the Member States adjust their national laws and regulations in order to achieve this aim. It applies to the 'working population' (Article 2), who are listed as 'self-employed persons, workers and self-employed persons whose activity is interrupted by illness, accident or involuntary employment and persons seeking employment', and to 'retired or invalided workers and self-employed persons'. It covers only certain specified categories of risk (Article 3), sickness, invalidity, accidents at work and occupational diseases, and old age.

Article 4 of Directive 79/7 sets out the basic principle of equal treatment: that there shall be no discrimination on grounds of sex, either directly or indirectly, by reference in particular to marital or family status. An example of the application of the Directive in a case concerning indirect discrimination is *Teuling*.[86] Under Dutch law all incapacitated workers were entitled to a benefit equal to 70% of the statutory minimum wage. This could be increased to 100% if the worker had a dependent spouse and children. Ms Teuling claimed that this was indirectly discriminatory against women because far fewer women than men were able to benefit from this rule. The ECJ held that, if a considerably smaller proportion of women than men were entitled to such benefits, it would be contrary to the Directive unless it could be justified by factors unrelated to sex. Although the decision whether it was justified on grounds of social policy was sent back to the national court, the ECJ appeared to accept the argument for its justification.

A number of exceptions are set out in Article 7. As well as the permanent exceptions of survivor's benefits, family benefits and occupational pension schemes, Article 7 provides for derogations. The most significant is in Article 7(1)(a), the determination of pensionable age for the granting of old age and retirement benefits and the consequences of this for other benefits.

Directive 86/378 provides for equal treatment in occupational pension schemes. Since the *Barber* judgment on occupational pensions as pay, this has limited significance. Directive 86/613 covers equal treatment in self-employment.

Treaty of Amsterdam

The Treaty of Amsterdam introduced a new article, Article 13, which enables the Community to take action concerning a wider range of discriminatory practices. It provides that:

> Without prejudice to the other provisions of this Treaty, and within the limits of the powers conferred by it upon the Community, the Council, acting unanimously on a proposal from the Commission, and after consulting the European Parliament, may take appropriate action to combat discrimination based on sex, racial or ethnic origin, religion or belief, disability, age or sexual discrimination.

Two Directives have been based on this new Article: Council Directive 2000/78 EC establishing a general framework for equal treatment in employment and occupation (the General Framework Directive) and Council Directive 2000/43 EC implementing the principle of equal treatment between persons irrespective of racial or ethnic origin (the Racial Equality Directive).

These two Directives were unanimously agreed within 18 months of the Treaty of Amsterdam coming into force. They share a number of

---

[86] Case 30/85 *Teuling v Bedrijfsvereniging voor de Chemische Industrie* [1987] ECR 2497.

features in common which distinguish them from the existing corpus of EC discrimination law. In particular, they make explicit reference to the human rights basis of non-discrimination and focus on the need to ensure effective equal treatment. Like the revised Equal Treatment Directive, there is the possibility for associations and other entities with a legitimate interest to 'engage, either on behalf or in support of the complainant, with his or her approval, in any judicial and/or administrative procedure provided for the enforcement of obligations under this Directive'. Sanctions have to be effective and proportionate.

The burden of proof is the same as in the Burden of Proof Directive. Both include specific measures to combat harassment, which is defined as 'unwanted conduct . . . with the purpose or effect of violating the dignity of a person and of creating an intimidating, hostile, degrading, humiliating or offensive environment'.

Racial equality

The Racial Equality Directive 2000/43/EC implements the principle of equal treatment between people irrespective of racial or ethnic origin. It covers discrimination in a wide range of areas: employment (including access to jobs, working conditions, rates of pay and the rights and benefits linked to employment); training; education; social security; healthcare; and access to goods and services (Article 3). Member States should have implemented it by July 2003. Its passage was in response not only to a perceived increase in racism and xenophobia in Europe but also to the inclusion of the right-wing Freedom Party in the Austrian government in February 2000.

Mark Bell[87] views the Racial Equality Directive as signally a highly significant development: 'it does not seem an overstatement to describe this instrument as one of the most significant pieces of social legislation recently adopted by the European Union'. For the first time, anti-discrimination legislation is extending beyond the sphere of employment to include discrimination in education and healthcare, both areas which until now have been largely the province of the national governments and where there has been very little scope for action by the Community.

The Framework Directive 2000/78/EC

The Framework Directive is similar in content to the Racial Equality Directive. It covers age, sexual orientation, religion or belief, and disability (Article 1). The difference between the two directives is that the scope of the Framework Directive is limited to employment and employment-related situations (Article 3). Limited exceptions are permitted – for

---

[87] M Bell 'Beyond European Labour Law? Reflections on the EU Racial Equality Directive' (2002) 8(3) *European Law Journal* 384–399 at p 384.

example, to preserve the ethos of religious organisations (Article 4) or to allow schemes designed to promote the integration of older or younger workers into the labour market (Article 6). Reasonable accommodation has to be made for disability (Article 5).

Conclusion

There is no doubt that discrimination now has a far higher profile within Community law than it did in the early years of the Community. The focus of concern has also shifted, from market integration to the rights of individuals. The new directives based on Article 13 EC certainly represent a considerable step forward in the legal protection of individuals against discrimination: the Framework Directive extends the grounds on which discrimination can be based beyond the established areas of nationality and gender; and the Racial Equality Directive takes the elimination of discrimination into new territory beyond the context of employment. Mainstreaming of an equality perspective into all aspects of Community action is explicitly provided for in the area of gender equality (Article 3(2) EC). The basis is in place for the development of a body of anti-discrimination legislation which will genuinely ensure that all citizens of the European Union are treated equally.

Further reading

Barnard, C *EC Employment Law* (2nd edn, Oxford University Press, 2000)

Bell, M *Anti-discrimination Law and the European Union* (Oxford University Press, 2002)

Craig, P and de Búrca, G *EU Law: Text, Cases and Materials* (3rd edn, Oxford University Press, 2003)

Craig, P and de Búrca, G *The Evolution of EC Law* (Oxford University Press, 1999)

Ellis, E *EC Sex Equality Law* (2nd edn, Clarendon Press, 1998)

Hervey, T *European Social Law and Policy* (Addison Wesley Longman, 1998)

Hervey, T and O'Keefe, D (eds) *Sex Equality Law in the European Union* (Wiley, 1996)

Szyszczak, E *EC Labour Law* (Pearson Education, 2000)

Journal articles

Barnard, C 'The principle of equality in the Community context: *Grant, Kalanke* and *Marschall*: four uneasy bedfellows' (1998) 57(2) *Cambridge Law Journal* 352

Bell, M and Waddington, L 'Reflecting on inequalities in European equality law' (2003) 28 *European Law Review* 349

Castro Oliveira, Á 'Workers and other persons: step by step from movement to citizenship – case law 1995–2001' (2002) 39 *Common Market Law Review* 77

Jacqueson, C 'Union citizenship and the Court of Justice: something new under the sun? Towards social citizenship' (2002) 27 *European Law Review* 260

McInerney, S 'Equal treatment between persons irrespective of racial or ethnic origin: a comment' (2000) 25 *European Law Review* 317

Reich, N with Harbacevica, S 'Citizenship and family on trial: a fairly optimistic overview of recent Court practice with regard to free movement of persons' (2003) 40 *Common Market Law Review* 615

Schiek, D 'A new framework on equal treatment of persons in EC law?' (2002) 8(2) *European Law Journal* 290

Waddington, L and Bell, M 'More equal than others: distinguishing European equality directives' (2001) 38 *Common Market Law Review* 587

The Commission campaign 'For Diversity – against Discrimination' www.stop-discrimination.info

Chapter 3

International law and discrimination

John Spencer and Maureen Spencer

Constitutional status of international law

In the United Kingdom national legislation has instituted an extensive framework for protection against discriminatory treatment. This framework is accompanied by two major European sources of law, namely the legislation derived from the European Union (EU) and the case law generated by the European Court of Human Rights. By virtue of the European Communities Act 1972 the former is an integral part of national law (see Chapter 2) and under the Human Rights Act 1998 the European Convention on Human Rights is given a defined status in UK law. Other international sources of law on discrimination are the Conventions generated by the United Nations and by the International Labour Organisation, neither of which feed directly into UK domestic law but which constitute significant treaty obligations.

For the most part, international law provisions in relation to social, political and economic rights set out minimum not maximum standards and it is generally the case that such standards will be separately acknowledged in existing UK national law. However, where the express or implied words of a national statute or prerogative order contradict international law provisions the former will prevail. In addition, unlike the position in relation to EU law, there is no court comparable to the European Court of Justice to enforce compliance with United Nations or ILO anti-discrimination measures. By virtue of s 2 of the Human Rights Act 1998 the case law of the European Court of Human Rights (ECHR) must be taken into account by national courts, but need not necessarily be followed. The ECHR cannot enforce its jurisdiction but clearly there is overwhelming political and moral pressure, as well as treaty obligations, for the United Kingdom to comply.

International treaty obligations may provide guidance when a court is called upon to interpret an ambiguous statute. There are also examples where legislation has been introduced to implement the Strasbourg

Court's rulings, one of the most recent being the Gender Recognition Bill, July 2003, which is expected to go before Parliament in 2004.

History

International law documents on discrimination fall into two groups: those emanating from the United Nations, including the provisions of the ILO; and various regional declarations and constitutions, including those of the Council of Europe.

United Nations

International human rights documents almost always include declarations in favour of equality. Thus the United Nations Charter, which came into force in October 1945, had the aim of achieving international co-operation 'in promoting and encouraging respect for human rights and for fundamental freedoms for all without distinction as to race, sex, language or religion' (Article 1(3)). The Universal Declaration of Human Rights 1948 states:

> Everyone is entitled to all the rights and freedoms set forth in this declaration without distinction of any kind, such as race, colour, sex, language, religion, political or other opinion, national or social origin, property, birth or other status.

The language of these documents is in marked contrast to that of UK legislation: UK law contains no general guarantee of equality and prohibits discrimination in a limited range of specific areas of activity. Outside these areas discrimination is lawful. By contrast, the documents of the United Nations in particular stress the need for equality alongside non-discrimination. Thus, a recognised aim of the United Nations is 'Promoting and encouraging respect for human rights and fundamental freedoms for all' (Article 3).

Before 1945 there was no general international law protecting individual rights. International law primarily regulated relations between states, not between states and their citizens. The main impetus towards setting out international yardsticks for the just treatment of the world's citizens was the Second World War and its aftermath, with western allied powers, above all the USA, taking the initiative in pressing for a new world organisation. As far as the United Kingdom was concerned, however, human rights declarations were not needed at home. As Brian Simpson (2001, p 39) puts it: 'the establishment of the United Nations, and the numerous references to human rights in its charter, had no direct impact on British domestic policy or legal culture'. They were an aspect of foreign relations, particularly engagement in the Cold War, not domestic government.

It is hardly a matter of surprise that the leading powers were initially opposed to any mechanism for enforcing rather vague and aspirational formulations such as that in Article 55(c) of the United Nations Charter which states:

> [the] United Nations shall promote . . . universal respect for human rights and fundamental freedoms for all without distinction as to race, sex, language or religion.

The United States still tolerated anti-black legislation in the South, the United Kingdom and France were then suppressing colonial uprisings and the Soviet Union was deporting national minorities and imprisoning dissidents.

Nonetheless, the Charter articulated concepts of human rights and specifically condemned discrimination on specific grounds. In effect, the impetus was being given to the growth of a body of customary international law. The next stage was an effort to define the rights set out in the Charter. The history of the second half of the twentieth century shows the gradual extension of concepts of human rights and their acknowledgement by the international community. In pursuit of the aims of the United Nations its Economic and Social Council (ECOSOC) is empowered to 'make recommendations for the purposes of promoting respect for and observance of human rights and fundamental freedoms for all' (Article 62(2)) and also to 'prepare draft conventions for submission to the General Assembly with respect to matters falling within its competence' (Article 63(3)). In January 1946, ECOSOC established the Commission on Human Rights (CHR) whose job was to draw up an international bill of rights.

Declarations of the General Assembly are not formally legally binding on members although they form strong normative provisions. In the case of the Universal Declaration on Human Rights, its provisions form an integral part of every human rights instrument. Strictly, however, it is only those instruments that are endorsed and ratified by state signatures which have legal force as international treaties, namely Covenants and Conventions, Protocols, Charters and Pacts.

One task of the Human Rights Commission, which it delegated to a drafting committee, was to compose a comprehensive equality and non-discrimination clause which would be legally binding on those states who endorsed it. The drafting was a matter causing a great deal of controversy between states. The United Kingdom delegation was opposed to a free-standing non-discrimination provision and wanted to confine its scope to the listed Covenant rights. Finally, however, agreement was reached on what was to be Article 26 of the International Covenant on Civil and Political Rights (ICCPR) adopted by the General Assembly of the United Nations in 1966. It reads:

> All persons are equal before the law and are entitled without any discrimination to the equal protection of the law. In this respect, the law

shall prohibit any discrimination and guarantee to all persons equal and effective protection against discrimination on any ground such as race, colour, sex, language, religion, political or other opinion, national or social origin, property, birth or other status.

It is not the only provision on discrimination. Article 2(1) obliges states to ensure the rights of the Covenant to all individuals within their jurisdiction without distinction of any kind. Article 3 guarantees equal rights of men and women in enjoyment of all rights of the Covenant and other Articles contain specific obligations on non-discrimination.

Human Rights Committee

The task of monitoring the provisions of the ICCPR lies with a Human Rights Committee (HRC), which scrutinises the reports submitted by state parties and hears individual communications from states that have accepted the Optional Protocol. The United Kingdom signed the ICCPR in September 1968 but, unlike many states, has not ratified the Protocol. The HRC, in its Reports and General Comments and through the system of appointment of expert Rapporteurs who scrutinise compliance, has with the CHR developed the application of Article 26.

Article 26 is distinguished from UK law in a number of ways:

(1) It is striking that the Article lists a number of prohibited grounds of discrimination and also contains an open category of 'other status'. Its coverage is thus very comprehensive (although some groups such as the aged are not separately listed). By contrast, UK law prohibits only specific forms of discrimination in defined areas of activity. The HRC has not developed clear guidelines on which groups are eligible to come under the heading of 'other status', but has acknowledged the inclusion of a wide range of areas, including sexual orientation, family responsibility, being a grandparent, illegitimacy and citizenship.

(2) There has been some controversy over the extent of the rights protected by Article 26, which has resulted in the acknowledgement by the HRC that Article 26, unlike Article 2, is not limited to Covenant rights. This is important since it means, for example, that social and economic rights which are not included in the ICCPR are also covered. In addressing claims for discrimination in the schemes for property restitution in the former Soviet empire, the HRC has held that Article 26 applies although the ICCPR does not include a right to property. (See Choudhury (2003).)

(3) Article 26 endorses affirmative action in calling for states to guarantee all persons equal and 'effective protection' against discrimination. The HRC has stated in a General Comment that 'The principle of equality sometimes requires States parties to take affirmative action

in order to diminish or eliminate conditions which cause or help to perpetuate discrimination prohibited by the Covenant'.[1]

The HRC has also acknowledged in the General Comment that some differentiation of treatment may be acceptable if the criteria for it are reasonable and objective and if the aim is legitimate. However, some areas of discrimination are particularly suspect and claims for exceptions will require strict scrutiny. This is reinforced by other Articles in the ICCPR. The high degree of importance attached to tackling sex discrimination is shown in the wording of Article 3. Article 4 allows states to derogate certain Covenant articles in times of national emergency but prohibits derogation by measures that discriminate solely on grounds of 'race, colour, language, religion or social origin'.

Article 26 applies to indirect as well as direct discrimination. The HRC made it clear that unintended discrimination is covered. The General Comment, which stated that discrimination covers:

> . . . any distinction, exclusion, restriction or preference which is based on any ground such as race, colour, sex, language, religion, political or other opinion, national or social origin, property, birth or other status and which has the purpose or effect of nullifying or impairing the recognition, enjoyment or exercise by all persons on an equal footing, of all rights and freedoms.[2]

The comprehensive coverage of Article 26 is accompanied by other United Nations instruments which contain non-discrimination sections. Key documents are listed in Table 3.1 and some will be referred to in more detail in the sections below covering specific areas of discrimination.

The International Labour Organisation (ILO)

The International Labour Organisation was established by the signatories to the Versailles Treaty in 1919 and was in effect refounded as a United Nations specialised agency by the Philadelphia Declaration of 1944. It is the only surviving major creation of the Treaty of Versailles. Its opening statement of aims reads:

> All human beings, irrespective of race, creed or sex, have the right to pursue both their material well-being and their spiritual development in conditions for freedom and dignity, of economic security and equal opportunity.

The Organisation's objective became to ensure to all, men and women alike, a just share in the fruits of progress, in terms of wages and earnings,

---

[1] Human Rights Committee, General Comment 18, para 10.
[2] HRC, General Comment 18, para 7.

Table 3.1   UN documents containing non-discrimination provisions

1945	Charter of the United Nations
1948	Convention on the Prevention and Punishment of the Crime of Genocide
1948	Universal Declaration of Human Rights
1952	Convention on the Political Rights of Women
1959	Declaration of the Rights of the Child
1963	United Nations Declaration on the Elimination of All Forms of Racial Discrimination
1966	International Convention on the Elimination of All Forms of Racial Discrimination
1966	International Covenant on Civil and Political Rights
1966	International Covenant on Economic, Social and Cultural Rights
1967	Declaration on the Elimination of Discrimination against Women
1973	International Convention on the Suppression and Punishment of the Crime of Apartheid
1979	Convention on the Elimination of All Forms of Discrimination against Women
1980	Declaration on the Elimination of All Forms of Intolerance and of Discrimination based on Religion or Belief
1989	United Nations Convention on the Rights of the Child
1993	General Assembly Standard Rules on the Equalisation of Opportunities for Persons with Disabilities
1999	Optional Protocol to the Convention on the Elimination of All Forms of Discrimination against Women
2000	Protocol to Prevent, Suppress and Punish Trafficking of Persons, especially Women and Children, supplementing the United Nations Convention against Transnational Organised Crime.

hours and other conditions of work; to provide child welfare and maternity protection; and to guarantee equality of educational and vocational opportunity.

As a result of its particular historic status, the ILO lacks coercive machinery to enforce its standards, in the sphere of discrimination as in other areas. It is frequently thus driven back on moral exhortation and exposure of discrimination.

From its foundation the ILO campaigned against racism and racial discrimination in the workplace. The pre-war ILO adopted a series of Conventions against forced labour and slavery. It played a part in the international campaign to stamp out the crime of apartheid. More recently it has paid particular attention to the position of vulnerable and disadvantaged groups and migrant workers. It has responded to campaigns by lesbian and gay communities against discrimination on grounds of sexual orientation. Discrimination against HIV-positive workers is also a problem which the ILO has sought to address. And the ILO has recently begun pressing for an end to discrimination against older workers, taking the view that the challenges of a rising proportion of old people in the population, particularly in the developed world, require a new approach to the participation of older people in the work process.

The ILO's stance against discrimination is enshrined in the Discrimination (Employment and Occupation) Convention 1958, which aims to protect all workers against discrimination 'on the basis of race, colour, sex, religion, political opinion, national extraction, social origin', and such other criteria 'as may be determined by the Member concerned after consultation with representative employers' and workers' organisations'. There is thus potential for broadening into hitherto neglected areas such as age discrimination.

Discrimination is defined as:

> any distinction, exclusion or preference made on the basis of race, colour, sex, religion, political opinion, national extraction or social origin, which has the effect of nullifying or impairing equality of opportunity and treatment in employment or occupation.

Notably, this definition is not restricted to intentional discrimination: discrimination can be direct or indirect – what matters is the effect. States adhering to the Convention are required to establish and implement a national policy to promote equality of opportunity and treatment in employment and occupation with a view to eliminating discrimination, and to co-operate with workers' and employers' organisations in the preparation and implementation of national policy. The Convention has been ratified by 158 countries. In practice, however, the ILO is often marginalised by the industrialised nations. It has not, for example, been granted observer status at the World Trade Organisation – unlike the World Bank, the International Monetary Fund and the Organisation for Economic Co-operation and Development.

Council of Europe

The global institutional framework of the United Nations in relation to human rights was the impetus for a number of regional organisations, the most effective and prolific being the Council of Europe. The Council was set up in 1949 largely as a bulwark against communism. It promulgated the European Convention on Human Rights and Fundamental Freedoms in 1950, which came into operation in 1953. The Convention has three Articles: Article 1 defines the rights provided in the Treaty; Article 2 provides for the establishment of a court of human rights, a process of course not followed by the United Nations; and Article 3 covers miscellaneous provisions such as reservations, denunciations, signature and ratification. The Convention has been expanded by a number of additional Protocols. Article 14, covering prohibition of discrimination, provides:

> The enjoyment of the rights and freedoms set forth in this Convention shall be secured without discrimination on any ground such as sex, race, colour, language, religion, political or other opinion, national or social origin, association with a national minority, property, birth or other status.

Its wording, with the exception of 'association with a national minority', is the same as Article 26. However, unlike Article 26 of the ICCPR, Article 14 does not create a general prohibition on discrimination; it bars only discrimination relating to those rights included in the Convention. This is particularly significant since the Convention is deficient in social and economic rights. Another criticism of the Article is that it has been slow to acknowledge indirect discrimination (see *Stedman v United Kingdom*, below). However, since the Convention is a 'living instrument', the ECtHR has gradually expanded the concept of discrimination and has in recent years made a number of liberal decisions. One example is that of *Van Raalte v Netherlands*.[3] Married childless women but not men over the age of 45 were exempted from having to pay contributions towards child benefit. The applicant, who was an unmarried man over the age of 45, successfully claimed violations of Article 14 in conjunction with Protocol 1, Article 1 (the right to possessions). The Court held that there was no objective justification for the difference: women over 45 could, for example, become stepmothers.

The complication and limitations of Article 14 have been a matter of academic comment. As Livingstone (1997, p 25) puts it: 'The European Convention's anti-discrimination provision is not one beloved of many international human rights lawyers'. The weaknesses of Article 14 have led to calls for its amendment. The Council of Europe has been consistently opposed to changing the existing wording of any sections of the Convention, preferring development through Protocols. Protocol 12 is now part of the European Convention on Human Rights but is not yet in force because a sufficient number of Member States has not yet ratified it. Article 1 of the Protocol contains a general prohibition on discrimination in the following terms:

(1) The enjoyment of any right set forth by law shall be secured without discrimination on any ground such as sex, race, colour, language, religion, political or other opinion, national or social origin, association with a national minority, property, birth or other status.

(2) No one shall be discriminated against by any public authority on any ground such as those mentioned in paragraph 1.

Thus, the Protocol is a 'free-standing' prohibition of discrimination. It will eliminate the requirement under Article 14 that applicants link the facts of their case to another Convention right. This change will particularly empower victims of discrimination based on sex, race, disability or age.

The United Kingdom has refused to ratify the Protocol, maintaining its rooted opposition to a free-standing anti-discrimination clause. Its reluctance to embrace general equality provisions is shown in its complaint that with the Protocol in force 'the European Court of Human

---

[3] (1997) 24 EHRR 503.

Rights might hold that a right set out in an international agreement, but not incorporated into United Kingdom law, is covered by Protocol 12'. A spokesman noted 'new rights are not necessarily cost free (especially when they are economic, social and cultural rights) and may affect the rights of others, as many rights have to be balanced against each other'.[4]

The European Convention on Human Rights is deficient in social and economic rights. These are covered in the European Social Charter (ESC) adopted in Turin in 1961 by 11 Council of Europe Member States and subsequently amended. However, unlike the European Convention on Human Rights, this has no enforcement provisions. For the most part, its provisions mirror those of the International Covenant on Social, Economic and Cultural Rights. It has similar implementation procedures to those of United Nations Treaties, including collective but not individual complaints, and reporting systems through a Committee of Independent Experts; it has thus similar weaknesses of enforcement. The ESC coverage on discrimination issues is wide: its preamble states that 'enjoyment of social rights should be secured without discrimination on grounds of race, colour, sex, religion, political opinion, national extraction or social origin'. The rights of children and young persons, employed women and migrant workers are cited as requiring specific protection.

Discrimination on grounds of gender

United Nations

Although Article 26 sets out a wide range of grounds on which discrimination can be claimed, it does not treat all grounds in the same way. Discrimination on the basis of sex merits as a particular target, although paradoxically, out of all the human rights treaties, that outlawing discrimination against women has attracted the greatest number of reservations, particularly on grounds of religious and cultural relativism. In 1967, the UN adopted the Declaration on Elimination of Discrimination against Women and, in December 1979, the Convention on the Elimination of All Forms of Discrimination Against Women (CEDAW) was adopted by the UN General Assembly. It is now an international treaty (known as the Treaty for the Rights of Women) to which 174 countries have adhered. The Convention is the main international instrument outlawing discrimination against women.

Article 1 of CEDAW defines discrimination against women as:

> . . . any distinction, exclusion or restriction made on the basis of sex
> which has the effect or purpose of impairing or nullifying the recognition,

---

[4] *Hansard* HL, WA 14, 23 October 2000; WA 45, 25 October 2000. (See Choudhury and Moon, p. 295.)

> enjoyment or exercise by women, irrespective of their marital status, on
> a basis of equality of men and women, of human rights and fundamental
> freedoms in the political, economic, social, cultural, civil or any other field.

The Convention begins realistically by acknowledging the continued existence of extensive discrimination against women in violation of the principles of equality of rights and respect for human dignity which lie at the root of the United Nations ethos.

All states which are party to CEDAW are required by Article 3 to take 'all appropriate measures, including legislation, to ensure the full development and advancement of women, for the purpose of guaranteeing them the exercise and enjoyment of human rights and fundamental freedoms on a basis of equality with men'.

The Convention then sets out an agenda for equality, covering women's civil rights and legal status, but dealing in addition with the 'third dimension' – human reproduction and the impact of cultural factors on gender relations.

CEDAW consolidates a number of previous conventions on the rights and status of women. In 1952 the United Nations adopted a Convention on the Political Rights of Women, which guaranteed women the right to vote, to hold public office and to exercise public functions, including the function of representing their countries at international level. These rights, which are still a matter of contestation in many parts of the world, are reaffirmed in CEDAW.

Article 15 states that women should enjoy full equality in civil and business matters, and that all national laws directed at restricting women's legal capacity 'shall be deemed null and void'. Article 16 asserts women's equality with men in the choice of spouse, and in the sphere of parenthood, personal rights and command over property.

A major feature of CEDAW is its emphasis on women's reproductive rights. The principle asserted in the Convention is that 'the role of women in procreation should not be a basis for discrimination'. This concern is taken up at several points in the body of the Convention. Article 5, for example, advocates 'a proper understanding of maternity as a social function', stressing the need for both sexes to take an equal share of responsibility for child-rearing.

Maternity protection and child-care provisions are asserted to be essential rights, and the Convention links these rights into its provisions relating to employment, family law, health care and education. States should offer social services, especially child-care facilities, which allow individuals to combine family responsibilities with work and participation in public life. Article 4 recommends special measures for maternity protection and provides that such provisions 'shall not be considered discriminatory'.

The Convention also affirms women's right to reproductive choice. It is the only human rights treaty to mention family planning, obliging states parties to include advice on family planning in the education process and to develop family codes that guarantee women's rights 'to decide freely and responsibly on the number and spacing of their children and to have access to the information, education and means to enable them to exercise these rights'.

One of CEDAW's objectives is to enlarge understanding of the concept of human rights, by giving formal recognition to the influence of culture and tradition on restricting the scope of women's exercise of fundamental rights. The Convention emphasises that the stereotypes, customs and norms which embody these constraints on women's advancement cannot be overcome without a change in the traditional role of men.

States parties are therefore required to work towards the elimination of 'prejudices and customary and all other practices which are based on the idea of the inferiority or the superiority of either of the sexes or on stereotyped roles for men and women'. This includes the revision of textbooks, school programmes and teaching methods. In particular, CEDAW targets cultural patterns which define the public sphere as a man's world and the domestic sphere as a woman's domain. It aims to provide a comprehensive framework for challenging the social, economic and cultural forces that have created and sustained discrimination based upon sex.

Monitoring of the implementation of CEDAW is in the hands of a committee of 23 experts nominated by their own governments to receive regular reports from the states parties. The states are expected to set out the measures they have adopted to secure compliance with the Convention. Many of the signatory states – the United Kingdom included – have entered reservations against parts of the treaty. The United States has not signed the treaty, although the administration has listed it among treaties it believes to be 'generally desirable' and which should be approved.

The UK derogations are designed to protect existing provisions for succession to the throne, peerages and social precedence. The government has also signalled that it will not introduce sex equality into the armed forces. There was widespread international criticism of some of the derogations, particularly by states with a predominantly Islamic population. Saudi Arabia, for example, simply stated: 'In the case of contradiction between any term of the convention and the norms of Islamic law, the Kingdom is not under obligation to observe the contradictory terms of the convention.' A reservation in such wide terms was criticised as raising doubts about the signatory's commitment to the Convention. Non-governmental organisations monitoring human rights have highlighted the extent of discrimination against women in Saudi Arabia and some other Islamic states.

The gap between the rhetoric of international discourse and the situation on the ground has been repeatedly highlighted. For example, in its millennium report, 'Lives Together, Worlds Apart', the UN Population

Fund complained that, in countries all over the world, gender inequality, discrimination and violence are holding back not only women but entire communities, societies and, indeed, whole nations. A fund spokeswoman said:

> Today one women in three will be subjected to violence in her lifetime. Some two million girls between the ages of 5 and 15 are bought and sold worldwide, forced into marriage, slavery or prostitution. Every year 5,000 girls are the victims of so-called honour crimes [and] sometimes their dishonour is having been raped.

She pointed out: 'Studies show that societies where gender discrimination is greatest have more poverty and an overall lesser quality of life for their people.'[5]

States are required to take positive action to end discrimination against women. In General Comment 28, the HRC stated that states should 'review their legislation and practices and take the lead in implementing all measures necessary in order to eliminate discriminations against women, in all fields, for example by prohibiting discrimination by private actors in areas such as employment, education, political activities and the provision of accommodation, goods and services'.[6] Arguably, the Sex Discrimination Act 1975 does not fulfil these stringent requirements. For example, although the legislation allows positive action to be taken to encourage women workers and potential workers and to provide training this does not include providing jobs.[7]

The International Labour Organisation took a pioneering stance in relation to sex discrimination: in 1951 it adopted Convention No 100 on equal compensation for men and women for work of equal value. This established for the first time the legal principle that compensation rates for work of equal value must be set with no discrimination based on sex. The Convention provides that compensation includes regular, primary or minimum wages or minimum salaries, and any other compensation provided directly or otherwise in cash or in kind by the employer to the employee for work performed by the latter.

Council of Europe

Compliance with treaty requirements has been one of the motives for wide-ranging equality legislation introduced in Britain in the last quarter-century. This has been bolstered by decisions of the European Court of Human Rights, according only a very limited margin of appreciation to states in relation to sex discrimination.

---

[5] See www.unfpa.org/swp/2000/pdf/english.
[6] HRC, General Comment 28, Equality of Rights between Men and Women, para 31.
[7] See further Choudhury and Moon, p. 303.

The key case is *Schmidt v Germany*,[8] which concerned a regional provision requiring male but not female adults either to perform local fire brigade duties or to pay a financial levy. The German constitutional court had regarded the difference as objectively justified. However, the ECtHR found that, since women as well as men served in the fire brigade, there was no such justification and the provision constituted a breach of the Human Rights Convention. The Court observed that very strong reasons were required to justify difference of treatment on grounds of sex.

In relation to equal pay and employment conditions the European Human Rights Convention has been overshadowed by the far more robust provisions of the European Community, motivated in part by the aim of achieving a level economic playing field. However, the European Convention on Human Rights is having an increasingly important effect in the field of protecting the human rights of homosexuals. Thus, in *Smith and Grady v United Kingdom*,[9] the ECtHR held that sexuality is a private matter and rules which invade people's privacy as to their sexuality or which discriminate on the grounds of sexuality may be in violation of Article 8 of the European Convention. In this case, investigation into the applicants' homosexuality resulted in their discharge from the Navy, in pursuit of a policy of excluding homosexuals from the forces. The applicants complained of degrading treatment and violation of their right to a private life. They also complained that they had no effective remedy. The Court held that, although the interference with the applicants' right to respect for private life was 'in accordance with law' and could be said to pursue legitimate national security aims, the perceived problems of allowing homosexuals in the armed forces were founded solely on the negative attitudes of heterosexual personnel. Article 8 had been violated but the applicants' treatment was not so severe as to constitute degrading treatment. The case illustrates the importance of Article 8 – the right to respect for private and family life – in upholding discrimination claims on grounds of gender.

The importance of Article 8 in relation to discrimination is demonstrated also in the case of *Goodwin v United Kingdom*.[10] Two post-operative male to female transsexuals faced difficulties in matters such as pensions and national insurance because they were still regarded as legally male. The ECtHR held that there was a violation of Article 8 and the government could no longer rely on a margin of appreciation in view of changes in attitudes to transsexuals. The decision led the UK government to introduce the Gender Recognition Bill in July 2003 to allow transsexual people to gain legal recognition in their acquired gender.

[8]   (1994) 18 EHRR 513.
[9]   (2000) 29 EHRR 493.
[10]   (2002) 35 EHRR 18.

Racial discrimination

United Nations

The concept of equality and specifically non-discrimination on grounds of race is a recurrent theme in United Nations documents. In addition specific treaties on racial discrimination have been promulgated. The International Convention on the Elimination of All Forms of Racial Discrimination (the Race Convention) was adopted on 21 December 1965 and put into force on 4 January 1969. Member States have shown a great degree of unanimity on this issue and it is one of the most widely ratified treaties, support being in part inspired initially by the international campaign against South Africa's apartheid regime. The Convention defines 'racial discrimination' in Article 1(1) as 'any distinction, exclusion, restriction or preference based on race, colour, descent, or national or ethnic origin which has the purpose or effect of nullifying or impairing the recognition, enjoyment or exercise, on an equal footing, of human rights and fundamental freedoms in the political, economic, social, cultural or any other field of public life'.

Two specific controversial limitations of this definition should be noted. First, discrimination in Article 1 is apparently confined to 'public' places. It, however, appears that the Convention contains a broader scope in Article 2(1)(d) and Article 5. The former requires as follows:

> Each state party shall prohibit and bring to an end, by all appropriate means, including legislation as required by circumstances, racial discrimination by any persons, group or organisation.

Article 5 of the Convention obliges state parties to guarantee the enjoyment of civil, political, economic, social and cultural rights and freedoms without racial discrimination. A number of civil rights are listed but this is not an exhaustive list. Thus it is the case that, where private institutions or individuals influence the exercise of a right on the availability of opportunities, the state has an obligation to ensure that the result is not racially discriminatory.

The second controversial area is that of the scope of the Convention in relation to non-citizens. The Convention makes very clear exceptions. Article 1(2) reads: 'This Convention shall not apply to distinctions, exclusions, restrictions or preferences made by states party to this convention between citizens and non-citizens.' Article 1(3) reads:

> Nothing in this Convention may be interpreted as affecting in any way the legal provisions of states parties concerning nationality, citizenship or naturalisation, provided that such provisions do not discriminate against any particular nationality.

Thus, under international law non-nationals can be denied equal treatment and many states have used denial of citizenship as a means of discrimination.

Article 2 of the Convention imposes stringent specific obligations of action on the part of states:

> States parties condemn racial discrimination and undertake to pursue
> by all appropriate means and without delay a policy of eliminating racial
> discrimination in all its forms and promoting understanding among
> all races.

It lists specific forms of action. Thus, states have both positive obligations to introduce measures to combat racial discrimination and negative obligations to refrain from racially discriminatory practices. In addition, Article 1(4) permits affirmative action.

Article 4 has aroused a certain amount of controversy since, in condemning racist propaganda, it might arguably interfere with freedom of speech. In particular, states are required to 'declare illegal and prohibit organisations, and also organised and all other propaganda activities which promote and incite racial discrimination, and shall recognise participation in such organisations or activities as an offence punishable by law'.

Less controversially, Article 6 requires states to ensure that victims of discrimination have means of redress. Article 7 requires states to promote anti-racism actively: they should adopt immediate and effective measures, 'particularly in the field of teaching, education, culture and information, with a view to combating prejudices which lead to racial discrimination and to promoting understanding, tolerance and friendship among nations and racial or ethnical groups as well as to propagating the purposes and principles of the Charter of the United Nations, the Universal Declaration of Human Rights, the United Nations Declaration on the Elimination of All Forms of Racial Discrimination and this Convention'.

The International Convention on the Elimination of All Forms of Racial Discrimination was the first human rights instrument to include measures for the implementation of its content. Article 8 of the Convention established the Committee on the Elimination of All Forms of Racial Discrimination (CERD), which reviews the states' performance of the Convention and its implementation. The 18 members are 'experts of high moral standing and acknowledged impartiality elected by States Parties from among their nationals . . .'; they serve for four years. The key implementation mechanism is the reporting procedure whereby states send annual reports to the CERD, which in turn reports annually to the General Assembly through the Secretary-General. It is generally acknowledged that the CERD's scrutiny of the state reports is successful. Rehman (2003, p 291) writes:

> Despite the often considerable delay in receiving State reports, with frequent
> and significant omissions or lack of information, the flexibility and ingenuity
> with which the Committee has performed its task has made the reporting
> procedure a success. Its flexibility in receiving delayed reports, the use of
> a variety of sources of information alongside the content of the report,

providing guidance as to the content of the state reports, and accommodating a system of examination of reports have all contributed towards a positive element.

There are other procedures open to the committee, including individual or group Communications, and the inter-state complaints procedure, but they are less frequently employed. A number of states, including the United Kingdom, have not ratified the Communications procedure.

It goes without saying that recent world events, as well as racial and ethnic tensions in some UK cities underline that bringing an end to racial discrimination is far from achieved. The United Kingdom has come under criticism from the CERD, specifically in 1996 on the submission of its 13th periodic report. Specific causes for concern included the higher unemployment rate of ethnic minorities and the fact that 'not enough has been done to inquire into causes of [racist] attacks and the manifestation of racist ideas'. (See Parratt and Foley (1996, p 385).) Overall, the CERD has received applause for its work: Egon Schwelb (1966, p 1057), for example, has described the Convention as 'the most comprehensive and unambiguous codification in treaty form of the idea of the equality of races'.

Council of Europe

The European Convention on Human Rights protects against racial discrimination in a number of ways. Such discrimination may amount to degrading treatment under Article 3. In *East African Asians v United Kingdom*[11] the Commission was asked to decide whether the discriminatory effect of United Kingdom immigration legislation could be regarded as degrading treatment under Article 3 on the grounds that 'to single out a group of persons for different treatment on the basis of race may constitute a special form of affront to human dignity and might therefore be capable of constituting degrading treatment'. The applicants were citizens of the United Kingdom and colonies and husbands of Commonwealth citizens who were already resident in the United Kingdom. Although the legislation would have permitted wives to come into the United Kingdom to join their husbands, the husbands were refused entry. The Commission held that in relation to one group of applicants 'the racial discrimination' to which they had been publicly subjected by the legislation constituted 'an interference with their human dignity which amounted to ... degrading treatment in the sense of Article 3 of the Convention'. This group had been promised free entry to the United Kingdom and their continued residence in East Africa was illegal and they were stateless. With regard to another group of 'protected persons' who were not British subjects, since the legislation did not distinguish between categories of

---

[11] (1981) 3 EHRR 76.

persons on any racial basis there was no violation of Article 3. Thus, although the use of immigration controls is not in itself a violation of the European Convention on Human Rights, controls based on racial discrimination could amount to degrading treatment.

However, the ECHR found sexual but not racial discrimination in *Abdulaziz, Cabales and Balkandali v United Kingdom.*[12] The husbands of three women immigrants who were lawfully and permanently settled in the United Kingdom were not allowed to join them. Again, the rules then in place applied more strictly to men wishing to join partners than women or nationals of EU Member States. The Court held that the difference of treatment complained of did not denote any contempt or lack of respect for the personality of the applicants and was not designed to, and did not, humiliate or debase but was intended solely to achieve policy aims. Article 3 was accordingly not violated; nor was Article 8 standing alone violated since the obligation to respect family life could not be held to extend to a right of couples to live where they chose. However, since the state had extended the right to bring a family into the country to non-national men, Article 14 taken with Article 8 was breached. There had been violations of Articles 13 and 14 on the grounds of sexual discrimination, although the rule was not racially discriminatory.

These cases illustrate that, although Article 14 is formally parasitic on the other Convention Articles, the ECHR has in fact allowed it an autonomous existence to some extent. In *Abdulaziz, Cabales and Balkandali v United Kingdom*, for example, there was no breach alone of a substantive Article but the Court found a breach of Article 14. At the other extreme, where there has been a breach of the substantive article the Court will often conclude that it is not necessary to consider Article 14 as in the *East African Asian Case.*

The limitations of the European Convention on Human Rights in relation to racial discrimination are illustrated in the case of *Smith v United Kingdom.*[13] The applicant was a gypsy who claimed that as a result of a UK law she was criminalised in relation to accommodation. The offence of parking a caravan outside a designated area was arguably discriminatory since it applied only to gypsies. She alleged breaches of Articles 8, 11 and 14. The Commission held that, since the applicant had not proved that the law had a real and direct effect on her way of life, there were no breaches of Article 8 or 11. Since there were no substantive breaches it followed that Article 14 was not breached.

By contrast, a more robust approach to racial discrimination is illustrated in the case of *Sander v United Kingdom.*[14] After a trial where the Asian applicant was the defendant, a juror had transmitted a note to the judge indicating that another juror had made racist comments in the

---

[12] (1985) 7 EHRR 471.
[13] (1993) 18 EHRR CD 65.
[14] (2000) 8 BHRC 2791.

jury room. The judge had given the jury a redirection. The applicant was convicted and alleged a violation of Article 6. The ECtHR held that a tribunal must be impartial from a subjective as well as an objective point of view. Racial comments by jurors are a very serious matter in today's multi-cultural Europe. This was not redressed by the judge's redirection to the jury; the judge should have reacted in a more robust manner. There was a violation of Article 6(1), the right to a fair trial.

Discrimination on grounds of religion and political belief

United Nations

A number of international documents condemn intolerance on grounds of religion or belief. Thus, Articles 1(3) and 13 of the United Nations Charter condemn discrimination on grounds of religion or belief. Other references are contained in the Universal Declaration on Human Rights and the International Covenant on Civil and Political Rights. In 1981, the United Nations made a Declaration on the Elimination of All Forms of Intolerance and Discrimination based on Religion or Belief. This is a non-binding General Assembly resolution. In practice, these statements have not led to vigorous action to combat religious or political discrimination. In some ways there has been a watering-down of protection. For example, the ICCPR granted the 'freedom to have or to adopt' a religion or belief but the 1981 Declaration makes no reference to this. There is no international consensus on what constitutes a religion or a religious minority; and, while some religious groups are protected, others within the same state are persecuted.

As Rehman (2003, p 275) points out:

> there is a strong tendency among religions to invoke complete and absolute submission and in the process they are likely to affect many aspects of human life including matrimonial and family affairs, family planning, care of children, inheritance, public order, food and diet, and freedom of expression and association. The collective dimension of religious freedom raises complex issues within the individualistic framework of human rights in domestic and international law.

The outcome has been that international human rights law has had limited effect on safeguarding religious freedom. Divisions and acrimony dogged this sensitive issue in contrast to the more widespread consensus on racial discrimination. Thus, there has been no international treaty on the elimination of discrimination based on religion or belief. There are, however, some positive developments. The Human Rights Committee has used Article 18 of the ICCPR to invoke the reporting, individual communication and general comment procedures to spell out the ambit of religious tolerance. In 1992, the General Assembly passed the Declaration on the Rights of Persons Belonging to National, Ethnic, Religious and Linguistic Minorities, thus highlighting the need for protection of religious minorities. The Convention on the Rights of the Child 1989 enshrines the principle of non-discrimination against children whatever their religious beliefs. Finally, the Rapporteur system has been employed to highlight instances of discrimination and to encourage religious toleration within states. The United Kingdom has no legislation outlawing discrimination on grounds of political belief. The Employment Equality (Religion or Belief) Regulations 2003 make it unlawful to discriminate on grounds of religion or belief in employment.

The International Labour Organisation has also taken a characteristically principled stand: in 1989 it passed Convention No 169 on Indigenous and Tribal Peoples, which calls for states to protect the beliefs of indigenous peoples.

Council of Europe

Article 9 of the European Convention on Human Rights states:

1. Everyone has the right to freedom of thought, conscience and religion; this right includes freedom to change his religion or belief, and freedom, either alone or in community with others and in public or private, to manifest his religion or belief, in worship, teaching, practice and observance.

2. Freedom to manifest one's religion or beliefs shall be subject only to such limitations as are prescribed by law and are necessary in a democratic society in the interests of public safety, for the protection of public order, health or morals, or the protection of the rights and freedoms of others.

It follows that individuals should not be penalised or discriminated against on these grounds unless one of the limitations applies. The Strasbourg court has held that the article protects atheist views. Thus, in *Kokkinakis v Greece*[15] it stated that Article 9 'is in its religious dimension one of the most vital elements that go to make up the identity of believers and their conception of life, but it is also a precious asset for atheists, agnostics, sceptics and the unconcerned'. In this case the applicant and his wife were Jehovah's Witnesses who were sentenced to prison for proselytising. He complained of breaches of Articles 7, 9 and 10 on the grounds that no clear dividing line could be drawn between proselytism and freedom to change one's religion or belief and to manifest it. The Court held that the applicant's conviction was not justified by a pressing social need, proportionate to the legitimate aims of maintaining social order or 'necessary in a democratic society . . . for the protection of the rights and freedoms of others'. On the other hand, professional or contractual

[15] (1994) 17 EHRR 397.

obligations may justify apparently discriminatory treatment. In *Stedman v United Kingdom,*[16] the applicant was dismissed after 22 months' employment because she refused to accept an amendment to her contract of employment requiring that she work on Sundays. She complained that the exercise of her Christian faith had been interfered with and claimed violations of Articles 6, 8, 9 and 14. The Commission, however, rejected her case on the grounds that her dismissal was not based on her religious conviction. The case illustrates that the Court is slow to accept the concept of indirect discrimination.

Arguments have been put that, by uniquely protecting the Christian religion, the English blasphemy laws infringe Articles 9 and 14. In *Choudhury v United Kingdom,*[17] the applicant had sought unsuccessfully to prosecute the publisher of Salman Rushdie's *Satanic Verses* for blasphemy. The English courts ruled that the offence applied only to attacks on Christianity and did not protect Islam. The applicant complained under Articles 9 and 14. However, the Commission found no link between freedom from interference with Article 9 rights and the applicant's complaints, and so the discrimination complaint was also rejected. Arguably, a pluralist society should not accept a criminal law which protects just one religion; but neither would it be acceptable to criminalise attacks on all religions.

Discrimination against public sector employees on political grounds may be a violation of Articles 10 and 11. In *Vogt v Germany,*[18] a teacher had been sacked from her post because her active membership of the Communist Party was considered incompatible with her duties. In a landmark decision, the ECHR held that Articles 10 and 11 were violated. In another blow against discriminatory practices in public sector employment, the Court has held that the right not to be discriminated against on grounds of religious belief or political opinion in employment is a civil right within the meaning of Article 6(1). In *Devlin v United Kingdom,*[19] the applicant was a Catholic and a member of the Irish National Foresters who had been unsuccessful in his application for the post of administrative assistant with the Northern Ireland Civil Service. Following several appeals, the Secretary of State for Northern Ireland issued a certificate stating that the refusal was an act 'done for the purpose of safeguarding national security and protecting the public'. The applicant was refused permission to challenge this by judicial review. He complained that his rights under Article 6(1) were infringed. Previous decisions of the ECHR had held that, where the incumbent of a public post is 'wielding a portion of the state's sovereign power', Article 6(1) did not apply. The post of administrative assistant was held not to fall

---

[16] (1997) 23 EHRR CD 169.
[17] (Application No 17439/90) (1991) 12 HRLJ 172.
[18] (1995) 21 EHRR 205.
[19] (2002) 34 EHRR 43.

into this category. There was no independent scrutiny of the facts and no evidence as to why the applicant was a security risk. Article 6(1) was breached.

National minorities and indigenous peoples

United Nations

The presence within a state of ethnic, religious or linguistic minorities may give rise to particular problems. Such minorities have suffered historically from discrimination and repression, but the issue has received comparatively little attention until recently. Among the reasons for this relative neglect are the conceptual conflicts between the presence of minorities and the theory of the nation-state, developed during the nineteenth century. Constitution makers tended to ignore the specific needs of minorities within the state, and generally made little provision for them, perhaps fearing that to do so might encourage separatism. A related but somewhat different set of problems is raised by the presence within a national state of indigenous peoples, such as Aboriginals in Australia, Maoris in New Zealand, Amerindians in much of the New World, with particular demands and grievances.

A complete exposition of the international law relating to minorities and indigenous peoples is outside the scope of this chapter and it is sufficient to highlight the main relevant international instruments. These are the United Nations Declaration on the Rights of Persons Belonging to National or Ethnic, Religious or Linguistic Minorities 1992. Article 1 of this declaration provides:

> States shall protect the existence and the national or ethnic, cultural, religious and linguistic identity of minorities within their respective territories, and shall encourage conditions for the promotion of that identity.

The declaration sets out the right of persons belonging to minorities to enjoy their own culture, to profess and practise their own religion, and to use their own language, in private and in public, freely and without interference or any form of discrimination. Such persons have the right to participate effectively in cultural, religious, social, economic and public life and in decisions on the national and, where appropriate, regional level concerning the minority to which they belong. They have the right to establish and maintain their own associations and can also maintain, without any discrimination, free and peaceful contacts with other members of their group and with persons belonging to other minorities, as well as contacts across frontiers with citizens of other states to whom they are related by national or ethnic, religious or linguistic ties.

It will be noted that the rights are accorded, not to the minority as an entity, but to the members of the minority. This limitation arises from an unwillingness, already noted, to trespass too far on the purlieus of the national state. Since the passage of the declaration, a monitoring mechanism has been established, consisting of a five-member working group.

In the final quarter of the twentieth century many indigenous peoples powerfully asserted their specific demands for human rights, forcing their specific requirements onto the international law agenda. Indigenous peoples seek the right to self-determination and rights of self-government, autonomy, territorial integrity and exclusive enjoyment of their lands and resources. Generalisation is dangerous, but it is safe to say that the representatives of indigenous peoples have in many cases recognised that their right to self-determination is unlikely to be fulfilled by the creation of new nation states, a form of national organisation that is regarded by many with distrust, in the light of their national experience. The emphasis is rather on freedom to be themselves.

Particular attention has focused on the effect of environmental change on indigenous peoples, who require to control the use of natural resources if their way of life is to survive. Autonomy has been chosen for indigenous peoples in such countries as Greenland, Canada, Nicaragua and Panama, with some success, but the search for a satisfactory constitutional form which can accommodate the indigenous peoples' demands is ongoing.

Council of Europe

In 1995 the Council of Europe passed the Framework Convention for the Protection of National Minorities.

Discrimination on grounds of trade union membership

United Nations

The right to form and join trade unions is formally protected in international human rights documents, including those emanating from the United Nations, the Council of Europe and the International Labour Organisation. United Kingdom trade unions have been awarded favourable decisions most frequently by the ILO. Protection from discrimination on grounds of trade union membership is embedded in the International Covenant on Economic, Social and Cultural Rights, which includes a right to strike provision.

Labour rights particularly are vulnerable to changes in the national political climate. As new liberal and monetarist views have prevailed, a number of developed countries (including the United Kingdom) have eroded rights such as freedom of association and the right to bargain. The current Labour government has failed to repeal much of the legislation which undermined trade union rights (see Chapter 10).

Council of Europe

Trade union members have found in a number of cases that the protection afforded by Article 11 of the European Convention on Human Rights is limited. Article 11 specifies that:

> Everyone has the right to freedom of peaceful assembly and to freedom of association with others, including the right to form and to join trade unions for the protection of his interests.

The ECHR has held that discrimination on grounds of trade union membership should protect the right not to join as well as the right to join, although arguably the former negative position has no social value, being regarded by some critics as similar to the right not to vote. In *Young, James and Webster v United Kingdom*[20] the applicants were dismissed by British Rail because they were not in the union and the enterprise operated a 'closed shop'. The ECHR held that the applicants thereby suffered a breach of their right to freedom of association under Article 11. Thus, the European Convention was chiefly concerned with the rights of individuals, seen as needing defence against trade union might.

On the other hand, in the recent case of *Wilson v United Kingdom, Palmer v United Kingdom*,[21] the ECHR unanimously found a breach of Article 11 in a case arising out of union de-recognition. Wilson was an NUJ member at the *Daily Mail* and the other applicants were employees of Associated British Ports. The applicants had refused to accept new contracts based on individual pay scales when the employers 'de-recognised' the unions. The House of Lords had upheld the employers' stance. The Strasbourg court found that the United Kingdom did effectively frustrate the trade unions' ability to protect their members. In allowing employers to use financial incentives to encourage employees to give up their union rights, the United Kingdom had not observed Article 11. The decision illustrates that states have positive obligations to ensure that trade union members are not subject to discrimination.

Civil and political rights, including trade union rights, are comprehensively protected in the European Social Charter. It sets out policy areas and a number of substantive rights, particularly in Article 5 (the right to organise) and Article 6 (the right to bargain collectively).

---

[20] [1983] IRLR 35.
[21] (2002) 35 EHRR 20.

Discrimination on grounds of disability

United Nations

International treaties have not specified protection for the disabled except in relation to disabled children. Thus, Article 23 of the Convention on the Rights of the Child, first adopted in 1989, requires that states parties recognise the rights of mentally and physically disabled children to have a decent living and ensure that they have a life of dignity and self-reliance and are enabled to participate in the life of the community. The Article also requires resources to be directed to this end.

In addition, a number of Declarations have been made on disability discrimination, particularly after the International Year of the Disabled and the adoption by the General Assembly of the World Programme of Action concerning Disabled Persons. This programme promoted the rights of persons with disabilities to the same opportunities as other citizens and to an equal share in the improvements in living conditions resulting from economic and social development. In June 1993 the World Conference on Human Rights in Vienna affirmed that: 'Special attention needs to be paid to ensuring non-discrimination, and the equal enjoyment of all human rights and fundamental freedoms by disabled persons, including their active participation in all aspects of society.'

Standard Rules on the Equalisation of Opportunities for Persons with Disabilities were adopted by the General Assembly in December 1993. These are not legally binding but are an important measure of areas of discrimination and underline the moral and political basis of the need for governments to take action to prevent discrimination on grounds of disability. The rules form a basis for national policymaking and for technical and economic co-operation. They document different areas of disability, including physical, intellectual or sensory impairment, medical conditions or mental illness, both permanent and temporary. Handicap is 'the loss or limitation of opportunities to take part in the life of the community on an equal level with others. It describes the encounter between the person with a disability and the environment.' The term is used in the Rules to emphasise the focus on the shortcomings in the environment and in many organised activities in society – for example, information, communication and education – which prevent persons with disabilities from participating on equal terms.

The Rules stress that current terminology recognises the necessity of addressing both the individual needs (such as rehabilitation and technical aids) and the shortcomings of the society (various obstacles to participation). The 22 Rules concerning disabled persons are grouped into four chapters covering preconditions, target areas, implementation measures and monitoring mechanisms. Target areas include accessibility, education, employment, income maintenance and social security, and family life and personal integrity.

The fact that there is, as yet, no specific United Nations Convention on the rights of the disabled suggests that protection in this area is weaker than, for example, in relation to racial discrimination. The Commission for Social Development has the prime responsibility for monitoring the Rules. There is provision also for the institution of a special Rapporteur with relevant extensive experience and for the formation of an advisory panel of experts for organisations representing persons with disabilities.

Additional protection against discrimination of the disabled arises from the decision that the Committee on Economic, Social and Cultural Rights has responsibility 'to monitor the compliance of states parties to the Covenant with their obligation to ensure the full enjoyment of the relevant rights by persons with disabilities'. Significantly, however, the Covenant on Economic, Social and Cultural Rights does not refer explicitly to persons with disabilities, and the lack of awareness of what needs to be done to redress imbalances is shown by a failure to direct adequate resources to combat disability discrimination.

Added encouragement to states to address disability discrimination is provided by the International Labour Organisation, which has developed wide-ranging instruments covering work-related rights of persons with disabilities. Consultation No 159 (1983) deals with vocational rehabilitation and employment of persons with disabilities.

An area of growing concern in discrimination terms is discrimination against HIV-positive people. The United Nations has become seized of the matter primarily through the World Health Organisation, but its human rights aspect arises from concerns about the availability of treatment for HIV-AIDS, particularly in third world countries where infection with the HIV virus is widespread. The campaign to make cheap retroviral drugs available in Africa and elsewhere has led to some relaxation of trade rules to permit generic production under controlled conditions. The ILO has expressed concern about such practices as mandatory HIV testing in the workplace, breaches of confidentiality of HIV-related information and stigmatisation of HIV-positive workers.

Council of Europe

The European Convention on Human Rights provides no freestanding right not to be discriminated against on grounds of disability. In *Botta v Italy*[22] the physically disabled applicant found that there were no adequate facilities at his holiday resort. Under Italian law private beaches are required to facilitate the access of disabled people. There were no proceedings against the local authorities for failing to enforce the relevant law. The applicant alleged violations of various Articles including Article 14, the prohibition of discrimination. The Commission declared admissible the applications under certain of the Articles, including Article 14,

[22] (1998) 26 EHRR 241.

but the ECtHR held that on the facts the case did not fall under any Convention right. Article 14 therefore could not apply.

The European Social Charter does specify employment protection for the disabled. Part 1 includes the following provision: 'Disabled persons have the right to vocational training, rehabilitation and resettlement, whatever the nature and origin of their disability.'

Conclusion

The above account illustrates that from 1945 onwards (or 1919 in the case of the ILO) international human rights documents have proclaimed both the general principles of equality and non-discrimination and also specific protections for what were held to be particularly vulnerable groups. Some significant aspects of these proclamations are listed below:

1. Hierarchy of protection

In both international and domestic anti-discrimination law the highest and most general levels of protection expressly and impliedly are given to discrimination on grounds of race and sex. Less protection is given in more controversial areas such as religion.

2. Weakness of enforcement measures

The European Convention has its own court to ensure compliance but even there no sanctions are available, by contrast to the position in EU law. In relation to the UN and the ILO the enforcement procedure is even weaker. The Human Rights Committee, made up of experts nominated by Member States, has developed a body of jurisprudence arising from its right to hear individual and group petitions about discrimination by a state party. However, the Committee's powers are limited to reminding the state party that it is under an obligation to provide an effective remedy for abuses or requesting an amendment to discriminatory legislation. The Human Rights Commission, by a process of public procedures, reports, working groups and Special Rapporteurs, has also carried out valuable work. In essence, the reporting procedure is the leading mechanism for the implementation of the Covenant.

3. The United Kingdom fails to meet some international standards

The United Kingdom has refused to incorporate Article 26 into domestic law on the grounds that Covenant rights are protected by domestic legislation but, even after the passing of the Human Rights Act 1998, the United

Kingdom lacks a general non-discrimination provision. Arguably, the incorporation of the European Convention on Human Rights still leaves some areas of weakness. In *R (S) v Chief Constable of South Yorkshire*, Lord Woolf CJ indicated the limitations of Article 14. In this case claimants, who were suspects investigated by police but never convicted of any offence, argued that the decision of the Chief Constable to retain their fingerprints and DNA samples was discriminatory. Lord Woolf said:

> It is important to note that Article 14 does not prohibit all discrimination . . . It is difficult to treat discrimination based on a difference in the treatment between those from whom fingerprints or samples have been lawfully taken from those from whom they have not been taken as falling within the language of the Article.[23]

4. Article 26 is a clearer statement of equality than exists in UK law

United Kingdom law has no clear equality provision and the very complexity of UK law in comparison with the clear statement in Article 26 arguably hampers public understanding of the law. Choudhury and Moon (2003, p 307) comment:

> Not only is discrimination law within the United Kingdom varied in its provisions and coverage between the different grounds for protection but it is also inaccessible and difficult to understand. In 2000 it was calculated that to get a comprehensive picture of our discrimination law you would have to consult 30 Acts, 38 statutory instruments, 11 codes of practice and 12 EC Directives and Recommendations. The complexity of the current law and proposed legislation has led to a gulf between what people think equality is about and what the law actually is.

5. Affirmative action is protected in international law

Articles 26 and 14 allow positive action to be taken to assist groups against discrimination. Since UK law is based on non-discrimination rather than equality, there is only limited scope for such action except where the legislation specifies it (e.g. as in the Race Relations (Amendment) Act 2000). The protection afforded to disabled persons is particularly weak in this regard.

The other chapters in this book indicate that UK law on discrimination is in substantial compliance with international obligations – although some gaps remain (e.g. in the area of political belief). In fact, where there is protection in domestic legislation this can go beyond requirements of international law; and, in the area of age discrimination, domestic law will give specific protection where UN and Council of Europe provisions are lacking. However, the current government reluctance

---

[23] [2002] 1 WLR 3223, 3233.

to incorporate Protocol 12 is a measure of official lack of enthusiasm for broad sweeping equality provisions.

Further reading

Bindman, G 'When will Europe act against racism?' [1996] 2 EHRLR 143

Brownlie, I *Basic Documents in International Law* (5th edn, Oxford, 2002)

Choudhury, T 'The drafting of Article 26 of the International Covenant on Civil and Political Rights: Part I' [2002] 5 EHRLR 591

Choudhury, T 'Interpreting the right to equality under Article 26 of the International Covenant on Civil and Political Rights' [2003] 1 EHRLR 24

Choudhury, T and Moon, G 'Complying with its international human rights obligations: the United Kingdom and Article 26 of the International Covenant on Civil and Political Rights' [2003] 3 EHRLR 283

Fredman, S 'Why the government should sign and ratify Protocol 12' (2002) 105 *Equal Opportunities Review* 21

Gandhi, PR *Blackstone's International Human Rights Documents* (3rd edn, Oxford, 2002)

Hegarty, A and Leonard, S *Human Rights. An Agenda for the 21st Century* (Cavendish Publishing, 1999)

Lester, A 'Equality and United Kingdom law: past, present and future' (2001) *Public Law* 77

Livingstone, S 'Article 14 and the Prevention of Discrimination in the European Convention on Human Rights' [1997] 1 EHRLR 25

McColgan, A 'Principles of Equality and Protection from Discrimination in Human Rights Law' [2003] 2 EHRLR 158

Nowak, M 'Civil, political, economic, social and cultural rights' in J Symonides (ed) *Human Rights: Concept and Standards* (UNESCO, Ashgate, 2000), pp 69–106

O'Dempsey, D, Allen, A, Belgrave, S and Brown, J *Employment Law and the Human Rights Act 1998* (Jordans, 2001)

Parratt, L and Foley, C 'The United Kingdom's thirteenth periodic report to the UN Committee for the Elimination of Racial Discrimination (CERD)' [1996] 4 EHRLR 384

Rehman, J *International Human Rights Law. A Practical Approach* (Longman, 2003)

Schwelb, E 'The International Convention on the Elimination of All Forms of Racial Discrimination' (1966) 15 *International and Comparative Law Quarterly* 1996

Simpson, AWB *Human Rights and the End of Empire* (Oxford University Press, 2001)

Steiner, HJ and Alston, P *International Human Rights in Context* (2nd edn, Oxford University Press, 2000)

Symonides, J (ed) *Human Rights: Concept and Standards* (UNESCO, Ashgate, 2000)

Wallace, RMM *International Human Rights Text and Materials* (2nd edn, Sweet & Maxwell, 2001)

Chapter 4

Sex and race discrimination

Sam Middlemiss

Introduction

This chapter will involve detailed consideration of the legal protection available to victims of sex and race discrimination. These are the areas of discrimination law that are by far the longest standing in the United Kingdom and a working knowledge of these areas is instrumental to an understanding of discrimination law.

What follows is a description of the current law in these areas, including the legal rules covering discrimination on grounds of sexual orientation, gender reassignment and racial and sexual harassment (aspects relating to the European Union are considered in Chapter 2).

Sex discrimination

Historical background

> The sexual division of labour was predetermined by the division of labour that had existed in the family when the household was the unit of production. The epoch of modern industry far from challenging this division further demarcated it.[1]

The starting point for sex discrimination within employment in the United Kingdom is commonly identified as the Industrial Revolution, when for the first time the home was separated from the place of

---

[1] S Alexander *Women's Work in 19th Century London. A Study of Years 1820–1850* (Journeyman Press, 1983), p 5.

work[2] and women were expected to stay at home and out of the workplace.[3]

> The productive role which women had played as part of the economic unit of a family was largely forgotten in the economic and social changes brought about by the Industrial Revolution.[4]

When economic necessity forced women to enter employment they were faced with a wide variety of discriminatory behaviour.[5]

> Gendered patterns of occupational segregation can be explained by the pervasive domestic or patriarchal ideology prescribing certain work roles as appropriate for women and others not: an ideology shared by employers, male workers and even many women themselves.[6]

The fact is that, where women were brave enough to enter employment in the face of a general opposition, they were regarded by paternalistic employers as second class workers. They were consequently restricted to low-paid and unskilled occupations,[7] required to work for long hours in bad working conditions and often subjected to sexual harassment. Employers would be unlikely to promote women for a number of reasons. Women often worked part-time and promoted posts would often only be available to full-time workers. 'In general working-class women did not regard full-time work as something they would undertake for the whole of their adult lives, while married women continued to firmly believe that their primary commitment was to home and family.' Where promotion was available only to persons with a considerable length of service, women would find it difficult to qualify where they had taken breaks in employment to fulfil their parental role.[8]

The trade unions were the only force capable of gaining improvements in women's rights from employers but they were traditionally driven by male interests. They failed to encourage women to join the union and did not consider women's issues: this was because unions were restricted to craft or skilled workers for most of the nineteenth century, which excluded almost all female workers.[9]

---

[2] In the agrarian society prior to the Industrial Revolution men and women worked alongside each other on an equal basis and the place of work, the farm, was also the home. The process of alienation of work from home brought about by changing work patterns caused by the process of industrialisation has become known amongst sociologists as the 'social division of labour'.

[3] E Durkheim *The Division of Labour in Society* (The Free Press, 1997).

[4] S Boston *Women Workers and the Trade Unions* (Lawrence and Wishart, 1997), pp 13–14.

[5] For the equivalent position in the United States, see J Matthaei *An Economic History of Women in America: Women's Work, the Sexual Division of Labour and the Development of Capitalism* (Schocken Books, 1988).

[6] J Zeitlin 'The sexual division in the Chartist family' (1989) 54 *British Society of Social Labour History Journal* 6.

[7] Sexual division of labour and job segregation.

[8] I Pinchbeck *Women Workers and the Industrial Revolution* (Frank Cass & Co Ltd, 1969).

[9] Note 4 above, pp 15–28.

Although in more recent times things have improved for women in terms of representation by trade unions,[10] it is only relatively recently that mechanisms have been put in place to ensure that women receive equality of treatment with men in employment. The position of women began to change in the 1970s, with the passing of the Equal Pay Act 1970 (EPA 1970) and the Sex Discrimination Act 1975 (SDA 1975) (equal pay issues are dealt with in Chapter 5).

The main legislative provisions dealing with sex discrimination in the United Kingdom are as follows (see Chapter 2 for EU aspects):

- SDA 1975
- SDA 1986
- Sex Discrimination and Equal Pay (Remedies) Regulations (SI 1993/2798)
- Sex Discrimination (Gender Reassignment) Regulations 1999, SI 1999/1002
- Sex Discrimination (Indirect Discrimination and Burden of Proof) Regulations 2001, SI 2001/2660
- Sex Discrimination Act 1975 (Amendment) Regulations 2003, SI 2003/1657.

Sex Discrimination Act 1975

Despite the fact that the United Kingdom had already joined the European Community (EC) when this legislation was introduced, little or no account was taken of the EC equality agenda at the time. 'It is doubtful too, whether the EEC Directive had much influence upon the structure of the U.K. Act.'[11] The Equal Treatment Directive 76/207 clearly came into being after the SDA 1975 was enacted, although details of its content were available to the legislators and they could easily have included its main provisions. The major influence on the legislation came from further afield than Europe: 'The main foreign influence on the UK Legislation was clearly from the United States.'[12] Concepts borrowed from the US legal system included the concept of indirect discrimination[13] and the role of the Equal Opportunities Commission.[14] Reference to American discrimination cases has been deemed relevant by courts in the United Kingdom and the European Court of Justice (ECJ).[15]

The threshold requirement in the SDA 1975 and the Race Relations Act 1976 (RRA 1976) is that an applicant in a case of sex or race

---

[10] General and Municipal Workers Union, USDAW, NALGO, NUPE and the AUEW.

[11] C McCrudden (ed) *Women, Equality and European Equality Law* (Eclipse Publications, 1987), p 36.

[12] Ibid p 37.

[13] As defined by the United States Supreme Court in *Griggs v Duke Power Company* 401 US 424 [1971].

[14] Based on the role of the Employment Equal Opportunities Commission (EEOC) in the United States.

[15] *Jenkins v Kingsgate* [1981] IRLR 228, ECJ.

discrimination must show that his or her employer is vicariously liable for the actings of the perpetrator of the discriminatory act.[16] So, if, for example, a female employee is harassed in the workplace by a male colleague, is the employer then vicariously liable under the SDA 1975? On the basis of case law dealing with sexual harassment (considered below), it seems likely.

The employee could, in these circumstances, also sue the perpetrator of the discriminatory act or persons that assist him. Under s 42 of the SDA 1975 and s 33 of the RRA 1976, a person who knowingly aids another person to commit an act which is unlawful under the Act shall be treated as himself doing an unlawful act of the like description. In *Hallam v Avery and Lambert*,[17] the Court of Appeal held that it is not enough that the person assisted with a complete act of discrimination. It must be established that the person knew that the perpetrator was treating or was about to treat someone less favourably on racial grounds and proceeded to provide them with aid.[18] In *Anyanwu and another v South Bank Student Union and another*,[19] the House of Lords held that a person aids another to do an unlawful act under the RRA 1976 if he or she helps or assists that other, whether or not that help is substantial and productive, provided it is not negligible.

One of the main aims of the SDA 1975 is to combat stereotypical assumptions about women and to make unlawful any behaviour by an employer that is based upon such assumptions. In *Skyrail Oceanic v Coleman*,[20] an assumption that a man was the 'breadwinner' in a marriage, resulting in the dismissal of a female employee, was held by the Court of Appeal to be discriminatory. In *Hurley v Mustoe*,[21] the employer's general assumption that employees with young children are unreliable was held to be directly discriminatory against women and also indirectly discriminatory on the grounds of marital status.[22]

Which types of workers are protected?

The SDA 1975 offers protection against discrimination to both men and women, although the legislators rightly anticipated that women would need more protection. The protection offered by the discrimination laws is not restricted to employees and applies to a much wider constituency. The SDA 1975 and the RRA 1976 offer protection to job applicants against

---

[16] SDA 1975, s 41; RRA 1976, s 32.
[17] [2001] ICR 408.
[18] For some background to this provision, see S Middlemiss 'Aiding a Discriminatory Act of the Employer (*AM v WC and SPF* [1999] IRLR 410)' *Scots Law Times*, Issue 1, 7 January 2000, pp 1–4.
[19] [2001] IRLR 305.
[20] [1981] ICR 864.
[21] [1981] IRLR 208.
[22] See also *Horsey v Dyfed County Council* [1982] IRLR 395.

discriminatory recruitment and selection practices (under section 6 and section 4 respectively).

Employment for the purposes of the SDA 1975 is defined widely by section 82(1) to include women working under a contract of service or of apprenticeship or a contract personally to execute any work or labour. This last category of person includes the self-employed, independent contractors, certain agency workers and trainees working under a training contract with the employer.[23]

Direct discrimination

Direct discrimination is a relatively straightforward concept whereby an employer directly and usually blatantly discriminates against persons of one sex in terms of his process of recruitment and selection or in his employment policies. Section 1(1) states:

> A person discriminates against a woman in any circumstances relevant for
> the purposes of any provision of this Act if –
> (a) on the grounds of her sex he treats her less favourably than he treats or
> would treat a man . . .

In respect of direct discrimination as defined above, the motive or intention of the discriminator is irrelevant, as determined by the House of Lords in *James v Eastleigh Borough Council.*[24] Mr and Mrs James, both aged 61, went for a swim in Eastleigh Borough Councils baths. Mrs James was allowed in free because she had reached the 'pensionable age' of 60, while Mr James had to pay 60p. Mr James, with the support of the Equal Opportunities Commission, brought a claim of direct sex discrimination as per s 1(1)(a) of the SDA 1975. Lord Bridge said 'pensionable age' is a convenient shorthand expression that refers to 60 for women and 65 for men. Thus, this was a case of direct discrimination – which is in breach of s 1(1)(a) of the SDA 1975 – and *but for* the fact that Mr James was a man he could swim free of charge in Eastleigh Borough Council's baths.

James v Eastleigh Borough Council establishes the '*but for*' test and also confirms that laudable motives are of no significance in determining if the employer is guilty of direct discrimination. In order to find direct discrimination under section 1(1)(a), the complainant must show that he has been treated less favourably by the discriminator than the discriminator treats or would treat other persons in the same circumstances. However, in certain cases the comparison need not be demonstrated by evidence as to how a comparator was or would be treated, because the very action complained of is in itself less favourable treatment on sexual or racial grounds.[25]

---

[23] *Daley v Allied Suppliers Ltd* [1983] IRLR 14, EAT.
[24] [1990] IRLR 288, HL.
[25] *Sidhu v Aerospace Composite Technology Ltd* [2000] IRLR 602, CA.

Indirect discrimination

Indirect discrimination is defined in section 1(1):

> A person discriminates against a woman in any circumstances relevant for the purposes of any provision of this Act if –
> (b) he applies to her a requirement or condition which he applies or would apply equally to a man but –
>   (i) which is such that the proportion of women who can comply with it is considerably smaller than the proportion of men who can comply with it, and
>   (ii) which he cannot show to be justifiable irrespective of the sex of the person to whom it is applied, and
>   (iii) which is to her detriment because she cannot comply with it.

A different definition of indirect discrimination is provided by section 1(2), which applies to certain aspects of the SDA 1975, including those relating to employment.[26] Under section 1(2)(b) a person discriminates against a woman if he applies to her a provision, criterion or practice which he applies or would apply equally to a man but:

> (i) which is such that it would be to the detriment of a considerably larger proportion of women than of men, and
> (ii) which he cannot show to be justifiable irrespective of the sex of the person to whom it is applied, and
> (iii) which is to her detriment.

In *Price v Civil Service Commission*,[27] Mrs Price applied for a job as an executive officer in the Civil Service but she was told that she was too old at 32 as the age requirement for candidates was between 17 and 28. She claimed that this requirement represented indirect discrimination as less qualified women in the job market would be able to comply with it than men (as many women were absent from the sphere of work during this time, bringing up their families). It was held on appeal that it was a case of indirect discrimination that was not justifiable and the Civil Service were liable for damages. The Civil Service altered their age requirements for executive officer posts following this decision.

In *Home Office v Holmes*,[28] Mrs Holmes had worked full-time for the Civil Service but after maternity leave she found this difficult and asked her employer for part-time work. Her employer refused to employ her part-time on the basis that all their posts were full-time. She claimed indirect discrimination on the basis that it was more difficult for women to comply with the full-time requirement than men, given that women are more likely to have primary parental responsibility. It was held that in this case

---

[26] Any provision of Part 2, ss 35A and 35B, any provision of Part 3 so far as it relates to vocational training.
[27] [1978] ICR 27.
[28] [1984] IRLR 299, EAT.

there was indirect discrimination. The tribunal at the initial stage of the legal process summarised the position as follows: 'it is still a fact that the raising of children tends to place a greater burden on women than it does on men'. The Employment Appeal Tribunal (EAT), however, took the view that this ruling was not to be treated as a precedent that women are entitled to work part-time in all such circumstances. Whether or not a woman would be entitled to be offered part-time employment would depend on the circumstances in the case.

Issues in indirect discrimination cases

(1) The meaning of the terms 'requirement or condition' is clarified in *Falkirk Council v Whyte*,[29] where these terms were broadly interpreted by the EAT. In this case three women brought a claim of indirect discrimination when they were refused employment in a managerial post at Cortonvale Prison. The job specification stated that management training and supervisory experience were desirable qualities. It was clear that possession of these qualities was a decisive factor in being selected for the job. It was more difficult for women than men to comply with as all women were employed at basic grades.[30] It was held that a desirable quality could be a requirement or condition in this case.

A very different conclusion was reached in a race discrimination case, *Perera v Civil Service Commission (No 2)*,[31] where it was stated that for a requirement or condition to be treated as discriminatory it must be an absolute bar to the employee gaining equal rights with their comparator. There have been recent changes to the definition of indirect discrimination under the Sex Discrimination (Indirect Discrimination and Burden of Proof) Regulations 2001, SI 2001/2660 (considered below). Under the Regulations, the terms 'requirement or condition' were replaced with the much broader terms of 'provision, criterion or practice' for certain important sections of the SDA 1975. This will make it easier for applicants and employees in indirect discrimination cases to establish they have been subject to inequality in their treatment by their employer.

(2) It is important that, in deciding the relevant 'pool' for comparison for the purposes of an application, one tries to second-guess the pool that the employment tribunal will choose. In *Jones v University of Manchester*,[32] the applicant was excluded from employment as a careers adviser as the University (wanting someone close to the age of the students) had restricted eligibility for this post to graduates aged 27–35. She was 46 years of age and the basis of her claim was that the requirement was indirectly

---

[29] [1997] IRLR 560.
[30] See also *Meer v London Borough of Tower Hamlets* [1988] IRLR 399.
[31] [1983] IRLR 166.
[32] [1993] IRLR 218.

discriminatory as female mature students tended to be older than male mature students and, by definition, fewer women could comply with the age requirement than men. The Court of Appeal rejected this argument, claiming that the appropriate comparators were all persons meeting the relevant criteria: 'It is, in effect, the total number of all those persons, men and women, who answer the description contained in the advertisement, apart from the age requirement. Here, that means all graduates with the relevant experience.'[33] In the event that an applicant chooses a pool for comparison which is incorrect, he or she will lose the case.[34] The relevant pool is a matter of fact for the employment tribunal to determine[35] but, as illustrated in the *Jones* case, it does often prefer to choose a broad pool (e.g. all women in the United Kingdom eligible to apply for a job). The tribunal will expect statistical evidence to be produced and led to support assertions of indirect discrimination. One solution is to provide statistical evidence for a number of different pools and, instead of the employment tribunal turning down the case, if deemed appropriate, it can decide which statistical evidence is most apt and accept that as evidence of discrimination.

(3) It is a defence to a claim for indirect discrimination to show that the types of discriminatory activity were 'objectively justifiable' by an employer on a ground other than sex. The question is, can the provision, criterion or practice be shown to be justifiable?

In *Clarke v Eley (IMI) Kynoch Ltd*[36] it was not justifiable under a redundancy procedure to choose part-timers for dismissal before full-time staff. In *Ojutiku v MSC*[37] the Court of Appeal said that the standard for proving a justifiable reason other than sex should be 'what was acceptable to right thinking people as sound and tolerable reasons for adopting the practice in question'.[38] This was not a very helpful definition for employment tribunals and the ECJ in *Bilka-Kaufhaus*[39] provided clarification of the standard of proof required. The employer must demonstrate objectively justified factors which are unrelated to discrimination based on sex. The employer must show that there is a real business need for the discriminatory outcome and that the means chosen to achieve the outcome are suitable and necessary.[40]

---

[33] Ibid, per Evans LJ at 228–291.
[34] *Pearce v City of Bradford Metropolitan Council* [1988] IRLR 378, EAT.
[35] *Kidd v DRG (UK) Ltd* [1985] IRLR 190, EAT.
[36] [1982] IRLR 482, EAT.
[37] [1982] IRLR 418, CA.
[38] Ibid at p 422. In *Rainey v Greater Glasgow Health Board* [1987] IRLR 26, the House of Lords held that the concepts of justification in indirect discrimination and equal pay cases should be interpreted in the same way.
[39] *Bilka-Kaufhaus GmbH v Weber Von Hartz* [1986] ECR 1607.
[40] S Anderman *Labour Law – Management Decisions and Workers' Rights* (Butterworths, 2000), ch 8. J Dine and B Watt (eds) *Discrimination Law. Concepts, Limitations and Justifications* (Longman, 1996), pp 103–109.

(4) The applicant must show that their inability to meet or comply with the provision, criterion or practice caused them to suffer a detriment. The degree of detriment needed to substantiate a discrimination claim for the purposes of this Act and other equality legislation was until recently unsettled.[41] In *Ministry of Defence v Jeremiah*[42] it was defined as merely 'putting under a disadvantage'. In other cases, however, something more had been looked for. In *Schmidt v Austicks Bookshops Ltd*[43] it was not sufficient detriment for a woman to be required to wear a dress under the company rules.[44]

To establish a detriment it is not necessary to establish a breach of contract but it is necessary to show that the applicant had been disadvantaged in the circumstances in which he or she had to work.[45] In *Insitu Cleaning Co Ltd v Heads*[46] a single sexist comment made to a female manager in a meeting was sufficient to constitute a detriment. In *Shamoon v Chief Constable of the Royal Ulster Constabulary*[47] the House of Lords heard an appeal from a decision of the Northern Ireland Court of Appeal that a female chief inspector whose power to undertake staff appraisals had been withdrawn by her employer had not suffered sufficient detriment for the purposes of the Sex Discrimination (Northern Ireland) Order 1976. The Court of Appeal's finding, that for a detriment to be established there must be some physical or economic consequence as a result of the discrimination, which is material and substantial, was overturned. The House of Lords emphasised that the word detriment should be given its broad ordinary meaning and there was no requirement to show that the employee suffered some economic or physical consequence.[48]

Victimisation

Under s 4 of the SDA 1975 it is unlawful to discriminate against persons by way of victimisation when they try to assert a right under the SDA 1975 or take part in proceedings to assert such a right for someone else or themselves. To establish victimisation the applicant must show that the following three elements are present:

(1) The victim must have brought an action for sex discrimination to an employment tribunal, given evidence in a sex discrimination case or alleged that sex discrimination has taken place.

---

[41] *Shamoon v Chief Constable of the Royal Ulster Constabulary* [2003] IRLR 285, HL.
[42] [1979] IRLR 436, CA.
[43] [1977] IRLR 360, EAT.
[44] In *De Souza v Automobile Association* [1986] IRLR 103, CA, a racial insult made in a conversation overheard by a typist was insufficient detriment.
[45] Sexual harassment will represent a suitable detriment in most cases.
[46] [1995] IRLR 4, EAT.
[47] [2003] IRLR 285.
[48] *Chief Constable of West Yorkshire v Khan* [2001] IRLR 830.

(2) It must be shown that the applicant experienced less favourable treatment compared to a person not involved in sex discrimination proceedings.[49]

(3) It must also be established that the less favourable treatment is a direct result of the involvement in sex discrimination proceedings.

In *Coote v Granada Hospitality Ltd (No 2)*,[50] a woman who had left her employment claimed she had been subjected to victimisation by her employer because it refused to provide her with a reference. This matter was referred to the ECJ by the EAT to determine if she had a right of action under European Law. The ECJ ruled that Article 6 of the Equal Treatment Directive did provide a right to bring an action for discrimination after the contract had come to an end. The EAT decided it could give effect to the ECJ judgment without distorting the language of the SDA 1975 and it was possible to construe the Act in a way that is in conformity with the Directive.[51]

The application of the SDA 1975 to relationships which have come to an end is dealt with by reg 3 of the Sex Discrimination Act 1975 (Amendment) Regulations 2003, and similar provisions are made under the Employment Equality (Sexual Orientation) Regulations 2003 (reg 21)[52] and the Race Relations Act 1976 (Amendment) Regulations 2003 (inserting s 27A into the RRA 1976, which includes only grounds of race, ethnic or national origin).[53] Where a 'relevant relationship' has come to an end it will be unlawful for the 'relevant party' to discriminate so as to subject another party to a detriment or to harass such a party 'where the discrimination or harassment arises out of and is closely connected to that relationship'.

Unlawful activities

The Act specifies what type of discriminatory activities should be treated as unlawful. These cover discriminatory practices in recruitment and selection, within employment and dismissal on the ground of sex. Under s 6 of the SDA 1975 it is unlawful for an employer to discriminate against a woman:

- *in the arrangements made for the purpose of determining who shall be offered employment* (s 6(1)(a)). In *Brennan v Dewhurst*[54] the EAT held that it

---

[49] Ibid.
[50] C-185/97; [1998] ECR I-5199, ECJ.
[51] The legislation introduced to implement the Race Discrimination Directive and the Framework Directive makes it unlawful for an employer to discriminate against a former employee where the discrimination is closely connected to the employment relationship.
[52] Employment Equality (Sexual Orientation) Regulations 2003, SI 2003/1661.
[53] SI 2003/1626.
[54] [1983] IRLR 357, EAT.

was irrelevant that the employer did not intend to discriminate and clarified that 'in all stages in applying for and obtaining employment a woman should be on an equal footing with a man'.

- *or in the terms in which employment is offered* (s 6(1)(b)). Although inequality in pay and other terms and conditions between men and women in employment is covered by the EPA 1970, where the inequality applies to terms and conditions offered at the selection stage of employment the SDA 1975 will apply. It will also apply where there is no opportunity to bring a case under the EPA 1970 (e.g. where there is no suitable male comparator in the same employment). 'Under the EPA 1970 a female applicant must normally point to a male comparator with whom to compare her terms and conditions of employment, whereas in an equivalent claim under the RRA 1976 the applicant need only point to a hypothetical comparator of a different racial group.'[55] In *Macarthys Ltd v Smith*[56] it was decided by the ECJ that a woman was entitled to receive the same terms and conditions as her male predecessor under Article 119 (now Article 141).

- *by refusing or deliberately omitting to offer her employment* (s 6(1)(c)). This will be difficult to prove because the information needed to make a comparison is in the hands of the employer and the applicant needs to show that they are the best candidate and were refused employment on the basis of their sex.[57] The employer has a managerial prerogative to decide who is chosen for employment and, unless there is clear evidence of discrimination, the employment tribunal may be reluctant to intervene.

- *in the way in which she is afforded access to promotion, transfer or training or to any other benefits, facilities or services or by refusing or deliberately omitting to afford access to them* (s 6(2)(a)). This is a wide-ranging measure capable of covering most kinds of discrimination arising within the employment relationship.

- *by dismissing her or subjecting her to any other detriment* (s 6(2)). The term detriment has been interpreted by the courts as including sexual harassment (discussed below). Where a woman is dismissed on the ground of her sex then she may have a choice of bringing a claim under this part of the Act or for unfair dismissal.[58] The benefit for her pursuing the former option rather than the latter is that she will not need to establish that she has continuous service of one year with the employer and the damages that she can be awarded are unlimited. The term

---

[55] R Townshend-Smith *Discrimination Law: Text, Cases and Materials* (Cavendish, 1998), p 331.

[56] [1980] IRLR 210, ECJ.

[57] An order for the discovery of documents (see *Nasse v Science Research Council; Vyas v Leyland Cars* [1979] IRLR 465, HL) and a questionnaire procedure under s 74 of the SDA 1975 and s 65 of the RRA 1976 will assist the applicant in proving his or her case.

[58] Under s 95 of the Employment Rights Act 1996.

'dismissal' here and under s 4(2)(c) of the RRA 1976 has been extended to cover constructive dismissal.[59]

Genuine occupational qualifications

There are certain situations prescribed by s 7 of the SDA 1975 where it is permissible to discriminate in terms of recruitment and selection and these are known as genuine occupational qualifications (GOQs). The onus is on the employer to show that this defence applies and he need only show that part of the job is covered by a GOQ.

Discrimination in recruitment and selection may be permissible where:

- it is for physiological reasons (other than physical strength or stamina). This would allow someone of a particular sex to be chosen for a job where the physical characteristics of a person of that sex are needed for reasons of authenticity (e.g. acting, modelling).[60]
- the job needs to be held by a man or a woman to preserve decency or privacy as it is likely to involve physical contact with a man and it is reasonable for them to object. In *Wylie v Dee & Co (Menswear) Ltd*[61] a woman applied for a job as a sales assistant in a men's tailors. She was refused employment on the basis that part of the job involved taking the inside leg measurements of male clients and they would object if a woman did this (GOQ). It was held that the refusal to employ her was sex discrimination and the GOQ did not apply because this was a small part of the job that could be undertaken by one of the six male assistants.
- men or women will be in a state of undress.[62]
- there is single-sex accommodation – it is impractical for the job-holder to live anywhere other than in the employer's premises and the only such premises available are for one sex and these are not equipped with separate sleeping accommodation or sanitary facilities and it is not reasonable for an employer either to equip those premises with such accommodation and facilities or to provide other premises (e.g. manned lighthouses).
- the job is in a single-sex establishment which is a prison, hospital or other establishment for persons requiring special care, supervision and attention and it is reasonable having regard to the essential character of the establishment or that part of the job should be held by a person of a specified sex.

---

[59] SDA 1975 (as amended), s 82(1A) and *Derby Specialist Fabrication Ltd v Burton* [2001] IRLR 69, EAT.

[60] G Pitt 'Madam Butterfly and Miss Saigon: Reflection on Genuine Occupational Qualifications' in J Dine and B Watt (eds) *Discrimination Law. Concepts, Limitations and Justifications* (Longman, 1996), pp 198–206.

[61] [1978] IRLR 103.

[62] *Etam plc v Rowan* [1989] IRLR 150.

- the holder of the job provides individuals with personal services promoting their welfare or education or similar personal services and those services can most effectively be provided by a person of a specified sex.
- the job is one of two held by a married couple.
- the job involves working outside the United Kingdom in a country whose law and customs are such that the duties could not or could not effectively be carried out by a person of a specified sex.

Remedies

A complaint of sex discrimination must be brought to an employment tribunal within three months of the discriminatory act. Where a complaint is made out of time the tribunal can consider it when it is just and equitable to allow the case to proceed to a hearing.

Where a claim for sex discrimination is successfully brought against the employer there are three possible remedies that an employment tribunal can award to the applicant:

(1) A declaratory order from the employment tribunal, setting out the rights and obligations of the parties in relation to the act to which the complaint relates (SDA 1975, s 65(1)(a)).[63]

(2) Recommendations can be made by a tribunal, recommending that an employer take action to remove the discriminatory effect of its behaviour on the complainant. This might consist of transferring a harasser away from his victim, introducing training for managers on equal opportunities policies and procedures, changing procedures for recruitment and selection to ensure equality of treatment, and providing a fair and accurate reference to someone that is dismissed because of his or her sex. When an employer fails to comply with the recommendation without reasonable justification, then the amount of compensation it has been required to pay to the complainant can be increased; or, where no provision for compensation has been made, an order for compensation can be issued against the employer.

(3) Compensation is the most common remedy sought by and awarded to complainants. The compensation is unlimited as a consequence of the ruling of the ECJ in *Marshall v Southampton and South West Hampshire Health Authority (No 2)*[64] and the Sex Discrimination and Equal Pay (Remedies) Regulations 1993. In some instances, the amount of damages awarded have been considerable.[65] The headings of financial loss which the complainant can be compensated for

---

[63] For a critique of the remedies, see L Lustgarten 'Racial inequality and the limits of the law' (1986) 49 *Modern Law Review* 68.

[64] [1993] IRLR 445.

[65] M Nichols 'Analyst wins over £1m for sex discrimination' *The Scotsman*, Friday 31 January 2002, p 5.

by way of restitution include injury to feelings, loss of earnings (including future earnings), loss of pension rights, interest due on the award, and expenses associated with the legal claim.

Positive or affirmative action[66]

The SDA 1975 and the RRA 1976 both make provision for positive action for sexual or racial groups who are under-represented in terms of employment, training or promotion. Most commentators agree that the provisions in both Acts are inadequate as a positive force for combating inequality.[67] The provisions in equality law encourage two types of positive discrimination: the first is to encourage more persons in a disadvantaged group to apply for jobs and to provide such groups with the opportunity to gain such skills and experience to allow them to compete for these jobs.[68]

The second type, which is the right to positively discriminate in favour of one sex or a racial group, will not apply unless it can be shown that the group it is sought to discriminate in favour of is under-represented as per s 47(1) of the SDA 1975 – in other words, within that group, no one has been employed in that particular job during the last 12 months or the number of persons doing that work is comparatively small.[69] Under sex discrimination law, in determining whether the number of employees in a particular job is comparatively small, the comparator will be all women in a population. The issues related to this are highlighted in the following quote:

> One of the difficulties with legal intervention, perhaps inevitably, is that there is no sliding scale of what is permissible . . . In policy terms, the greater the degree of under-representation, the greater and more varied the steps an employer should be encouraged and permitted to take.[70]

In race discrimination cases the comparator in determining under-representation is much narrower, being the numbers employed by a particular employer, and this presents less difficulty for employers from an evidential point of view.[71]

Sex Discrimination Act 1975 (Amendment) Regulations 2003

This very short piece of legislation deals with two main issues, one of which has been dealt with elsewhere. Sections 1 and 2 clarify that a

---

[66] These terms can be used interchangeably.

[67] RJ Townshend-Smith *Discrimination Law: Text, Cases and Materials* (Cavendish, 1998), p 539. For the contrary view, see B Parekh 'A case for positive discrimination' in B Hepple and E Szyszcak (eds) *Discrimination: Limits of the Law* (Mansell, 1993), pp 261–280.

[68] V Sacks 'Tackling Discrimination Positively in Britain' in ibid, pp 357–383.

[69] RRA 1976, s 37(1).

[70] *Hughes v London Borough of Hackney*, below.

[71] *Hughes v London Borough of Hackney* [1986] unreported, London Central Industrial Tribunal; see 7 *Equal Opportunities Review* 27.

police constable (despite being an office holder) should be treated as an employee for the purposes of the SDA 1975 and deemed to be working for the chief officer of police.[72] Further, anything done by a person holding such an office shall be treated as done in the course of employment. Given that the police are increasingly respondents in discrimination cases, it is not surprising that the liability of both parties arising under the SDA 1975 should be clarified.

Under sections 3 and 4 the rules are set out dealing with discrimination after an employment relationship has come to an end (see the *Coote*[73] case). Where there is a relevant relationship and the discriminatory act that arises after the employment has ceased is closely connected with that relationship, then protection is provided (ss 20A and 35C are inserted into the SDA 1975).

Sexual harassment

Article 2(2) of the Equal Treatment Amendment Directive provides that harassment is unwanted conduct related to the sex of a person that occurs with the purpose or effect of violating the dignity of that person. Harassment is defined as occurring where, on grounds of sex, A engages in unwanted conduct which has the purpose or effect of (a) violating B's dignity or (b) creating an intimidating, hostile, degrading, humiliating or offensive environment for B. The conduct is deemed to have the required effect if, having regard to all the circumstances, including in particular the perception of B, it should reasonably be considered as having that effect. Under the new legislative rules implementing the amendments, harassment will no longer be a type of discrimination but a distinct type of unlawful conduct.

Sexual harassment has been described as:

> Conduct of a sexual nature, or other conduct based on sex affecting the dignity of women. It is unacceptable, if it is unwanted, unreasonable and offensive to the recipient and such conduct creates an intimidating, hostile or humiliating working environment for the recipient.[74]

In *Porcelli v Strathclyde Regional Council*[75] Mrs Porcelli was subjected to a campaign of harassment by two male colleagues to get her to leave her job, including sexual comments and sexual innuendoes, threatening gestures, etc. She applied for and was given a transfer and claimed that the behaviour constituted sex discrimination under SDA 1975. It was held for the first time that sexual harassment was sex discrimination under

---

[72] Similar measures were brought in for race discrimination cases under the Race Relations (Amendment) Act 2000.
[73] *Coote v Granada Hospitality Ltd (No 2)* [1998] ECR I-5199.
[74] Council of Ministers of EU, Code of Practice, definition of sexual harassment.
[75] [1986] IRLR 134, Ct Sess.

s 6(2)(b) of the Act and fell under the term 'any other detriment'. The behaviour was discriminatory as a man similarly placed who was equally disliked would not have suffered the same fate. Treatment is on grounds of the woman's sex as per s 1(1)(a). Sexual harassment by itself without any accompanying threat to terms and conditions of employment is sufficiently detrimental to be treated as sex discrimination (working environment).

While it was originally believed that harassment must involve a continuous mode of conduct, this was refuted by two cases: *Bracebridge Engineering Ltd v Darby*,[76] where a single incident of harassment was capable of constituting sufficient detriment (a serious assault by her supervisor and another); and *Insitu Cleaning Co Ltd v Heads*,[77] where a single verbal comment of a sexist nature made by a fellow manager at a meeting was sufficient detriment.

In the following two cases sufficient detriment was not established. In *British Telecommunications v Williams*[78] an interview by a male manager of a female applicant for a job in a very confined space was not treated as sex discrimination; and in *Stewart v Cleveland Guest (Engineering) Ltd*[79] pornographic images displayed in the workplace were not deemed to be discriminatory against women as working in an environment tainted by pornography was gender neutral (a man would have been equally offended).

In *Waters v Commissioner for Police of the Metropolis*[80] a female police officer was sexually assaulted by a colleague outside working hours in her home. She reported the incident to her employer but after an enquiry no action was taken against the harasser. She then experienced victimisation by her employer and made a claim under s 4 of the SDA 1975. It was held that no legal action could be taken against the employer under the Act for the assault (not vicariously liable as per section 41 because the harasser was acting outside the scope of his employment); correspondingly, there was no right to bring a claim for victimisation, which is dependent on the action complained of following a complaint under s 41 of the SDA 1975. The case was eventually taken to the House of Lords and they upheld Ms Waters' claim that the employer's failure to offer her support and to prevent harassment and victimisation of her amounted to breach of its duty of care under the law of contract and tort:[81]

> If an employer knows that acts being done by employees during their employment may cause physical or mental harm to a particular fellow employee and he does nothing to supervise or prevent such acts, where it is

[76] [1990] IRLR 3, EAT.
[77] [1995] IRLR 4, EAT.
[78] [1997] IRLR 668, EAT.
[79] [1994] IRLR 440, EAT.
[80] [1995] IRLR 531.
[81] *Waters v Metropolitan Police Commissioner* [2000] IRLR 720.

in his power to do so, it is clearly arguable that he may be in breach of his duty to that employee. It seems to me that he may also be in breach of that duty if he can foresee such acts may happen, and if they do, that physical or mental harm may be caused.[82]

The employer should have anticipated that Ms Waters' persistent complaint about the assault by a fellow officer would lead to retaliatory action.

I consider the person employed under an ordinary contract of employment can have a valid cause of action in negligence against her employer if the employer fails to protect her against victimisation and harassment which cause physical or mental injury. This duty arises both under the contract of employment and under the common law principles of negligence.[83]

In the course of employment

Anything done by a person *in the course of their employment* shall be treated for the purposes of the SDA 1975 as having been done by the employer as well as him, whether or not it is done with the employer's knowledge or approval. The term 'in the course of their employment' must be given its everyday meaning.[84]

It is a defence for an employer to show he has done all that was reasonably practicable to prevent an employee's discriminatory act. In *Chief Constable of the Lincolnshire Police v Stubbs*[85] the employer was held liable under s 41 of the SDA 1975, for a discriminatory act perpetrated outside the workplace. On two occasions outside work, a female police officer socialising with her colleagues was sexually harassed physically and verbally by a fellow officer. A question arose concerning the liability of the employer for these acts. It was held by the EAT that the employer was liable:

these incidents are connected to work and the workplace. They would not have happened but for the applicant's work. Work-related functions are an extension of employment and we can see no reason to restrict the course of employment to purely what goes on in the workplace.

The courts adopted a similar approach to determining whether the vicarious liability of an employer applied under the law of tort. In *Lister v Hesley Hall Ltd*[86] a warden at a school for children with emotional or behavioural difficulties was sexually abusing his charges. The House of Lords held that the employer was vicariously liable for the acts of its employee because the well-being of the children in its care was part of

---

[82] Ibid, per Lord Slynn at 721.
[83] Ibid, per Lord Hutton at 724.
[84] See race discrimination cases redefining rules concerning vicarious liability, below.
[85] [1999] IRLR 81.
[86] [2001] IRLR 472.

the school's responsibility that it delegated to its employee. The torts were connected to the performance of the employee's duties under his contract.

Sexual orientation and gender reassignment

Until recently, victims of discrimination based on sexual orientation were denied any protection under discrimination law. There were no rights available to homosexual or lesbian employees facing discrimination under the equality laws of the United Kingdom or the European Union. They were denied protection because sexual orientation was not included within the ambit of section 1 of the SDA 1975, Article 141 of the EC Treaty or Article 5 of the Equal Treatment Directive 76/207 EEC. The position in the United Kingdom was summarised by the Court of Appeal in the case of *Smith v Gardner Merchant* [87] in the following way:

> ... discrimination on grounds of sexual orientation is not discrimination on the ground of sex within the meaning of the SDA 1975. A person's sexual orientation is not an aspect of his or her sex.

It was the view of the judiciary that homosexuality derived from someone's sexual proclivity rather than their gender and only gender-based discrimination was acceptable for comparison in sex discrimination cases.

A similar interpretation of Community law was provided by the ECJ in *Grant v South-West Trains,* [88] although they were apologetic for reaching such a conclusion: 'While the European Parliament ... has indeed deplored all forms of discrimination based on a person's sexual orientation, it is nevertheless the case that the Community has not yet adopted rules providing for such equivalence.' [89]

Even if homosexuals and lesbians could overcome this jurisdictional hurdle they would still be faced with the related problem of finding an appropriate comparator that meets the evidential requirement of the judiciary in these cases. The courts had ruled that the correct approach in determining if inequality of treatment applied was to compare a homosexual's treatment against a hypothetical comparator, namely a lesbian in the same situation. In the case of lesbians pursuing their rights, a homosexual would be the comparator. Only if they could satisfy the court that their gay comparator would be subjected to discrimination in the same circumstances would an action lie. [90] This intractable view of the judiciary on this issue has recently been given the added support of the Scottish Court of Session in the case of *Secretary of State for Defence v*

---

[87] [1998] IRLR 510.

[88] [1998] IRLR 206.

[89] Ibid at p 218; this reasoning was followed in *R v Secretary of State for Defence, ex parte Perkins (No 2)* [1998] IRLR 508.

[90] Referred to as the 'equality of misery' in sexual discrimination, this can now apply to gays: Employment Law News from Tolley, 23 October 2000, available on www.personneltoday.net/pt_legal/legal_features.

MacDonald.[91] It removed any hope in the short term for lesbians and gay men obtaining equal rights with heterosexual employees under UK employment law.

They overturned an ambitious but ill-considered judgment of the EAT (discussed below) which resulted in short-lived protection being provided for employees suffering discrimination on the basis of their sexual orientation.[92] It is important to remember that, despite this setback for these employees, legal developments in the law of the European Union in the form of a Directive providing protection against discrimination on the ground of sexual orientation, and consequent implementation in the United Kingdom through the Employment Equality (Sexual Orientation) Regulations 2003, will bring about a change in their legal position.[93]

European Convention on Human Rights

The European Convention on Human Rights became part of the law of the United Kingdom with the passing of the Human Rights Act 1998 (HRA 1998).[94] The HRA 1998 came fully into force in most of the United Kingdom on 2 October 2000.[95] The precise impact of the legislation is still uncertain; however, it does offer the prospect of legal rights being provided for various categories of victims of discrimination not catered for by UK employment law (Article 8 – homosexuals and lesbians; Article 9 – covering religious discrimination; and Article 14 – a more general discrimination provision).

It was successfully argued before the Scottish EAT in *MacDonald v Ministry of Defence*[96] that, as the European Convention had directly impacted on interpretation of domestic legislation, domestic equality legislation (the SDA 1975) should therefore be deemed to include sexual orientation within the term 'sex' as the basis for a claim under the Act in view of relevant case law of the European Court of Human Rights (ECHR). The justification for this conclusion came from the decision of the ECHR in *Salguiero da Silva Mouta v Portugal.*[97] Article 14 was interpreted (the right not to be discriminated against) as extending a direct right of action for discrimination on the basis of sexual orientation. In light of this

---

[91] [2001] IRLR 431.

[92] The Court of Appeal's decision was recently upheld by the House of Lords.

[93] In the Employment Equality (Sexual Orientation) Regulations 2003, SI 2003/1661 it is left suitably vague concerning the appropriate comparator in direct and indirect discrimination cases; and under reg 3 they are referred to as 'other persons', leaving the employment tribunal with a wide choice of comparator.

[94] K Ewing 'The Human Rights Act and Labour Law' (1998) 27(4) *Industrial Law Journal* 276.

[95] In s 57(2) of the Scotland Act 1998, the Scottish Parliament was called on to recognise the impact of the Convention and the Human Rights Act 1998 in fulfilling its legislative function.

[96] [2000] IRLR 749.

[97] Case 33290/96 [2001] Fam LR 2, ECHR.

judgment, the EAT interpreted UK domestic legislation as incorporating this right. The Court of Session, on appeal, regarded this reasoning as flawed and rejected this hypothesis in favour of the reasoning adopted in earlier cases such as *Smith* and *Grant*:

> On the whole matter I am satisfied that this statute and in particular this provision is concerned with gender and not sexual orientation. Section 3(1) of the 1998 Act does not in my opinion enable or oblige us to adopt any other reading.[98]

This judgment must be considered in the light of developments in the European Union: the Framework Directive 2000/78/EC has been implemented in the UK Employment Equality (Sexual Orientation) Regulations 2003 and this has had a direct impact on the rights of victims of sexual orientation discrimination. The Regulations will make it unlawful to discriminate on various grounds not directly covered by existing legislation, including sexual orientation.

HRA 1998 and Secretary of State for Defence v MacDonald

The case against the Ministry of Defence was as follows: Mr MacDonald was initially commissioned into the Territorial Army Intelligence Corps and then employed by the Royal Air Force. He applied for a transfer to the Scottish Air Traffic Control centre at Prestwick on compassionate grounds. Mr McDonald was subjected to a rigorous vetting procedure for the job, under which he was asked if he was a homosexual. After heavy questioning about his sexuality, he confirmed that he was a homosexual and notified his commanding officer of this fact. His declarations led to his compulsory resignation under Queen's Regulations 2905. He claimed that he was sexually harassed and unlawfully dismissed on the ground of his sex.

Although the legislative rules in the United Kingdom and the European Union offered him no chance of success, as his employer was the Ministry of Defence (a public body), he was entitled to seek appropriate protection under the HRA 1998. The argument that the effect of the HRA 1998 was expansion of the scope of existing domestic legislation to cover discrimination on these grounds was rejected by the Court of Appeal.

In *Smith and Grady v United Kingdom*[99] the ECHR was satisfied that the introduction and application of the Ministry of Defence's policy to discharge homosexuals from the services when their sexual orientation became known to them (e.g. following an investigation into the personal affairs of the accused) was contrary to Article 8 (right to respect for private life) and Article 13 (right to an effective remedy before a national

---

[98] *Secretary of State for Defence v MacDonald* [2001] IRLR 431, per Lord Prosser at p 436.
[99] [1999] IRLR 735.

authority). The issue of the applicability of Article 14 to discriminatory acts based on someone's sexual orientation was raised but was considered inadmissible.

The EAT in *MacDonald* considered the following question: who should be the appropriate comparator in these cases? It was decided that it should either be a heterosexual man where a lesbian is bringing a claim or a heterosexual woman where the applicant is a homosexual man.

> If comparators are relevant, the issue is not as between male and female simpliciter but between a male or female homosexual and a male or female heterosexual in order to determine not whether one homosexual is being treated less favourably than another but whether homosexuals of either gender in this context are being treated less favourably than heterosexuals of the opposite gender which is the true comparator in the context of sexual orientation.[100]

The use of inter-sex comparison as the basis of a discrimination claim is already undertaken in the enforcement of rights under the SDA 1975, whereby heterosexual comparisons are carried out between the sexes.

It is questionable whether an inter-sex or intra-sex comparator (e.g. comparing a lesbian with a heterosexual female) is likely to be the best option. In *P v S and Cornwall County Council*,[101] however, the ECJ ruled that transsexuals should be compared with persons of the same sex not considering or undergoing gender reassignment. The EAT in the *MacDonald* case suggested that in serious cases of discrimination based on sexual orientation (such as those involving physical harassment or bullying) no comparator should be required: 'In circumstances where the behaviour complained of is both "blatantly unacceptable" and "sexually related" then there is no need for a comparator.' A similar approach was taken by the Court of Appeal in *Clark v Novacold Ltd*,[102] where it was decided, in respect of disability discrimination, that the 'sick person' comparison was invalid and no comparator was required to establish discrimination against a disabled employee on the ground of his or her disability.[103] In the Court of Appeal, the majority reverted to the original basis for comparison in these cases – a homosexual man or lesbian. However, Lord Prosser (in his dissenting judgment) said that the appropriate comparator was a person of the opposite sex, regardless of any question of sexual orientation.

---

[100] M Rubenstein (2000) 29(11) *Industrial Relations Law Reports* 745.
[101] [1996] IRLR 347.
[102] [1999] IRLR 318, CA.
[103] For an interesting discussion on the appropriate comparators in gender reassignment cases, see R Wintemute 'Recognising new kinds of direct sex discrimination, transsexualism, sexual orientation and dress codes' (1997) 60 *Modern Law Review* 334 at pp 340–341. The intra-sex comparison is now part of the Sex Discrimination (Gender Reassignment) Regulations 1999, SI 1999/1002.

Employment Equality (Sexual Orientation) Regulations 2003[104]

Sexual orientation is widely defined under regulation 2 to mean orientation towards persons of the same sex (homosexuals), persons of the opposite sex (heterosexuals), and persons of the same sex and the opposite sex (bisexuals). This means that homosexuals, heterosexuals and bisexuals are protected under the legislation.

> They cover discrimination on grounds of perceived as well as actual sexual orientation (i.e. assuming – correctly or incorrectly – that someone is lesbian, gay, heterosexual or bisexual). The Regulations also cover association, i.e. being discriminated against on grounds of the sexual orientation of those with whom you associate (for example, friends and/or family).[105]

The Regulations provide protection against direct and indirect discrimination and victimisation. Regulation 3 states:

(1) For the purposes of these Regulations, a person ('A') discriminates against another person ('B') if –
  (a) on grounds of sexual orientation, A treats B less favourably than he treats or would treat other persons; or
  (b) A applies to B a provision, criterion or practice which he applies or would apply equally to persons not of the same sexual orientation as B, but –
    (i) which puts or would put persons of the same sexual orientation as B at a particular disadvantage when compared with other persons,
    (ii) which puts B at that disadvantage, and
    (iii) which A cannot show to be a proportionate means of achieving a legitimate aim.
(2) A comparison of B's case with that of another person under paragraph (1) must be such that the relevant circumstances in the one case are the same, or not materially different, in the other.

The key provisions of this legislation are the same as or similar to existing equality legislation. Regulation 4 deals with victimisation and provides protection against such behaviour where it occurs for the reason that a person has brought an action against another or proceedings against, or given evidence or information in connection with proceedings against another, etc.

The definition of harassment in regulation 5 is similar to that found in other legislation, making it unlawful for A to engage in unwanted conduct on the ground of sexual orientation, which has the purpose or effect of violating B's dignity or creating an intimidating, hostile, degrading, humiliating or offensive environment for B. Under regulation 6(3)

---

[104] SI 2003/1661.
[105] DTI website, www.dti.gov.uk/er/equality/eeregs_a.html.

'it is unlawful for an employer . . . to subject to harassment a person whom he employs or who has applied to him for employment.' Regulation 6 sets out the types of activities that will be treated as unlawful under the Regulations, which are largely identical to those under s 4 of the RRA 1976 and s 6 of the SDA 1975. Dismissal of a person includes expiry of a fixed-term contract or constructive dismissal.

Regulation 7(2) sets out a general occupational requirement in favour of employees of a particular sexual orientation that can exempt an otherwise discriminatory act, including unlawful dismissal of someone not of that sexual orientation. Under regulation 7(3), where employment is for the purpose of organised religion the employer can impose a requirement that it is difficult for a person (because of their sexual orientation) to meet and consequently can discriminate against them (including undertaking dismissal). This can apply where such a requirement is necessary to comply with the doctrine of a religion, or where, because of the nature of the employment (or the context in which it is carried out), the requirement is necessary to avoid conflicting with the strongly held convictions of a significant number of the religion's followers.

There has been little research into the extent of this type of discrimination within employment in the United Kingdom. However, where research has been undertaken the results show that discriminatory practices in employment against this type of employee are commonplace.[106]

While at the present time it is impossible for victims of discrimination based on sexual orientation to bring a successful claim for discrimination, there may be other statutory claims (working time, wages, breach of contract, harassment) and common law actions (e.g. actions in tort) they could pursue.[107] Where they are dismissed because of their sexual orientation, this action could be deemed to be reasonable by an employment tribunal.[108] There is clearly a deficiency in equality legislation, which will hopefully be addressed by the Employment Equality (Sexual Orientation) Regulations 2003. It will be interesting to see how successfully the new regulations fulfil this role. Employees may be reluctant to pursue claims against their employers for fear of stigmatisation, victimisation (regulation 4) or harassment (regulation 5), despite legal protection being provided against these activities; and the issue of choosing the appropriate comparator may still cause problems for employment tribunals.

---

[106] Stonewall, a national lobbying organisation on behalf of lesbians, bisexuals and gay men, undertook a survey of 2,000 employees in 1993. They found that 16% of respondents had experienced discrimination, 48% had been harassed because of their sexual orientation and 68% felt the need to conceal their sexual orientation from co-workers. In an independent survey carried out by the Social and Community Planning Group in 1995, similar results were obtained.

[107] S Middlemiss and N Busby 'The equality deficit, legal protection for homosexuals and lesbians in employment?' (2001) 8(4) *Gender Work and Organisation* 387.

[108] *Saunders v Scottish National Camps Association Ltd* [1980] IRLR 14.

Transsexuals

Legal protection against discrimination has been provided for transsexuals at work. Transsexuals are persons convinced that their physical anatomy is different from their true gender.[109] They will often undertake operations to redress this perceived imbalance (by changing their sex) and will dress in the clothes of someone of the opposite sex and want to use facilities provided for the opposite sex. This will often cause practical problems for employers[110] and possibly persons working alongside an employee who is a transsexual.[111] Transsexuals themselves may often experience various kinds of discrimination at work at the hands of their employer or co-workers, including harassment, social and professional isolation, dismissal and ostracism.

Judicial recognition of the right of transsexuals not to be discriminated against was first achieved in the ECJ's decision in *P v S and Cornwall County Council*.[112] When the applicant was initially employed as a general manager he was male but after about a year he announced that he was intending to undergo an operation for gender reassignment. He was dismissed. The tribunal felt that this case fell outside the scope of the SDA 1975 but referred the case to the ECJ to determine if the Equal Treatment Directive offered protection. The ECJ found that:

> such discrimination is based, essentially, if not exclusively, on the sex of the person concerned. Where a person is dismissed on the ground that he or she intends to undergo, or has undergone, gender reassignment, he or she is treated less favourably by comparison with persons of the sex to which he or she was deemed to belong to before undergoing gender reassignment.[113]

The treatment of the employee in this case was deemed to be contrary to Article 5(1) of the Equal Treatment Directive.

Following this case, the EAT ruled in *Chessington World of Adventures v Reed*[114] that the definition of sex discrimination in the SDA 1975 could be interpreted (in light of the judgment in *P v S*) as including gender reassignment. The response of the Government was to introduce legislation in the form of the Sex Discrimination (Gender Reassignment) Regulations 1999.[115] These Regulations expressly prohibit discrimination on the grounds of gender reassignment in the fields of employment and vocational training. Where a person receives less favourable treatment than another person on the ground that the individual intends to undergo, is undergoing or has undergone gender reassignment, then a case will be

---

[109] Referred to as gender dysphoria or gender identity disorder.
[110] *A v Chief Constable of the West Yorkshire Police* [2003] IRLR 32.
[111] In *Croft v Consignia plc* [2002] IRLR 851 a refusal to allow a pre-operative male to female transsexual to use a ladies' toilet was not contrary to the SDA 1975.
[112] [1996] IRLR 347.
[113] Ibid at p 354.
[114] [1997] IRLR 556.
[115] SI 1999/1002.

established, unless a GOQ applies.[116] As a result of the permanent GOQs, it will now be permissible to discriminate against an individual who intends to undergo, is undergoing or has undergone gender reassignment and the job involves the holder of the job being liable to be called upon to undertake physical searches[117] or work or live in a private home and objection might reasonably be taken to allowing that person a degree of physical or social contact with a person living in the home (or knowledge of their intimate details).

The impact of these Regulations can be seen in *Goodwin v United Kingdom*,[118] where the ECHR held that the United Kingdom was in breach of Article 8 of the Convention (dealing with the right to family life, etc.) because, as part of certain procedures set up to implement legal rules in the United Kingdom (e.g. dealing with national insurance, employment and social security), someone's sex was recorded as that of their birth, thereby discriminating against transsexuals.

In *A v Chief Constable of West Yorkshire Police*[119] the complainant was a male to female transsexual who applied to become a police constable. She was refused employment on the basis that legislation affected the carrying out of searches by transsexuals and, accordingly, the complainant would not be able to carry out the full duties of a police constable. The Chief Constable argued that 'she was legally male and conformity of legal and apparent gender was a genuine occupational qualification within the meaning of section 7 of the Sex Discrimination Act 1975'. The employment tribunal found in favour of the complainant; however, the Employment Appeal Tribunal allowed the appeal. The case went on appeal to the Court of Appeal, where it was held that a post-operative male to female transsexual was to be regarded as female, except where there were significant factors of public interest to weigh against the interests of the individual applicant in obtaining legal recognition of her gender reassignment. This might include the situation where a transsexual wanted her transsexualism to remain undisclosed, although that was not the position in this case.

Race discrimination

Background to the legislation

The large-scale influx of racial and ethnic minorities into the United Kingdom in recent times started with recruitment of cheap migrant

---

[116] For details of supplementary temporary and permanent GOQs in the legislation and relevant case law, see (2002) 104 *Equal Opportunities Review* 17.
[117] See *A v Chief Constable of West Yorkshire Police* [2003] IRLR 32, where this right was qualified.
[118] [2002] IRLR 664.
[119] [2003] ICR 161.

labour from the New Commonwealth territories such as the West Indies and India and other countries in Europe in the 1950s and 1960s. These immigrants were used to fill the labour shortages caused by post-war industrial expansion in the United Kingdom.

Following this period there was an economic recession which led to a substantial decrease in primary immigration, although the process of secondary immigration (whereby the families of existing migrants were allowed into the country to join their relatives) continued throughout the 1970s and 1980s. Substantial numbers of refugees from Eastern Europe and Africa sought asylum from the 1980s onwards and this phenomenon continues today.[120] Overall, the introduction of people with different backgrounds, cultures and physical characteristics often led to racism within British society and particularly in the workplace.[121]

> In societies such as Britain racism is produced and reproduced through political discourse, the media, the educational system and other institutions. Within this wider social context racism becomes an integral element of diverse social issues such as law and order, crime, the inner cities and urban unrest.[122]

The following quote summarised the traditional view of most employers in respect of employment of persons from racial minorities:

> Despite the need for their labour, their presence aroused widespread hostility at all levels . . . Employers only reluctantly recruited immigrants where there were no white workers to fill the jobs . . . At this time the preference for white workers was seen as quite natural and legitimate – immigrants were seen as an inferior but necessary labour supply.[123]

It was necessary to combat racism[124] through application of the law and the first attempt to do this in an employment context was the RRA 1968. There were inherent defects in this Act, however, which meant that it was ineffective in its attempt to combat racism within employment (e.g. there was no scope for direct complaint about employers by victims of discrimination and there was no facility to bring a case for indirect discrimination). These deficiencies became apparent and pressure was put on the government by various bodies to bring in new legislation in the form of the RRA 1976.

It is interesting to note that race discrimination in employment was not part of the agenda of the European Union until very recently. In the past, however, where changes in the legislation dealing with sex discrimination came about through EU legislation or case law, governments

---

[120] M MacEwen *Tackling racism in Europe: an examination of anti-discrimination law in practice* (Berg Publishing, 1995), pp 3–6, 155–159.
[121] B Wiley *Employment Law in Context* (2nd edn, Prentice Hall, 2003), pp 194–199.
[122] J Solomos *Race and Racism in Britain* (2nd edn, Macmillan, 1993), pp 183–185.
[123] J Solomos and L Back *Racism and Society* (Macmillan, 1996), pp 67–69.
[124] Ibid, pp 194–198 for useful definitions of race, ethnicity, colour and racism.

tended to introduce equivalent changes to legislation dealing with race discrimination shortly after (e.g. Race Relations (Remedies) Act 1994). The Amsterdam Treaty introduced the power to adopt a Directive to implement the principle of equal treatment on grounds of race or religion.[125] The power to adopt measures to deal with discrimination is now contained within Article 13 of the EC Treaty (see Chapter 2).[126]

Race Relations Act 1976

There are strong similarities between the legislation dealing with race and sex discrimination in most areas. As a result, there is no need to give detailed consideration to sections of the RRA 1976 where this applies because reference can be made to the relevant provision in the SDA 1975.

> The RRA takes its form from the SDA; the two are substantially equivalent, except that in one case discrimination on grounds of gender is being dealt with, whereas in the other it is discrimination on racial grounds which are proscribed.[127]

The case law arising under sex discrimination law can not only alter interpretation of that law but also the equivalent legal rules dealing with race discrimination, and vice versa.

Under s 3(1) of the RRA 1976 racial grounds are defined as meaning 'colour, race, nationality or ethnic or national origins'.[128]

There is no explicit protection against religious discrimination, although certain religions have protection under the Act (e.g. Sikhs and Jews) and all religions are covered by the Employment Equality (Religion or Belief) Regulations 2003[129] which came into effect in December 2003.

The term 'nationality' refers to race and citizenship. Thus it is unlawful to discriminate against nationals of countries in the European Union. It is now clear that the Scots and the English can be regarded as a separate national grouping for the purposes of the RRA 1976.

Direct discrimination and the RRA 1976

Section 1(1)(a) of the RRA 1976 provides: 'A person discriminates against another in any circumstances relevant for the purposes of any provision in this Act if . . . on racial grounds he treats that other less favourably

---

[125] Council Directive 2000/43/EC.

[126] E Guild 'The EC Directive on Race Discrimination: surprises, possibilities and limitations' (2000) 29 *Industrial Law Journal* 416.

[127] C Bourn and J Whitmore *Anti-Discrimination Law in Britain* (3rd edn, Sweet & Maxwell, 1996), p 11.

[128] The new regulations implementing the EU Race Discrimination Directive – the Race Relations Act 1976 (Amendment) Regulations 2003 – insert a new section 1A in the RRA 1976 that covers only discrimination based on race or ethnic or national origin, not on colour or nationality.

[129] SI 2003/1660.

than he treats or would treat other persons.' As in sex discrimination cases, the motive of the employer is irrelevant. It is enough to show that the employee suffered less favourable treatment. The assumption is that the applicant will cite a comparator of a different racial group in a similar position to him or her who has been given (or would have been given) preferential treatment by the employer. In the event that a comparator in the workplace cannot be found, reference may be made to a hypothetical comparator.[130]

The less favourable treatment may be on the ground of the race of a third party. In *Zarzynska v Levy*,[131] a female barperson was dismissed when she refused to follow an order not to serve drinks to persons of a particular racial group. It was held that this represented direct discrimination as per s 1(1)(a) of the RRA 1976.[132]

Indirect discrimination

Section 1(1)(b) of the RRA 1976 provides:

> A person discriminates against another in any circumstances relevant for the purposes of any provision of this Act if . . . he applies a requirement or condition[133] which he applies or would apply equally to persons not of the same racial group as that other but –
> (i) which is such that the proportion of persons of a racial group that can comply with it is considerably smaller than the proportion of persons not of that racial group who can comply with it; and
> (ii) which he cannot show to be justifiable irrespective of the colour, race, nationality or ethnic or national origins of the person to whom it is applied; and
> (iii) which is to the detriment of that other because he cannot comply with it.

Under section 1A[134] a person also discriminates against another if, in any circumstances relevant for the provision referred to in section 1B[135] (which includes discrimination in the employment field):

> he applies to that other a provision, criterion or practice which he applies or would apply to persons not of the same race or ethnic or national origins as that other but –
> (a) which puts or would put persons of the same race or ethnic or national origins as that other at particular disadvantage when compared with other persons,

---

[130] *Balamoody v United Kingdom Central Council for Nursing, Midwifery and Health Visiting* [2002] IRLR 288.
[131] [1978] IRLR 7, EAT.
[132] See also *Weathersfield v Sargent* [1998] IRLR 14, EAT.
[133] It used to be necessary to show that a discriminatory condition or requirement applied and this represented a high standard of proof for the applicant in these cases.
[134] Added by the Race Relations Act 1976 (Amendment) Regulations 2003, SI 2003/1626.
[135] Part II, ss 17–18D; s 19B so far as it relates to social security, health care, any form of social protection or social disadvantage which does not fall within s 20; ss 20–24, ss 26A and 26B; ss 76 and 76ZA; and Part IV in its application to the provisions referred to above.

(b) which puts that other at that disadvantage, and
(c) which he cannot show to be a proportionate means of achieving a
     legitimate aim.[136]

There are therefore two different definitions of indirect discrimination which apply under the RRA 1976 (the second definition having narrower grounds but a less stringent evidential requirement) and determining which one of these definitions is appropriate is dependent on which section of the Act applies. The evidential aspect of these definitions is best illustrated by consideration of indirect discrimination cases.

In *Perera v Civil Service Commission (No 2)*[137] the complainant was a Sri Lankan by birth. He had a legal qualification and had practised at the bar in his own country, and for several years in the United Kingdom he had practised at the bar and obtained ICMA qualifications. Despite this, he had failed after numerous attempts to be transferred into the legal service or accountancy section, or to obtain a promotion in his post as executive officer. He brought a case against his employer, the Civil Service, alleging discrimination over the rejection of his application for the post of legal assistant. The selection board took into account four factors in determining suitability for selection: experience in the United Kingdom; command of English; whether the candidate had or had not applied for British nationality; and age. He claimed these requirements were indirectly discriminatory against people from his racial group. The Court of Appeal held: that the applicant had failed to establish that these were the requirements or conditions (must be *absolute* bar); and that the candidate's personal qualities were the significant factor in determining selection of staff:

> The whole of the evidence indicates that a brilliant man whose personal qualities made him suitable as a legal assistant might well have been sent forward on a short list by the interview board in spite of being, perhaps, below standard on his knowledge of English and his ability to communicate in that language.[138]

It is doubtful that the Court would reach the same conclusion now, given that the definition of indirect discrimination has been amended.[139]

In *Hussein v Saints Complete House Furnishers*[140] an employer made it part of the specification for a job that applicants could not be residents in the city centre of Liverpool. Evidence was led which showed that 50% of the population of the city centre were black, whereas only 12% of the residents in the acceptable area were black. There was no justification for this

---

[136] RRA 1976, s IA.
[137] [1983] ICR 428, CA.
[138] Ibid, per Stephenson LJ at p 147.
[139] See *Raval v Department of Health and Social Security and Civil Service Commission* [1985] IRLR 370, where various questions were set for tribunals to help them analyse claims of indirect discrimination.
[140] [1979] IRLR 337.

discriminatory requirement. It was held that this was indirect discrimination as per s 1(1)(b) of the RRA 1976.

Victimisation

Under s 2 of the RRA 1976 anyone involved in enforcing the Act by bringing proceedings, making allegations or giving information is protected against victimisation by his employer or its employees.[141] It is now possible, as a result of the *Coote*[142] decision, to claim victimisation where an employer takes retaliatory action against an ex-employee (e.g. refusing to give a reference) because he or she brought a claim against the employer under the RRA 1976. Section 27A of the Act is concerned with 'relationships that have come to an end'.[143] This section provides that an act of discrimination or harassment is unlawful even after the relationship has come to an end, provided that the discrimination or harassment arises out of, or is closely connected to, the relationship.

Genuine occupational qualifications

Under s 5 of the RRA 1976 it is permissible to discriminate in recruitment and selection where:

- the job involves participation in a dramatic performance or other entertainment in a capacity for which a person of that racial group is required for reasons of authenticity
- the job involves participation as an artist's or photographic model in the production of a work of art or visual image for which a person of that racial group is required for authenticity
- the job involves working in a place where food or drink is provided or served to and consumed by members of the public in a particular setting for which, in that job, a person of that particular racial group is required for reasons of authenticity (e.g. Chinese restaurant)
- the holder of the job provides persons of that racial group with personal services promoting their welfare and those services can be most effectively provided by persons of that racial group.

Enforcement of the Race Relations Act 1976

An employee or an employer or the tribunal itself can request a discovery of documents by an employment tribunal, whereby a party is ordered to produce documentation where such information is necessary for dealing with the complaint. In *West Midlands Passenger Transport Executive*

---

[141] *Chief Constable of West Yorkshire v Khan* [2001] IRLR 830, HL.
[142] C-185/97 *Coote v Granada Hospitality Ltd (No 2)* [1998] ECR I-5199, ECJ.
[143] Inserted by the Race Relations Act 1976 (Amendment) Regulations 2003, SI 2003/1626.

v Singh[144] the applicant needed statistical data from his employer to substantiate his claim for indirect discrimination. The applicant was denied promotion as a senior inspector and claimed racial discrimination and asked for a discovery of documents of statistics relating to the ethnic origins, qualifications and experience of all applicants applying for senior inspector posts over a two-year period.

> The suitability of candidates can rarely be measured objectively; often subjective judgements will be made. If there is evidence of a high percentage rate of failure to achieve promotion at particular levels by members of a particular racial group, this may indicate that the real reason for the refusal is a conscious or unconscious racial attitude which involves stereotyped assumptions about members of the group.
>
> We are satisfied that the statistical material ordered is relevant to the issues in this case, in that (1) it may assist the applicant in establishing a positive case that the treatment of coloured employees was on racial grounds, which was an effective cause of their, and his, failure to obtain promotion; (2) it may assist the applicant to rebut the employer's contention that they operated in practice an equal opportunities policy which was applied in his case.[145]

Under the Race Relations (Questions and Replies) Order 1977[146] the questions to put to an employer in the form of a questionnaire are set out.[147] A completed questionnaire can be used as evidence in the proceedings and where the employer fails to respond to the questionnaire or his answers reveal a discriminatory attitude on his part then the tribunal will draw appropriate inferences at the hearing of the case.

Remedies

The following remedies are available under the Race Relations Act 1976:

(1) Compensation: the headings of compensation can include lost earnings, loss of future earnings, injury to feelings, loss of other employment rights (including pensions) and aggravated damages (in England and Wales).

 The Race Relations (Remedies) Act 1994 came into force in July 1994 and repealed the upper limit for compensation (set out in s 56(2) of the RRA 1976). It also gave the Secretary of State the power to make regulations providing for interest to be included in any compensation award made under the RRA 1976.

(2) Recommendations can be made whereby an employer will be given a specified time to take action to remove or lessen the harmful effect

---

[144] [1988] ICR 614, CA.
[145] Ibid at 620.
[146] SI 1977/842.
[147] Under RRA 1976, s 65 and SDA 1975, s 74 the Secretary of State is given the power to prescribe a questionnaire which an aggrieved party can send to an employer, seeking further information about the reasons for its decisions and actions.

of the discrimination on the complainant (RRA 1976, s 56(1)(c)). If an employer fails without reasonable justification to comply, then the employment tribunal (if it thinks it is just and equitable to do so) can award additional compensation.

(3) A declaratory order states the rights of the parties in relation to the allegation of discrimination.

(4) In the course of a formal investigation the Commission for Racial Equality can, where satisfied that an unlawful act or practice has taken place, issue a non-discrimination notice in respect of the person concerned.[148] The CRE also has the power to bring proceedings against an employer where the employer has issued instructions to or put pressure on an employee to discriminate. Under s 29(1) of the RRA 1976 it is unlawful to publish discriminatory adverts and the right to take action is placed in the hands of the CRE.

Burden of proof – vicarious liability

Under s 32 of the RRA 1976 and s 41 of the SDA 1975 (discussed above) an employer can be vicariously liable for the actions of an employee undertaking a discriminatory act. 'Anything done by a person in the course of his employment shall be treated . . . as done by his employer as well as by him, whether or not it was done with the employer's knowledge or approval.' In deciding if the employee was acting in the course of his employment for the purposes of the definition, the tribunals and courts referred to the interpretation of this phrase by the judiciary in tort cases under the common law.

In *Irving v Post Office*,[149] the Post Office was not liable for racially abusive words written on an envelope destined to be delivered by a postman, to his neighbour, since the postman was not acting in the course of employment. His employment provided the opportunity for his misconduct, but the misconduct formed no part of the performance of his duties, was in no way directed towards the performance of his duties and was not done for the benefit of his employer.

In *Tower Boot Co v Jones*[150] an employee was racially harassed at work, suffering severe physical and verbal abuse from his colleagues. The employer argued that the acts were not committed in the course of the harassers' employment and that there was therefore no liability. The EAT held:

> The nub of the test of whether an act is done in the course of employment is whether the unauthorised wrongful act of the employee is so connected with that which he was employed to do as to be a mode of doing it.

---

[148] SDA 1975, s 67; RRA 1976, s 58.
[149] [1987] IRLR 289, CA.
[150] [1995] IRLR 529, EAT.

The racial harassment did not represent a mode of carrying out their employment. The case of *Lister v Hesley Hall Ltd*[151] (discussed above) broadened considerably the scope for the employer to be vicariously liable under the common law for the actions of its employees.

The approach for determining the vicarious liability of an employer under both statutes was set out by the Court of Appeal in *Jones v Tower Boot Co Ltd*.[152] The Court rejected the EAT's approach of resorting to common law rules and said that the words 'in the course of employment' as set out in s 41 of the SDA 1975 should be given a purposive construction and interpretation should be on the basis of everyday speech. The employer was held liable for the actions of its employees. Where attempting to avoid vicarious liability, an employer's primary defence in race and sex discrimination cases is provided under s 41(3) of the SDA 1975 and s 32(3) of the RRA 1976:

> In proceedings brought under this Act against any person in respect of an act alleged to have been done by an employee of his it shall be a defence for that person to prove that he took such steps as were reasonably practicable to prevent the employee from doing that act, or from doing in the course of his employment acts of that description.

What shall be reasonably practical steps will depend on the circumstances. However, the following types of behaviour might in part or in full represent such steps: the employer undertaking training on equal opportunities for supervisory employees; having an equal opportunities policy (or more specific policies dealing with different kinds of discrimination, e.g. sexual harassment), the content of which is notified to all staff; providing adequate supervision to control discriminatory acts; and introducing disciplinary measures for dealing with perpetrators of sex or race discrimination under the employer's disciplinary procedure.

Race Relations (Amendment) Act 2000

This substitutes a new section 71 to the RRA 1976 and imposes a statutory duty on public authorities to have due regard, when performing their functions, to the need to eliminate unlawful racial discrimination and to promote equality of opportunity and good relations between persons of different racial groups. It therefore outlaws for the first time direct and indirect discrimination in the carrying out of public authority functions and places duties on public bodies to promote racial equality.[153] The CRE has new enforcement powers in the form of compliance notices, which

[151] [2001] IRLR 472.
[152] [1997] ICR 254, CA.
[153] The CRE has issued a code of practice for assisting public authorities in taking appropriate action to comply with the Act.

can be issued to public authorities failing to comply with any of their specific duties under the Act.[154]

Justification defence

The employer has a defence that the discrimination is justifiable on grounds other than race, nationality, ethnic origins, etc. It must show that there is a real need which can be objectively justified for the practice, criterion or condition. In *Singh v Rowntree Macintosh Ltd*[155] a 'no beard' rule was found to represent indirect discrimination against Sikhs; however, it was justified on the ground of health and safety.[156]

Race Relations Act 1976 (Amendment) Regulations 2003

The EU Race Discrimination Directive (2000/43/EC) is the first Directive to provide rights to employees in Member States. In the United Kingdom, this was transposed by the Race Relations Act 1976 (Amendment) Regulations 2003,[157] which include a statutory definition of racial harassment, introduce changes to the burden of proof and provide a new definition of indirect discrimination.

Definitions of direct and indirect discrimination were amended to comply more closely with the Burden of Proof Directive. With respect to indirect discrimination, the wording used in defining indirect discrimination as it applies to certain sections in the RRA 1976 changed to 'provision, criterion or practice' instead of 'requirement or condition' (discussed earlier). Also, for the first time racial harassment was defined under statute and treated as directly unlawful.

As in the case of sexual harassment, the legal protection against racial harassment has derived from creative interpretation of the RRA 1976 by the judiciary: it was decided that harassment was a detriment for the purposes of s 4(2)(c) of the Act.

In *De Souza v Automobile Association*[158] a black female employee overheard a racist comment about her in a conversation between two managers. This was not deemed to be sufficient detriment[159] by the Court of Appeal for the purposes of the RRA 1976. The Court of Appeal did take the opportunity to clarify that liability can arise in cases of sexual or racial harassment where the only detriment suffered by the employee is

---

[154] For detailed coverage of the Act's main provisions, see *Industrial Relations Law Bulletin* (March 2002) pp 2–8.
[155] [1979] IRLR 199, EAT.
[156] In *Panesar v Nestle Co* [1980] ICR 144, CA, a rule forbidding the wearing of beards in a chocolate factory, although discriminatory against Sikhs, was justifiable on hygiene grounds.
[157] SI 2003/1626.
[158] [1986] IRLR 103, CA; see also *Thomas and another v Robinson* [2003] IRLR 7.
[159] Defined as 'putting under a disadvantage' in *Ministry of Defence v Jeremiah* [1979] IRLR 436, CA.

having to work in a hostile or unwelcome working environment caused by the harassment.[160] The legal rules developed in sexual harassment cases such as *Strathclyde Regional Council v Porcelli*[161] and *Insitu Cleaning Co Ltd v Heads*[162] (covered earlier) also apply to racial harassment cases.

The leading case of *Jones v Tower Boot Co*[163] illustrates an extreme form of racial harassment involving physical assault and verbal abuse of a 16-year-old boy by a group of colleagues. The legal significance of this case was that employers could potentially be held vicariously liable for the actions of all their employees in cases of racial or sexual harassment or in other discrimination cases.

As a result of EU intervention, for the first time racial harassment is now defined and directly treated as unlawful under statute.[164] The Race Relations Act 1976 (Amendment) Regulations 2003 insert a new section 3A into the RRA 1976:

> A person subjects another to harassment . . . where, on grounds of race or ethnic or national origins, he engages in unwanted conduct which has the purpose or effect of –
> (a) violating that other person's dignity; or
> (b) creating an intimidating, hostile, degrading, humiliating or offensive environment for him.

This effect is said to have occurred 'if and only if, having regard to all the circumstances, including in particular, the perception of that other, it should reasonably be considered as having that effect'.[165] This takes into consideration the impact of the behaviour on a particular victim, which caters for differences in the reaction of victims to racial harassment. There is no longer any requirement for a comparator in harassment cases.

Further reading

Dine, J and Watt, B *Discrimination Law. Concepts, Limitations and Justifications* (Longman, 1996)

Fredman, S (ed) *Discrimination and human rights: the case of racism* (Oxford University Press, 2001)

MacEwen, M *Tackling racism in Europe: an examination of anti-discrimination law in practice* (Berg Publishing, 1995)

Rubenstein, M *Discrimination: a guide to the relevant case law on sex, race and disability discrimination and equal pay* (16th edn, Butterworths/Michael Rubenstein, 2003)

Townshend-Smith, RJ *Discrimination Law: Text, Cases and Materials* (Cavendish Publishing, 1998)

---

[160] For a critique of this case, see RJ Townshend-Smith *Discrimination Law: Text, Cases and Materials* (Cavendish Publishing, 1998), pp 239–240.
[161] [1986] IRLR 134, Ct Sess.
[162] [1995] IRLR 4, EAT.
[163] [1997] IRLR 168, CA.
[164] For detailed coverage of the legal rules, see generally the *Equal Opportunities Review*.
[165] *Reed and Bull Information Systems Ltd v Stedman* [1999] IRLR 299 at 302.

Chapter 5

Equal pay

Richard Benny

Introduction

Historically, there has been a longstanding pay disparity between men
and women which continues to the present day.[1] This has varied over the
years but is still substantial: broadly speaking, women earn on average
80% of men's pay.[2] Pay disparities based on gender constitute sex discrimination, and the equal pay legislation and case law (both domestic
and European) considered in this chapter concern the elimination of
such discrimination, unless it can be justified on grounds other than sex.

Equal pay claims in this jurisdiction may be made under either domestic
or European Community law. The Equal Pay Act 1970 (EPA 1970) represents the former, whereas Article 141 of the EC Treaty (formerly
Article 119), together with the Equal Pay Directive,[3] represent the latter.
One of the most interesting and perplexing areas of equal pay concerns
the interplay between these two legal systems, which has meant that the
law in this area is quite complex.

Equal pay is essentially an aspect of sex discrimination law and, as such,
is often considered together with another key piece of domestic discrimination legislation, the Sex Discrimination Act 1975 (SDA 1975). Although
the EPA 1970 has been on the statute books since 1970, it has been in force
only since 1975.[4] The EPA 1970 and the Sex Discrimination Act 1975

---

[1] In recent years, the average hourly female earnings have been estimated to be about 79%
of male earnings, while weekly earnings of full-time manual female workers amounted to
just over 72% of those of full-time manual men. (See S Fredman *Women and the Law*
(Clarendon Press, 1997); M Rubenstein 'The Equal Treatment Directive and UK Law'
in C McCrudden (ed) *Women, Employment and European Equality Law* (Eclipse Publications),
1987.)

[2] See C Collins *Employment Law* (Clarendon Law Series, OUP, 2003); Office for National
Statistics *New Earnings Survey 2001* (this indicates that female full-time employees earn on
average 82% of the average hourly earnings of male full-time employees).

[3] Directive 75/117/EEC.

[4] It came into force on 29 December 1975. This delay was intended to allow employers a
period in which to eliminate discrimination voluntarily before it became illegal.

(SDA 1975) together are supposed to form one homogeneous code of domestic legislation,[5] although the rights conferred by these two Acts are mutually exclusive. The EPA 1970 is concerned with *contractual* matters only. However, it is not limited only to pay, despite its short title, but covers *all* contractual benefits, including pay. The SDA 1975 covers matters *outside* contractual rights and benefits, such as appointment to a job, promotion, transfer, etc. (at least, where these are not contractual matters). Of course, non-contractual benefits may consist of the payment of money, in which case the SDA 1975 would apply.[6] It should be noted that the EPA 1970 applies equally to men as well as women,[7] although because of the 'gender pay gap' referred to above, most of the cases concern claims brought by women. The remainder of this discussion assumes a female claimant.

It is worth noting that the EPA 1970's objective is to eliminate gender-based pay discrimination. It is not about securing fair wages for women.[8] Pay disparities between men and women are permissible, so if the employer establishes a defence showing that the pay disparity is due to factors other than sex, the claimant fails.

The EPA 1970 gives effect to this principle (eliminating sex discrimination in pay) by providing that the equality clause will *not* operate where the employer can show that a disparity between the contract of a woman and her comparator is attributable to factors other than sex.

Discovering information on which to base an equal pay claim

One question often glossed over or avoided in books on the subject of equal pay is how the claimant may actually discover gender-based pay disparities in the first place, in order to bring a claim. The ECJ in *Danfoss*[9] indicated that pay systems should be 'transparent', meaning that the criteria upon which pay or pay increments are awarded should be clear to those affected by them. This is not always the case. In any event, knowing the criteria does not necessarily mean that the woman will uncover gender-based pay practices, unless other information is to hand. Occasionally, there may be open, informal discussion by individuals at work about their pay, so that such matters become common knowledge, although this is likely to be rare.

Failing the woman securing a vital piece of information in this regard by pure chance, there are two ways to discover pay inequality. The first concerns an aspect of collective labour law, i.e. the provisions contained

---

[5] See *Shields v E Coomes (Holdings) Ltd* [1978] ICR 1159.
[6] See comments of the Court of Appeal in *Peake v Automotive Products Ltd* [1977] ICR 480.
[7] See s 1(13).
[8] See the remarks of Lord Browne-Wilkinson in *Strathclyde Regional Council v Wallace* [1998] IRLR 146, HL, at 149: 'The purpose of s.1 of the Equal Pay Act 1970 is to eliminate sex discrimination in pay not to achieve fair wages.'
[9] Case 109/88 [1989] IRLR 532.

in ss 181–185 of the Trade Union and Labour Relations (Consolidation) Act 1992. These apply where an employer recognises a trade union for collective bargaining purposes. Under these provisions, employers recognising trade unions must give the union such information as it requires to bargain effectively, in accordance with good industrial relations practice. The union may thereby secure information concerning pay systems and rates, with statistics on the pay rates and sex of workers covered by the provisions.

Another approach is to use the Equal Pay Questionnaire, based on questionnaires which have been previously used for some time under the SDA 1975, the Race Relations Act 1976 (RRA 1976), and the Disability Discrimination Act 1995 (DDA 1995). This questionnaire procedure was introduced by the Employment Act 2002. Section 7B of the EPA 1970 and regulations[10] made under it allow the claimant (or proposed claimant) to ask the employer for relevant information which will help them to establish their complaint (or whether there are grounds to bring a complaint if no such complaint has been lodged). Employers are not under a statutory duty to supply answers to the questionnaire, but an employment tribunal (ET) will be entitled to draw inferences from a deliberate refusal to answer, or from a reply which is evasive or equivocal. Under the questionnaire procedure, the employer has eight weeks in which to respond.

The EAT has indicated that it is also possible for a claimant to use the discovery process to obtain disclosure of documents which might enable her to identify appropriate comparators, but only once a *prima facie* case has been established that her pay is lower than that of comparable male employees (see *Leverton v Clwyd County Council*[11]). However, this is a risky tactic because such a trawl may not turn up a comparator, or the tribunal might find that the selected comparator was not appropriate.

European Community law and equal pay

European Community law, particularly its interpretation by the European Court of Justice, has been immensely significant in the field of equal pay (see particularly Chapter 2). Article 141 of the EC Treaty states:

1. Each Member State shall ensure that the principle of equal pay for male and female workers for equal work or work of equal value is applied.
2. For the purpose of this Article, 'pay' means the ordinary basic or minimum wage or salary and any other consideration, whether in cash or in kind, which the worker receives directly or indirectly, in respect of his employment, from his employer.

---

[10] See the Equal Pay (Questions and Replies) Order 2003 (SI 2003/722), which came into force on 6 April 2003.
[11] [1985] IRLR 197.

This 'equal pay principle' is developed by Article 1 of the Equal Pay Directive,[12] which states:

> The principle of equal pay for men and women outlined in Article 119 [current Article 141] of the Treaty, hereinafter called 'principle of equal pay', means, for the same work or for work to which equal value is attributed, the elimination of all discrimination on grounds of sex with regard to all aspects and conditions of remuneration.
>
> In particular, where a job classification system is used for determining pay, it must be based on the same criteria for both men and women and so drawn up as to exclude any discrimination on grounds of sex.

Directives are enforceable against the state or emanations of the state (where they are sufficiently clear, precise, and unconditional, i.e. they require no detailed intervention from the state). Emanations of the state have been taken to include a health authority (*Marshall v Southampton and South West Hampshire Health Authority*),[13] British Gas (pre-privatisation),[14] and the governing body of a voluntary aided school.[15]

Article 141 is directly effective, i.e. it confers rights which can be enforced by an individual employee against his or her employer in the national courts (this was established by the decision of the ECJ in *Defrenne v Sabena (No 2)*[16]). The principle of direct effect means that Article 141 takes precedence over any provision of the EPA 1970 which is inconsistent with it.[17]

In its judgment, the ECJ in *Defrenne* stated that the right to equal pay is one of the fundamental principles of Community law. Article 141 (former Article 119) was a key principle in the Treaty of Rome, with a double goal: one economic, the other social. The economic aim was to prevent some Member States (who had an equal pay provision in their domestic legislation) being placed at a competitive disadvantage as against those Member States without such a provision in their domestic law. The social aim was to attain social progress and constantly to improve the living and working conditions of all the people of Europe, as stated in the Preamble to the Treaty of Rome. However, as stated in *Defrenne*, Article 141 is not retrospective, i.e. it could not be used for equal pay claims prior to the date of the judgment (8 April 1976). Article 141 applies to both direct and indirect discrimination.

It should also be remembered that under EC law any pay practice that is not gender-based may be successfully defended by the employer if it establishes that the practice is 'objectively justified'. The EPA 1970's 'genuine material factor' defence (discussed below) also provides a means of non-gender-based justification under domestic legislation.

[12] Council Directive 75/117/EEC.
[13] [1986] IRLR 140, ECJ.
[14] See *Foster v British Gas* [1990] IRLR 353.
[15] *National Union of Teachers v Governing Body of St Mary's Church of England Junior School* [1997] 3 CMLR 630; [1997] IRLR 242.
[16] [1976] ICR 547.
[17] See *Pickstone v Freemans plc* [1987] ICR 867.

Although EC law may be relied upon in employment tribunals by claimants bringing equal pay claims, it should be remembered that Article 141 is both wider and narrower in scope than the EPA 1970. It is wider in that it applies to all 'remuneration' which an employee receives from her employer, including contractual benefits, gratuitous benefits and any benefits which the employer is required to provide by statute. It is narrower than the EPA 1970 because Article 141 covers only pay, whereas the EPA 1970 covers all contractual terms, not only those relating to pay.[18]

Code of Practice on Equal Pay

Under s 56A of the SDA 1975, the Equal Opportunities Commission (EOC) is given the power to issue Codes of Practice containing such practical guidance as the Commission thinks fit to facilitate the elimination of discrimination in the employment field, and the promotion of equality of opportunity in employment between men and women. On 26 March 1997, the EOC issued a Code of Practice on Equal Pay ('the Code') whose objective is 'to provide practical guidance and recommend good practice to those with responsibility for or interest in the pay arrangements within a particular organisation'. The Code is admissible in evidence in proceedings under the EPA 1970.

The Code provides advice to employers on the steps they should take to identify and eliminate discriminatory elements in pay systems, including:

- performance pay;
- pay based on assessment of individual competencies; and
- grading systems.

The Code also gives guidance on the adoption of an equal pay policy, and a specimen policy is annexed to the Code.[19]

The equality clause (EPA 1970, s 1(1))

If successful under the EPA 1970, an equality clause is implied into the woman's contract of employment. This will only operate when the claimant is in the same employment as the selected comparator(s) of the opposite sex, who is/are engaged on like work (meaning work which is the same or broadly similar), work which has been given an equivalent

---

[18] The equality clause in EPA 1970, s 1(2) operates in respect of all contractual terms, 'whether concerned with pay or not'.

[19] There is also an EC Code of Practice: Code of Practice on the Implementation of Equal Pay for Work of Equal Value for Women and Men (COM (96) 336 final).

rating under a job evaluation study (JES), or work which is of equal value.[20] The comparator must be in the same establishment or one where the same terms and conditions apply, e.g. a national collective agreement covering workers across several establishments.

If any term of the woman's contract is or becomes less favourable, the equality clause modifies the woman's contract of employment by raising the less favourable term in her contract so that it is not less favourable when compared to that of her male comparator. Where there is no corresponding term in the woman's contract, it will be deemed to include one.[21] According to the House of Lords in the equal value case of *Hayward v Cammell Laird Shipbuilders Ltd*,[22] the individual contractual terms in the claimant's contract must be considered alongside individual terms in her comparator's contract, rather than looking at the contracts overall. After finding the equal value claim upheld, their Lordships stated that if there was any less favourable term in the woman's contract, the equality clause would operate to raise it so that it was not less favourable, i.e. there is upward equalisation.[23]

The comparator

A claimant must identify a comparator of the opposite sex who is engaged on like work, work rated as equivalent, or work of equal value.[24] Unlike the SDA 1975, where a hypothetical person may be used, under the EPA 1970 a woman must compare herself with an actual male worker; she cannot claim that a hypothetical male would be treated more favourably than she is. The choice of comparator is entirely up to the claimant, and selecting the wrong (i.e. inappropriate) comparator will mean that the claim fails (see *Ainsworth v Glass Tubes and Components Ltd*,[25] in which the EAT held that an industrial tribunal could not substitute for the applicant's choice of comparator another man whom it thought more appropriate).

Permitted comparators (EPA 1970, s 1(2))

Judicial interpretations of s 1(2) of the EPA 1970 mean that a claimant may select as a comparator a predecessor or successor, as well as one who is in some way anomalous.

---

[20] EPA 1970, s 1(2)(a), (b), (c), respectively.
[21] EPA 1970, s 1(2).
[22] [1988] ICR 464.
[23] Cf with the ECJ's approach to equalisation under Article 141 in the pensions case of *Smith v Avdel Systems Ltd* (C-408/92) [1994] IRLR 602, where the Court stated that equalisation could be secured by either upwards *or downwards* equalisation.
[24] EPA 1970, s 1(2).
[25] [1977] ICR 347.

Predecessors

In *Macarthys Ltd v Smith*,[26] the ECJ stated that what is now Article 141 (former Article 119) is directly effective only where a comparison can be made 'on the basis of concrete appraisals of the work actually performed by employees of different sex within the same establishment or service'. In this case, the applicant claimed equal pay with a male predecessor who had left his employment some four months earlier but who had been paid £10 per week more than she for the same job. The ECJ held that Article 119 did not require contemporaneous employment, and it therefore could apply in a case where a woman is paid less than a man who was employed on equal work prior to her period of employment. The EPA 1970 must be read in the light of this ECJ decision.

Successors

A claimant may select as a comparator a successor. In *Diocese of Hallam Trustee v Connaughton*,[27] Ms Connaughton left her employment as Director of Music in April 1994, with her notice period taking the actual date of termination to September 1994. The post was advertised in June 1994 at a salary some £2,000 greater than hers had been. A man was appointed to the post in January 1995, at a salary nearly double hers. The EAT allowed such a comparison, but stated that such comparisons are likely to raise greater evidential problems than those involving a contemporary or immediate predecessor. Furthermore, the EAT said that the tribunal would have to decide in the light of all the evidence whether the equal pay claim for equal work could truly be gauged by reference to the male successor's contract of employment, and it would also have to determine the period over which any such comparison could be sustained for the purpose of assessing compensation. In other words, the longer the gap between the claimant leaving employment and the successor being appointed, the less likely it would be that the claim would succeed.

Selecting more than one comparator

A claimant may select more than one comparator, but the courts are alert to prevent abuses of the equal value claims procedure by claimants adopting a 'scatter-gun' approach, i.e. where they identify too wide a range of comparators (*Leverton v Clwyd County Council*[28]).

[26] [1980] IRLR 210.
[27] [1996] ICR 860.
[28] [1985] IRLR 197.

Selecting a comparator who is less than the claimant's equal

In *Evesham v North Hertfordshire Health Authority*,[29] the claimant in an equal value claim (part of the aftermath of the long-running 'speech therapists' case', discussed below) selected a male comparator who was junior to her in terms of service. Her argument was that, as a speech therapist who had successfully compared herself to a clinical psychologist, she should have been put on a point on the pay scale higher than his, since she had more years of service. This was rejected by the Court of Appeal, which said that her successful claim under s 1(2)(c) of the EPA 1970 meant that she could establish only that she should receive the same pay as her comparator, not more. The woman's pay would be equalised but not allowed to exceed that of the male comparator. The Court held that section 1(2)(c) requires *equality* of treatment by the employer of the applicant and her selected comparator. The comparison was an individual one, not a general one, and the section did not require the employer to modify or include a term in her contract so that it became *more* favourable than the term in her comparator's contract.

Same employment

Under s 1(6) of the EPA 1970, men shall be treated as in the same employment as a woman if they are employed by her employer, or an associated employer,

- at the same establishment as the woman; or
- at establishments which include the establishment at which the woman is employed and at which common terms and conditions of employment are observed either generally or for the relevant classes of employee.

In *British Coal Corporation v Smith*,[30] some 1,286 female canteen workers and cleaners working in 47 different establishments chose as their equal value comparators 150 male workers who were either surface mineworkers or in clerical posts. Most of their terms and conditions were governed by a national agreement, although there were some local variations. The House of Lords held that section 1(6) required common terms to be observed not only at the other establishments but also at the establishments where the women worked, if employees of the comparator class worked there. If no such men worked at the place where the women worked, it would be necessary to establish that common terms would apply if such men did work there. Furthermore, the House of Lords stated that the terms of the comparator classes did not need to be identical or

[29] [2000] IRLR 257.
[30] [1996] IRLR 404.

essentially the same. They had only to be 'on a broad basis, substantially comparable'.[31] In this case, the comparators were held to be in the same employment.

Associated employers (EPA 1970, s 1(6)(c))

Section 1(6)(c) provides that two employers are to be treated as associated if one is a company controlled, either directly or indirectly, by the other employer (which need not be a company), or if both are companies of which a third person has control, either directly or indirectly.

Scope of the comparison permitted under the EPA 1970 and Article 141

It is clear from ECJ jurisprudence that a claim under Article 141 will succeed only where the terms of the claimant and those of the comparator emanate from a single source, such as will allow the employer to mount an explanation as to how the different pay rates arose, and therefore they would not be able to establish a defence. The scope of the comparison permitted under Article 141 was the issue before the ECJ in a case concerning the aftermath of a compulsory competitive tendering (CCT) exercise, following the successful claim of female school dinner ladies a few years earlier in a case arising from the same facts.[32] In *Lawrence v Regent Office Care Ltd*[33] the question was whether female workers employed by private companies who had successfully tendered for the catering and cleaning services in Yorkshire County Council schools could use as comparators male employees employed directly by the same Council who were carrying out equivalent work. The female workers had been employed by the County Council a few years earlier, but were now carrying out the work for their private employer on lower rates of pay than the Council had paid them.

The claimants' claim was that, when they were Council employees, an earlier job evaluation study had found that they were engaged upon work of equal value with their male comparators (who were still employed by the Council). The companies argued that, since the identity of the claimants' employer had changed, they, as completely different employers, would not be in a position to explain the rates of pay paid by the Council. They would, therefore, be unable to use the justification defence (discussed below). The ECJ held that Article 141 could not be relied upon

[31] At p 410.
[32] *Ratcliffe v North Yorkshire County Council* [1995] IRLR 439; [1995] ICR 833, popularly known as the '*Yorkshire Dinner Ladies*' case'.
[33] [2002] IRLR 822.

where the pay conditions cannot be attributed to a single source, i.e. there is no single body which is responsible for the pay inequality, and which could restore equal treatment.

Another case involving the range of permitted comparator allowed in equal pay claims is *Allonby v Accrington & Rossendale College*.[34] In this case, the college dismissed its part-time lecturers, of whom Ms Allonby was one, in order to reduce the financial impact of new employment legislation. She was then offered work as a self-employed subcontractor, through an arrangement with an agency, Education Lecturing Services (ELS), at lower pay and without a number of benefits. Ms Allonby brought a series of claims for sex discrimination and equal pay, one of which was against ELS, which raised the question of whether a male full-time lecturer employed by the College was a permitted comparator. She contended that she and the comparator were employed in the same establishment or service under European law, despite the fact that they were employed under contracts with different employers.

Ms Allonby lost in the ET and the Employment Appeal Tribunal (EAT), on the basis that s 1(6)(c) of the EPA 1970 did not apply because the college had no control over the terms of the contract between ELS and Ms Allonby. The Court of Appeal referred this question to the ECJ. At the time of writing, judgment in this case is awaited, but the opinion of Advocate General Geelhoed, given on 2 April 2003, was that her selection of her male comparator was not permitted under Community law. Following the ECJ's decision in *Lawrence*, the Advocate General stated that the difference in pay could not be attributed to a single source, and therefore there was no body that could be held liable for that difference and for its elimination which, under the Court's case law, was a prerequisite for the application of the principle of equal treatment.

It is interesting to note that the Advocate General in *Allonby* highlighted as a concern (which he said he shared with the Commission)[35] the fact that there was a growing trend for employers to contract out services to specialised contractors, and that the classic employer–employee relationship was being supplanted by these new forms of relationship. He stated: 'As the expression of a progressive specialisation in the economy this development should not *per se* be regarded as undesirable from a social or societal point of view.'[36] While this had positive 'advantages of technical and functional specialisation and diversification',[37] it did raise a general question of how the Community legislature could confer protection on workers (whether employed or self-employed) in these new, flexible work relationships. His conclusion on this aspect of the issues raised by the case was interesting. He stated that, since the principle of equal treatment

---

[34] [2001] IRLR 364.
[35] Paragraph 53.
[36] At para 44.
[37] Ibid.

was a fundamental legal principle, and since under Community law specific protection was given to workers, whether employed or self-employed, under Articles 13 and 141 EC and Articles 21(1) and 23 of the Charter of Fundamental Rights of the European Union, 'specific action by the Community legislature under Article 141(3) EC'[38] was justified. Furthermore, 'such action may precede other measures to ensure the protection of workers for which under Article 137(2)(b) unanimity in the Council is required'.[39]

In *Morton v South Ayrshire Council*,[40] the Inner House of the Court of Session decided that a female primary headteacher who claimed equal pay with a male comparator who worked for a different local authority as a secondary school headteacher had selected an appropriate comparator, since the source of their contractual terms was a national collective agreement applying to all teachers in Scotland. This meant that the collective agreement came within the interpretation of Article 141 given in the ECJ's ruling in *Defrenne v Sabena*.[41]

Lord Johnston stated that, even though each local authority decided how salary scales agreed by the Scottish Joint Negotiating Committee were to be implemented, there was a sufficient connection in a 'loose and non-technical sense',[42] so that the applicant and her comparator could be said to be in the same 'service' of education in Scotland. Interestingly, this was the case despite the fact that the claimant's employer, South Ayrshire Council, had no power or control of the terms and conditions of employment of the comparator employed by the Highland Council.

In a later, related, case, *Milligan v South Ayrshire Council*,[43] male primary school headteachers were unable to make equal pay claims using secondary school headteachers as comparators, since all of the latter were also male. The Court of Session allowed the male claimant to make a contingent claim by comparing himself to a female primary school headteacher, and to have his claim stayed until resolution of his comparator's equal pay claim against a male secondary school headteacher. The Court of Session stated that, unless permitted to bring such a contingent claim, 'he would suffer real prejudice in relation to back pay since he could lodge a claim only after the comparator's claim succeeded'.[44]

---

[38] At para 53.
[39] Ibid.
[40] [2002] IRLR 256.
[41] Case 43/75 [1976] ECR 455. In *Defrenne (No 2)* the ECJ said, at para 21: 'Among the forms of direct discrimination which may be identified solely by reference to the criteria laid down by Article [141] must be included in particular those which have their origin in legislative provisions or in collective labour agreements and which may be detected on the basis of a purely legal analysis of the situation.'
[42] Per the EAT in *Lawrence*.
[43] [2003] IRLR 153.
[44] Ibid, per Lord Gill, the Lord Justice-Clerk, at p 156.

Like work; work rated as equivalent; work of equal value

Like work

Section 1(4) of the EPA 1970 defines 'like work' as follows:

> A woman is to be regarded as employed on like work with men if, but only if, her work and theirs is of the same or a broadly similar nature, and the differences (if any) between the things she does and the things they do are not of practical importance in relation to terms and conditions of employment; and accordingly in comparing her work with theirs regard shall be had to the frequency or otherwise with which any such differences occur in practice as well as to the nature and extent of the differences.

Same or broadly similar work

In order to decide whether the work is the same or broadly similar, the tribunal must make a broad judgment, looking at the type of work, and the skill and knowledge required to do it. A minute examination is not required. For example, in *Capper Pass Ltd v Lawton*,[45] the EAT held that the work of a cook who prepared lunches for the company's directors (between 10 and 20) was broadly similar to that of an assistant chef who worked in the canteen preparing meals for all the factory employees.

A comparison must be made between the things that the claimant and comparator actually do, and the frequency with which they are done. The question is whether the differences (if any) between the two jobs are of practical importance. If the work of claimant and comparator appears to be broadly similar, but the employer claims a difference between the jobs, it is for the employer to establish that that difference is of practical importance in relation to terms and conditions. For example, in *Shields v E Coomes (Holdings) Ltd*,[46] the employer claimed that male counter-staff at its betting shop received a higher hourly pay than female counter-workers because of risk of robbery. The men were employed for security reasons. The Court of Appeal held that, as the men had never been required to deal with any disturbance or attempted violence, there was no difference of practical importance in relation to the terms of the job.

A difference in the degree of responsibility between the woman and her comparator may be a difference of practical importance in relation to their terms and conditions of employment. For example, in *Eaton Ltd v Nuttall*,[47] a female scheduler claimed equal pay with a male scheduler. The EAT held that it was correct to take into account a different degree of responsibility, since an error by the man would have had more serious consequence for the employer than one of the woman's, because she

---

[45] [1976] IRLR 366.
[46] [1978] ICR 1159.
[47] [1977] ICR 272.

dealt with items worth about £2.50 each, whereas he dealt with items worth between £5 and £1,000.

The time the work is carried out is not necessarily a difference of practical importance in relation to the terms and conditons of the claimant's work and her comparators. In *Dugdale v Kraft Foods*,[48] the EAT held that the female claimant (a quality control worker) and her male comparator were engaged upon like work, despite the fact that he worked night shifts and Sundays, whereas she did not. The EAT said that the mere fact that the men's and the women's work is done at different times is not a difference of practical importance justifying unequal pay. The men could be compensated for unsocial hours by a shift payment or premium, applying the same basic pay or day-shift pay between them and the claimant, to ensure equality of treatment.

The ECJ has held that even where job functions are the same or similar, a difference in qualifications and experience between the claimant and the comparator could be a significant difference. In *Angestelltenbetriebsrat der Wiener Gebietskrankenkasse v Wiener Gebietskrankenkasse*,[49] psychotherapists employed by a health authority were drawn from graduate psychologists (largely women) and medical doctors (largely men). The doctors had a different training and experience from the psychologists, and they could be required to undertake a different range of duties. This was held to be sufficient to justify a difference in pay between the two groups.

Work rated as equivalent

An equality clause may be inserted under the EPA 1970, s 1(2) where there has been a job evaluation study (JES) under which the claimant's and the comparator's job have been rated as equivalent. Section 1(5) states:

> A woman is to be regarded as employed on work rated as equivalent with that of any men if, but only if, her job and their job have been given an equal value, in terms of the demand made on a worker under various headings (for instance effort, skill, decision), on a study undertaken with a view to evaluating in those terms the jobs to be done by all or any of the employees in an undertaking or group of undertakings, or would have been given an equal value but for the evaluation being made on a system setting different values for men and women on the same demand under any heading.

The JES is an essential part of the concept of work rated as equivalent under the EPA 1970.[50] The five main methods of job evaluation are known as:

---

[48] [1977] ICR 48.
[49] [1999] IRLR 804.
[50] The main methods of job evaluation are described in ACAS Advisory Booklet No 1 'Job Evaluation – An Introduction'. The EOC publishes a guide entitled 'Job Evaluation Schemes Free of Sex Bias'.

(a) 'job ranking',
(b) 'paired comparisons',
(c) 'job classification',
(d) 'points assessment' and
(e) 'factor comparison'.

Of these, only (d) and (e) satisfy the requirements of section 1(5), since it has been held in *Bromley and others v H & J Quick Ltd*[51] that the subsection requires an analytical and objective JES. 'Analytical' in this context means that the jobs of each worker covered by the study must have been valued in terms of the demand made on the worker under various headings.[52]

Requirement of objectivity in JES

The JES must be entirely objective: any subjective or discriminatory elements concerning the evaluation of the nature of the work done may lead to a finding that the JES does not satisfy the legislative requirements. The ECJ made this clear in *Rummler v Dato-Druck GmbH*[53] (a case brought under Article 1(2) of the Equal Pay Directive). A female printer in Germany claimed that she was wrongly classified under a job classification scheme based on a national collective agreement, because the system gave undue weight to muscular effort. The ECJ held that job classification schemes must use the same criteria for men and women, and they must be organised so that as a whole they do not in practice discriminate against one sex. A JES based on muscular effort *was* permissible, provided it was objectively measurable, and, if the JES as a whole was to be non-discriminatory, such criteria had to be accompanied by other criteria 'in relation to which women had a particular aptitude'. For example, if a job classification scheme had a high weighting for muscular effort and a lower weighting for manual dexterity (normally a more developed ability in women) it could be attacked on that ground. Furthermore, the measurement of effort under the scheme could not be based on the average performance of workers of one sex, and the methods of evaluating criteria must not disadvantage a group of workers of one sex, since that would run the risk of indirect discrimination.

Any direct discrimination in the JES will permit the employment tribunal (ET) to adjust the results of the JES to take this into account in its application. This is the effect of the wording of section 1(5): if her job would have been given an equal value with that of a man but for the fact that

---

[51] [1988] ICR 623.
[52] In *Bromley* itself, the method used by the employer in this case was not analytical, since no attempt had been made to evaluate their jobs by reference to the *demands* made on the workers under the selected factor headings.
[53] [1987] ICR 774.

the evaluation was made on a system which set different values for men and women on the same demand under any heading.[54]

Once accepted as valid by the parties, the JES can be relied upon by the claimant, even if it has not been implemented.[55]

However, any JES has limitations since, as Honeyball and Bowers comment: 'it classifies jobs, not the people who fill them. It must be followed by a subjective merit assessment of the individual's qualities. A [JES] merely provides a building block to indicate the underlying structure of wages on which individual variations may then be built.'[56]

Work of equal value

Where the claimant's work does not come under either of the two other categories, it may come under s 1(2)(c) of the EPA 1970, if it is work of equal value, in terms of the demand made on her. A claimant cannot bring an equal pay claim if her comparator is engaged on like work or work rated as equivalent.

As originally drafted, the EPA 1970 provided for equal pay only where the man and the woman were engaged on like work or work rated as equivalent. There was no requirement under the Act for the employer to conduct a JES, and no one could conduct one without the employer's consent. Therefore, in such circumstances, if an employer refused to conduct a JES, a woman employee who was engaged on work of equal value to that of a man was effectively barred from bringing an equal pay claim. Clearly, this was inconsistent with the principle of equal pay set out in former Article 119 [current Article 141] and the Equal Pay Directive. The Commission made an application to the ECJ for a declaration that the United Kingdom had failed to fulfil its obligations under Community law, which was upheld.[57] The EPA 1970 was subsequently amended by the Equal Pay (Amendment) Regulations 1983[58] to allow a claim for equal pay to be made where work is of equal value, now contained in section 1(2)(c).

Section 1(2) gives examples of the headings under which jobs considered under the equal value provisions may be assessed, e.g. 'effort,

---

[54] This power of the ET to adjust applies only where there is direct discrimination. If there is *indirect* discrimination in the JES, the claimant must bring an equal value claim under EPA 1970, s 1(2)(c).

[55] See *O'Brien v Sim-Chem Ltd* [1980] ICR 573, HL, where a JES had been carried out in co-operation with the unions and new salary ranges had been agreed. These had not been implemented because of a government pay policy. The three women claimants whose jobs had been given an equal rating under the scheme with jobs done by men claimed equal pay under EPA 1970, s 1(2)(b). The House of Lords held that the JES was effective despite the fact that it had not been implemented.

[56] S Honeyball and J Bowers *Textbook on Labour Law* (7th edn, Oxford University Press, 2002), p 291.

[57] *Commission v United Kingdom* (C61/81) [1982] ECR 261.

[58] SI 1983/1794.

skill, decision'. The claimant may choose her comparator, even if there is a male employee working in the same job as her and on the same pay. Therefore, it is not possible for the employer to block an equal value claim by having a 'token' male doing the same job as the woman. In *Pickstone v Freemans plc*,[59] a female warehouse operative chose as her comparator a male checker warehouse operative, although there was a male warehouse operative on the same pay. The House of Lords took a purposive interpretation of section 1(2)(c) to allow compliance with what is now Article 141 and the Equal Pay Directive, allowing the woman's claim to proceed.

Once an equal value claim is presented to the ET, it has the option of appointing an independent expert from an independent panel to write a report on the issue within 42 days, which is also sent to the parties.[60] This report is not binding on the ET. If the ET decides not to appoint an expert, the parties may appoint their own expert. An employer may conduct a JES after the presentation of an equal pay claim, provided it considers the jobs as they were at the time of the complaint.[61]

Genuine material factor (EPA 1970, s 1(3))

Once a claimant has established that she is paid less than her male comparator who is engaged on like work, work rated as equivalent, or work of equal value, the employer may raise the defence that the difference in pay is not due to sex discrimination, and is a material difference between the claimant's case and the comparator's. This is known as the genuine material factor defence (GMF). If the employer does so, the equality clause will not be implied to modify the claimant's contract. Where the complaint is based on like work or work rated as equivalent, the defence *must* be a material difference between the woman's case and the man's; where it is an equal value claim, it may be a material difference.

Defence requirements

The GMF defence requires the employer to point to a factor which is:

- the genuine cause of the difference in pay;
- material;
- not the difference of sex.

---

[59] [1988] IRLR 357.
[60] EPA 1970, s 2A(1).
[61] See *Dibro Ltd v Hore* [1990] ICR 370 and EPA 1970, s 2A(2).

Requirement of genuineness

In *Strathclyde Regional Council v Wallace,*[62] the House of Lords held that the requirement of reasonableness will be satisfied if the ET concludes that the reason put forward by the employer is not a sham or a pretence.

The material factor and sex discrimination

In *Wallace,* their Lordships held that, to be material, a factor must be 'significant and causally relevant'. In *Wallace,* the nine female teachers who brought equal value claims failed because they could not establish sex discrimination since they were in a category of 134 unpromoted teachers who were carrying out the work of principal teachers, of whom 81 were men and 53 women. The employers asserted that the pay disparities came about through different promotion structures of teachers and financial constraints. The House of Lords held that an employer is not required to justify its pay system in every case where unequal pay is alleged. The need to establish objective justification arises only where the factor relied upon is indirectly discriminatory.

In *Glasgow City Council and others v Marshall,*[63] a number of female instructors claimed that they were engaged on like work with a number of male teachers, and one male instructor claimed that he was engaged on like work with a female teacher. The employers argued that the pay structure had been arrived at by different collectively bargained agreements, and that there was an absence of sex discrimination in those agreements (this latter argument was not appealed against). The House of Lords held that, where a pay system was not tainted with sex discrimination, the EPA had no application, and the equality clause would not operate. In the absence of sex discrimination, the employer was not required to go further and to provide an explanation of how the pay disparity had come about. It is only where there is evidence of sex discrimination in the pay structure that the employer will be required objectively to justify the pay disparity.

However, where a pay disparity is clearly tainted with sex discrimination, the GMF will not discharge the employer. In *Ratcliffe v North Yorkshire County Council*[64] (the '*Yorkshire Dinner Ladies*' case'), the reduction by the Direct Services Organisation of the Council of the dinner ladies' wages in order to compete with private contractors in a compulsory competitive tendering (CCT) exercise was not sufficient to meet the requirements of the EPA 1970, s 1(3) since their jobs had been rated as equivalent to those of their male comparators under a JES.

---

[62] [1998] ICR 205.
[63] [2000] IRLR 272.
[64] [1995] ICR 833.

Market forces

In *Rainey v Greater Glasgow Health Board*,[65] the House of Lords held that the GMF defence was made out when the NHS prosthetic fitting service, facing staff shortages, engaged private sector recruits who were paid more than the female claimant. Ms Rainey was paid on the Witley Council scale whereas the comparators were paid the going rates in the private sector. The House of Lords held that the pay difference had been objectively justified, since market forces meant that in order to recruit from the private sector commercial rates of pay had to be offered.

The reasoning in Rainey is influenced by the ECJ's judgment in *Bilka-Kaufhaus GmbH v Weber von Hartz*,[66] in which a part-time, female worker who was denied access to an occupational pension scheme claimed that this infringed the former Article 119. The ECJ held that a pay practice which is apparently gender-neutral but which in fact affects a far greater number of women than men will be contrary to Article 119 unless it is shown to be based on objectively justified factors which are unrelated to any discrimination on grounds of sex. Objective justification will be established where the practice:

(a) corresponds to a real need on the part of the employer;
(b) is necessary to achieve the objective in question;
(c) is proportionate to that objective ('the principle of proportionality').

Therefore, the employer has to balance the discriminatory impact of the practice against the reasonable needs of its business.[67]

Where the pay system lacks 'transparency' – burden of proof

In pay systems lacking transparency (i.e. where employees do not know what criteria it involves or how they are applied), the ECJ has held that it is not necessary for the applicant to show that the employer's pay system operates in a way which is disproportionately disadvantageous to women. In the *Danfoss*[68] case, minimum rates of pay were set for each grade, but differentials were permitted according to merit. The applicants alleged that this pay system resulted in women generally being at the bottom of each grade, earning less on average than men. The ECJ held that lack of transparency was a potential breach of the Equal Pay Directive. The burden in such a case was on the employer to prove that pay differences

---

[65] [1987] ICR 129.
[66] [1987] ICR 110.
[67] See also *Hampson v Department of Education and Science* [1990] ICR 511.
[68] *Handels- og Kontorfunktionaerernes Forbund i Danmark v Dansk Arbejdsgiverforening (acting for Danfoss)* [1989] IRLR 532, ECJ.

were not discriminatory. Therefore, it was sufficient for a woman to show that the average pay of female employees is lower than the average pay of male employees to transfer to the employer the burden of proving that the pay system is not discriminatory.

Accounting for the variation in pay – examples of specific factors

Red circling

Various factors have been argued by employers as satisfying the GMF defence, with varying degrees of success. For example, in *Snoxell v Vauxhall Motors Ltd*,[69] the employer argued that red circling provided a GMF, (this is a practice whereby an employee is placed on a lower grade but who has his (higher) salary protected ('red circled')). The argument did not succeed here because it was based on past sex discrimination. Furthermore, the defence will not be available if the circumstances giving rise to the red circling come to an end.[70]

Collective bargaining

In *Enderby*[71] (the famous '*Speech Therapists'* case'), Dr Enderby, a speech therapist, claimed equal pay with male pharmacists and clinical psychologists. The employer argued, *inter alia*, that the pay disparity of the applicant and her comparators were determined by separate collective bargaining processes. Dr Enderby argued that the collective bargaining processes were themselves indirectly discriminatory, since, although the speech therapy profession was predominantly female, pharmacists and clinical psychologists in the grades to which her claim related were overwhelmingly male. She said that the employer's defence under s 1(3) of the EPA 1970 was therefore not valid.

The ECJ held that a *prima facie* case of sex discrimination will be established where 'significant statistics' show that a job performed almost exclusively by women attracts an appreciably lower rate of pay than a job carried out predominantly by men. On the question of whether separate collective bargaining structures could provide justification, it held that this was not sufficient to account for the pay disparity. Furthermore, the ECJ held that where only part of the pay disparity is justified, the defence would stand for such part of the difference as could be attributed to that reason.

---

[69] [1978] QB 11, QBD.
[70] *Benveniste v University of Southampton* [1989] IRLR 122.
[71] *Enderby v Frenchay Health Authority and another* [1992] IRLR 15, CA; [1994] ICR 112.

Enforcement and remedies

Bringing a claim for equal pay

Equal pay claims are brought in the ET by virtue of s 2(1) under the EPA 1970. The claimant may rely upon EC law in the ET as well as the domestic legislation. The ET's jurisdiction is not restricted to applications by individual employees: under section 2(1A) employers may apply to the ET for a declaration where there is a dispute over the effect of an equality clause. Under section 2(2), the Secretary of State can bring proceedings where it appears that the employer of any women is or has been in breach of a term modified or included by an equality clause and it is not reasonable to expect the women themselves to bring proceedings (e.g. because they do not have a union to support their claim). Section 73 of the SDA 1975 empowers the EOC to seek a ruling from a tribunal as to whether an employer has infringed a term modified or included by an equality clause, to enable the Commission to exercise its powers under sections 71 and 72 of that Act to apply for an injunction to restrain persistent discrimination.

High Court/county court claims for breach of contract (EPA 1970, s 2(3))

Since the equality clause provision in the EPA 1970 eliminates discrimination by modifying the claimant's contract of employment, she may also bring an equal pay claim in the county court or High Court in the form of an action for breach of contract. However, under section 2(3) the ordinary courts have the power to refuse to hear equal pay claims in two situations: (1) where it appears to the court that a claim or counterclaim in respect of the operation of an equality clause could more conveniently be disposed of by an industrial tribunal, the court can strike the claim out in its entirety; and (2) where a question regarding the effect of an equality clause is part of a wider dispute which is before the court, the court may on the application of one of the parties or of its own motion refer that question to an industrial tribunal (or direct one of the parties to do so) and stay proceedings in the meantime.[72]

Time-limits

Under s 2(4) of the EPA 1970, equal pay claims must be brought within six months of leaving the employment to which the claim relates. This six months' rule was challenged in *Preston and others v Wolverhampton Healthcare NHS Trust*,[73] as being incompatible with EC law. One of the

---

[72] Industrial tribunals were the predecessors of employment tribunals.
[73] [2000] IRLR 506.

questions in *Preston* was whether the six months' time-limit applied to the particular contracts of service or whether it applied to the entire employment relationship extending over a period of time. The claimants were part-time teachers employed on fixed-term contracts. They argued that the six months' limit applied to the entire employment relationship. The ECJ held that the six months' rule was not incompatible with EC law, provided that the limitation period was no less favourable for actions based on Community law than for actions based on domestic law.[74]

Under the EPA 1970, s 2(5) as originally worded, a claimant may claim remuneration or damages in respect of the two years prior to the institution of proceedings. In *Levez v TH Jennings (Harlow Pools) Ltd*,[75] the ECJ held that the two-year limitation in s 2(5) of the EPA 1970 on arrears of remuneration is precluded if the section infringes the Community law principle of 'equivalence', which requires that a procedural rule must not discriminate as between Community law rights and national law rights. The House of Lords followed this decision in *Preston and others v Wolverhampton Healthcare NHS Trust (No 2)*.[76] The ECJ in *Preston* held that this limitation of two years on recovering compensation retroactively from the date the claim was brought was incompatible with EC law, since it was a restriction on the right to have a full and effective remedy for breach of what is now Article 141 EC and the Equal Pay Directive. Section 2(4) and (5) of the EPA 1970 have now been amended in the light of these ECJ rulings.[77]

Conclusion

Although the EPA 1970 has been in force since 1975, there is still a gender pay gap, currently around 20% or so. The EPA 1970, as a discrimination statute, is concerned with the elimination of sex discrimination from contracts of employment, rather than securing fair wages for women. As we have seen, some aspects of domestic law have been shown to be incompatible with EC law, after challenges relying upon what is

---

[74] See also *National Power plc v Young* [2001] IRLR 32, where the Court of Appeal held that the word 'employment' in s 2(4) of the EPA 1970, which provides that an equal pay claim cannot be brought if the applicant has not been 'employed in the employment' to which the claim relates within the six months preceding the date of the reference, does not relate to the particular job on which the woman bases her claim to an equality clause but rather to the contract of employment.

[75] [1999] IRLR 36.

[76] [2001] IRLR 237.

[77] The Equal Pay Act 1970 (Amendment) Regulations 2003, SI 2003/1656, came into force on 19 July 2003. Special rules apply in certain cases: where the employee and the employer had a stable employment relationship (even though one or more individual contracts of employment had ended); where the employer deliberately concealed relevant facts from the employee; or where the employee was under a disability.

now Article 141 and the Equal Pay Directive. In this sense, EC law has given impetus to the development of non-discriminatory pay structures in the United Kingdom. However, individual applicants face considerable hurdles when bringing equal pay claims, particularly equal value claims. Despite Government proposals for reform of ET procedure in this regard, legislation implementing some of these proposals is still awaited.[78]

Further reading

Barnard, C 'Equality, non-discrimination and the labour market in the UK' (2002) 18(2) IJCLLIR 129

Busby, N 'Equal pay and contracting out: *Lawrence v Regent Office Care Ltd*' (2003) 7(2) *Edinburgh Law Review* 233

Cox, S 'Equal Pay: a guide to the law' (2002) 109 *Equal Opportunities Review* 1

'ECJ rules on equal pay comparators' (2003) 348 *European Industrial Relations Review* 32

'Employment law review 2002: sex discrimination and equal pay' (2003) 724 *IDS Brief* 5

'Equal pay – ECJ's judgment in *Lawrence*' (2002) 97 *Employment Lawyer* 21

'Equal pay – more questions than answers' (2003) 732 *IDS Brief* 2

'Equal pay: transferred workers cannot compare their pay with retained workers' (2003) 767 *IRS Employment Law* 46

Honeyball, S and Bowers, J *Textbook on Labour Law* (7th edn, Oxford University Press, 2002), ch 11

Sargeant, M (2002) *Employment Law* (2nd edn, Pearson, 2002), ch 6, pp 222–231

---

[78] The Government announced proposals to tackle 'red tape and bureaucracy involved in taking an equal pay case . . .' in May 2001 (see DfEE Press Release Pn 2001/0252, 8 May 2001). Five sets of draft 'equality' regulations have been issued, one of which concerned equal pay.

Chapter 6

Disability discrimination

Jeremy Cooper

The Disability Discrimination Act 1995 (DDA 1995) makes it unlawful to discriminate against disabled people in connection with: employment; the provision of goods, facilities and services; education; and the buying or renting of land or property.[1]

Discrimination in employment

The employment provisions of the DDA 1995 were implemented on 2 December 1996, and are supplemented by legally binding Regulations[2] and by Codes of Practice.[3] Although Codes of Practice are not legally binding, a failure to follow them can be raised by applicants in tribunal and court hearings as evidence of unreasonable practice.

---

[1] Discrimination in relation to the buying or renting of property is not covered in this chapter.

[2] Disability Discrimination (Services and Premises) Regulations 1996, SI 1996/1836; Disability Discrimination (Meaning of Disability) Regulations 1996, SI 1996/1455; Disability Discrimination (Employment) Regulations 1996, SI 1996/1456; Disability Discrimination (Exemption for Small Employers) Order 1998, SI 1998/2618; Disability Discrimination (Description of Insurance Services) Regulations 1999, SI 1999/2114; Disability Discrimination (Providers of Services) (Adjustment of Premises) Regulations 2001, SI 2001/3253; Disability Discrimination (Designation of Educational Institutions) Order 2002, SI 2002/1459; Disability Discrimination Act 1995 (Amendment) Regulations 2003, SI 2003/1673.

[3] Code of Practice for the Elimination of Discrimination in the Field of Employment against Disabled Persons or Persons who have had a Disability 1996; Code of Practice: Rights of Access: Goods, Facilities, Services and Premises, 1996, 1999, 2002; Codes of Practice for Providers of Post-16 Education and Related Services 2002; Code of Practice for Schools 2002. An additional Code of Practice is anticipated to be published in late 2004–early 2005, to incorporate the changes introduced by the Disability Discrimination Act 1995 (Amendment) Regulations 2003, SI 2003/1673.

There have been a large number of judicial decisions concerning actions brought under the DDA 1995, running into several hundred reported cases, and many thousands of unreported cases.[4] Early research revealed that the majority of cases were registered by men, and the most common disabilities leading to applications were (in order):

- problems connected with the back or neck;
- depression;
- bad nerves or anxiety; and
- problems connected with the arms or hand.[5]

Cases are heard in the employment tribunal at first instance, then subsequently in the Employment Appeal Tribunal, and occasionally in the Court of Appeal. Some have expanded, and others have narrowed the application of this law. However, research on the first four years of the operation of the DDA 1995 revealed that only 23% of cases disposed of at tribunal hearings were successful (i.e. won by the applicant).[6] In more recent years, not only have 'success' rates been slowly rising, the amounts of money paid out in compensation have been escalating dramatically. In 2000, a total of £639,255 was paid out in compensation, a 73% increase on 1999; and in 2001, a total amount of £1,182,621 was paid out in compensation, an 85% increase on 2000. The average award in a disability discrimination case is now significantly higher than in a sex or race discrimination case.[7]

In general terms, the concept of equality that the courts have tended to follow is one of equal opportunities, rather than one of equal rights or equal outcomes.[8] In many ways, the Act follows the parallel provisions of the Sex Discrimination Act 1975, and the Race Relations Act 1976 with regard to discrimination on the grounds of gender or race. Nevertheless, there are some significant differences: for example, a claim for indirect discrimination cannot currently be brought under the DDA 1995,[9] the special duty to make 'reasonable adjustments' to counter possible discrimination is unique to the DDA 1995, as is the availability of a defence

---

[4] For an account of some of the leading cases, see *50 Key Cases for the DRC* (Disability Rights Commission, 2002).
[5] N Meager *et al* 'Monitoring the Disability Discrimination Act 1995' (Research Report RR119, NDC/DfEE, 1999).
[6] Income Data Service 'Monitoring the DDA-Phase 2: First Interim Report to the Department for Education and Employment' (Income Data Services Ltd, 2000).
[7] *RADAR Bulletin*, February 2002, p 5; *Community Care*, 22–28 August 2002, p 13.
[8] On this point see G Quinn and T Degener *Human Rights and Disability* (New York: United Nations, 2002), ch 1.
[9] Note that the eventual full implementation of the EU Council Directive Establishing a General Framework for Equal Treatment in Employment and Occupation 2000/78/EC may bring about a change in this current position.

justifying direct discrimination in certain defined circumstances. These differences led to one expert commentary in 2001 observing that 'it has become increasingly apparent that this piece of legislation and its operation in the tribunals is very different from the race and sex discrimination legislation'.[10]

Although there was originally to be no equivalent central Commission to oversee the enforcement of the DDA 1995, a Disability Rights Commission (DRC) was established in April 2000.[11] The brief of the DRC is to assist disabled people by providing a central source of information and advice, via research, conciliation, investigation and a range of advisory powers.[12] The DRC, as the most recent of the specialist Commissions dealing with equality issues, is concerned that the Government intends to merge all the 'Equality Commissions' into one single Equality and Human Rights Commission. While supportive in principle of the idea – as a means of pooling resources and expertise, and addressing such issues as multiple discrimination – the DRC is nevertheless concerned that a single Equality Commission might in future dilute the impact achieved by the DRC in its brief history, and has made the following points:[13]

- A single equality body is a potentially exciting idea, but the Government's current thinking falls well short of that potential.
- A huge amount remains to be done to combat the discrimination and disadvantage faced by disabled people, and for them to secure comprehensive civil and human rights. The DDA 1995 and the DRC have only been in operation for a handful of years, in contrast to the legislation and Commissions on race and gender, which have all existed for over 25 years.
- The Government must first fulfil its manifesto commitment to progressive new disabilities legislation to put into force the recommendations of the Disability Rights Task Force and reflecting experience of the DDA 1995 in practice. It will take five to ten years for this legislation to come fully into force and be implemented successfully.
- The DRC provides a model for ways forward. From the start, alongside effective strategic use of its enforcement powers, the DRC has given priority to changing attitudes and cultures on discrimination, alternative means of resolving disputes, working effectively with employers and service providers, and empowering individuals.

---

[10] C Casserly and B Gor *Disability Discrimination Claims: an Adviser's Handbook* (Jordans, 2001), p iii.
[11] Disability Rights Commission Act 1999.
[12] For more information visit the DRC website at www.drc-gb.org. Added to its powers from October 1994 will be powers to enforce action against discriminatory advertisements, and to outlaw instructions and pressure to discriminate: DDA 1995, ss 16B and 16C.
[13] Available on DRC website: www.drc-gb.org.

- The Government should introduce a Single Equalities Act before establishing any single body, in order to ensure high and consistent standards of protection across all the forms of discrimination covered by a new body. Otherwise, any new body will be lumbered with a legislative mess and 'hierarchies of equality', seriously weakening its internal cohesion and external credibility.
- Consideration of the various options on the design, powers and resources of any new body must be evidence-based, and any changes must represent progress on the present position for disabled people. Options to be considered include an umbrella body, with responsibility for human rights as well as discrimination, coupled with distinct organisations, each concerned with the main specific forms of discrimination and including one to ensure disability equality.
- Meanwhile, disabled people and their organisations must be closely involved in the discussions on a single body. Disability discrimination is frequently distinct from other types, particularly given the importance of technical support and adjustments to the physical environment. Disabled people will not accept losing out under any new arrangement.

Definition of a person with a disability

The status protected by the DDA 1995 is that of 'a disabled person', defined as follows:

> a person who has a physical or mental impairment which has a substantial and long-term adverse effect on their ability to carry out normal day-to-day activities.[14]

The 'adverse effect' must also be long-term, that is have lasted for at least 12 months, or the period that it can reasonably be expected to last is at least 12 months or the rest of the person's life (whichever is the shorter).[15]

'Normal day-to-day activities' include:[16] mobility; manual dexterity; physical co-ordination; continence; the ability to lift, carry or otherwise move everyday objects; speech, hearing or eyesight; memory or the ability to concentrate, learn or understand; the perception of the risk of danger; the daily application of make-up by women. The focus is on what the applicant *cannot* do, rather than on what they *can* do.[17] This focus on the negative aspects of the disability has been criticised as exposing applicants to demeaning cross-examination to establish the veracity of their claim, and to significant costs in obtaining medical verification of their incapacity.

---

[14] DDA 1995, s 1(1).
[15] DDA 1995, Sch 1, para 2.
[16] DDA 1995, Sch 1, para 4(1), supplemented by case law.
[17] *Abadeh v British Telecommunications plc* [2001] ICR 156.

So far, cases involving acute vertigo, chronic pain in the legs and feet induced by fallen arches, transient epileptic fits, a sight loss in one eye, back strain with a continuing ability to carry out light duties, and rheumatoid arthritis, in the absence of independent medical evidence, have all failed the test of having 'a substantial adverse effect upon normal day-to-day activities'. In contrast, conditions causing pain from kidney stones and 'an undiagnosed cause', and sciatica in conjunction with a club-foot, have passed the test. Each case is ultimately decided on its particular facts. Increasingly, it is the practice for tribunals to hear medical evidence as to whether an impairment objectively exists, although determining whether the impairment is substantial remains a question of fact for the tribunal alone to determine.[18]

Although 'mental impairment' is not defined by the DDA 1995, the Act does state that, if the mental impairment emanates from mental illness, disability will be established only if it is 'from, or consisting of, a mental illness that is clinically well recognised', as set out in the *WHO International Statistical Classification of Diseases and Related Health Problems (ICD)*.[19] This restriction is thus likely to exclude not only 'controversial' mental disorders such as psychopathy,[20] but also 'recognised' mental disorders that are still not fully established in the patient, and illnesses whose symptoms have a psychosomatic basis.[21]

In addition to the above situations, the DDA 1995 covers a number of special situations, as follows:

- *Progressive conditions*: According to the DDA 1995, a person with a progressive condition causing an impairment that has 'some but not yet substantial' adverse effect on normal day-to-day activities is deemed to be a 'disabled person' for the purposes of the Act, if his or her condition is expected to produce, at a later stage, a substantial adverse effect. Sufferers from multiple sclerosis, some forms of cancer and HIV may come into this category. Not included in this definition are those with asymptomatic conditions, those who are not yet experiencing any impairment, and those who are genetically predisposed to such conditions but who have not yet acquired them. In a recent case[22] the applicant was diagnosed with prostate cancer and underwent surgery which left him suffering from mild incontinence. The Court of Appeal has however accepted the argument that the impairment of mild incontinence can be a consequence of the progressive condition of cancer, even though there has been intervening surgery that triggered its development.

---

[18] Ibid.
[19] *Morgan v Staffordshire University* [2002] IRLR 190.
[20] Kleptomania and pyromania are already excluded by regulation.
[21] *Rugamer v Sony Music Entertainment UK Ltd* [2001] IRLR 644. Note that the Queen's Speech of November 2003 announced the Government's intention to remove these exclusions in new legislation.
[22] *Kirton v Tetrosyl Ltd* [2003] IRLR 353.

- *Controlled or corrected conditions*: A condition that is controlled or corrected (for example, by medication or the use of a prosthesis or other aid) is still deemed to be a disability for the purposes of the DDA 1995 if, but for the control or correction, there would be a disability meeting the general definition of disability. The Act does, however, exclude sight impairment correctable by spectacles or contact lenses.[23]
- *Severe disfigurement*: A person with a severe disfigurement (for example, scars, birthmarks, a skin disease or a limb or postural deformation) is to be treated as falling within the definition of a disabled person for the purposes of the DDA 1995, although disfigurement caused by self-mutilation (for example, tattoos and body piercing) is excluded from this provision.[24]
- *Persons already registered as disabled*: As a general rule, under UK law, a person who meets a generic definition under one piece of legislation will not automatically satisfy that definition for other purposes. For example, a person deemed to be self-employed for the purposes of tax law will not automatically be deemed self-employed in employment law. Thus, a person who is on the local authority disabled person's register under the Chronically Sick and Disabled Persons Act 1970 (definition: 'a person suffering from a permanent and substantial disability') will not automatically be deemed to be 'disabled' for the purposes of the DDA 1995. The Government intends however to publish regulations to implement the 'Towards Inclusion'[25] proposal that persons who have been certified or registered as blind or partially sighted should be deemed to be disabled.

Notion of discrimination under current law

Under the DDA 1995,[26] it is unlawful for an employer to discriminate against a disabled person:

(a) in the arrangements made to determine to whom employment should be offered; or
(b) in the terms on which employment is offered; or
(c) by refusing to offer, or deliberately not offering, employment.

Furthermore it is unlawful for an employer to discriminate against a disabled person in their employment:

---

[23] DDA 1995, Sch 1, para 6(3)(a).
[24] DDA 1995, Sch 1, para 3.
[25] DfEE 'Towards Inclusion – Civil Rights for Disabled People' (March 2001), published as the Government's response to the report of a 24-member Disability Rights Task Force 'From Exclusion to Inclusion' (DfEE, December 1999).
[26] DDA 1995, s 5.

(a) in the terms of employment; or
(b) in the opportunities afforded to the employee for promotion, transfer, training or to receive other benefits; or
(c) by refusing to make available, or deliberately not making available, any such opportunity; or
(d) by dismissing the employee, or subjecting them to any other detriment.

An employer discriminates against a disabled person if:

(a) for a reason which relates to the disabled person's disability, that person is treated less favourably than the employer treats others to whom that reason does not, or would not, apply, and
(b) the employer cannot show that the treatment in question is justified.[27]

In determining whether less favourable treatment has occurred, it will be necessary to find a comparator. The correct test for a comparator is to ask the following questions:

(1) What was the material reason for the alleged less favourable treatment?
(2) Does this reason relate to a disability?
(3) Would the employer have treated someone else, to whom the material reason does not apply, in the same way?[28]

From October 2004, it will also be discriminatory, and therefore unlawful, for an employer to subject a disabled employee, or applicant employee, to harassment, which is defined as follows:

> unwanted conduct which has the purpose or effect of violating the disabled person's dignity or creating an intimidating, hostile, degrading, humiliating or offensive environment for that person.[29]

---

[27] From October 2004 the defence of justification will not be available in instances of 'direct discrimination' which fall within the definition to be inserted as DDA 1995, s 3A(5)–(6) as follows:

> A person directly discriminates against a disabled person if, on the ground of the disabled person's disability, s/he treats the disabled person less favourably than s/he treats or would treat a person not having that particular disability whose relevant circumstances, including his/her abilities, are the same as, or not materially different from, those of the disabled person.
> Nor will a person under a duty to make reasonable adjustments in relation to a disabled person, who fails to comply with that duty, be able to justify that treatment unless it would have been justified even if they had complied with that duty.

> See Disability Discrimination Act 1995 (Amendment) Regulations 2003, SI 2003/1673, reg 4.

[28] *Clark v Novacold* [1999] ICR 951. Also see below at p 139.
[29] Disability Discrimination Act 1995 (Amendment) Regulations 2003, SI 2003/1673, regs 4 and 5.

Definitions of employment, occupation and training

Under the DDA 1995 employment is defined ('subject to any prescribed provision') as 'employment under a contract of service or of apprentice-ship or a contract personally to do any work'.[30] Thus, any paid activity that falls within the above definition is *prima facie* protected by the Act unless specifically excluded.[31]

There is set out below a list of those areas of employment that are currently exempted from the provisions of the DDA 1995. It should, however, be noted that, following the introduction in 2000 of the EU Council Directive establishing a General Framework for Equal Treatment in Employment and Occupation,[32] the British Government has passed amending regulations which significantly reduce the range of exempted employments, with effect from 1 October 2004.[33]

The following areas of employment are currently excluded:

- employers with fewer than 15 employees (this exclusion removed from October 2004[34])
- employees working on board ships, aircraft or hovercraft (this exclusion removed from October 2004[35])
- prison officers (except a custody officer/prison custody officer), fire-fighting members of the fire brigade, members of the Ministry of Defence Police, British Transport Police, Royal Parks Constabulary, UK Atomic Energy Authority Constabulary (this exclusion largely removed from October 2004[36])

---

[30] DDA 1995, s 68(1).
[31] Note the proposal of the Disability Rights Commission that protection should be extended to unpaid volunteers (see below).
[32] Council Directive 2000/78/EC.
[33] Disability Discrimination Act 1995 (Amendment) Regulations 2003, SI 2003/1673. Of particular importance will be the repeal of the exemption for small employers, in para 7. The Government's desire to reduce significantly the number of exempted categories of employment was first stated in an important policy paper, 'Towards Equality and Diversity: Implementing the Employment and Race Directives', published in 2001, which stated:

> 'We are ending the exemption of small employers from the DDA [currently those employers with fewer than 15 employees] in October 2004, and also propose to make the other changes to the DDA required by the Employment Directive at the same time. These will include ending other occupational and employment exemptions and omissions from the DDA mentioned in "Towards Inclusion"'.

To this end, the Government published in the autumn of 2002 the (Draft) Disability Discrimination Act 1995 (Amendment) Regulations 2003, together with a set of Explanatory Notes and Supplementary Questions. The Government invited feedback on the [Draft] Regulations and has prepared a set of final Regulations which were placed before Parliament for July 2003 to come into effect on 1 October 2004: SI 2003/1673.
[34] Note that associated companies cannot be counted together for the purposes of determining the number of employees: *Hardie v CD Northern Ltd* [2000] IRLR 87; *Colt Group Ltd v Couchman* [2000] ICR 327; Disability Discrimination Act 1995 (Amendment) Regulations 2003, SI 2003/1673, reg 7.
[35] Disability Discrimination Act 1995 (Amendment) Regulations 2003, SI 2003/1673, reg 27.
[36] Ibid, reg 24.

- statutory office holders (e.g. police, judiciary, magistrates) (this exclusion largely removed from October 2004[37])
- employees working wholly outside Great Britain (this exclusion significantly modified from October 2004[38])
- serving members of the naval, military or air forces of the Crown.

The issue of whether employers, school and college managers, etc. are entitled to be informed whether a person has a disability is a little complex. The Code of Practice (Employment etc.)[39] states that an employer must do all they reasonably can be expected to do, in order to find out whether or not a person has a disability. The question 'Is actual knowledge of the disability a prerequisite of a discriminatory act?' remains unclear, and the case law is conflicting.[40] The Code of Practice (Education etc.) makes similar observations regarding good practice in education, whilst conceding that a request for confidentiality by a student within one part of the institution may have the effect of allowing another part of the institution to plead ignorance of a disability, if a discriminatory act is subsequently alleged.[41]

Vicarious liability of the employer for discrimination and harassment under current law

An employer may be vicariously liable for the discriminatory acts of an employee, if these acts are committed during the course of their employment.[42] The DDA 1995 does, however, provide a limited defence if the employer can prove that reasonably practicable steps were taken to prevent that employee from committing the unlawful discriminatory acts.[43] Vicarious liability may also be shared with another person who knowingly aids in the commission of an unlawful act of discrimination (for example, a personnel manager who, aware of the company's discriminatory acts, colludes in their perpetration).[44] However, in these latter circumstances, there is a specific defence, that a person does not knowingly aid another to carry out a discriminatory act, if they act in reliance on a statement made to them by that other person. The statement must be to the effect that the discriminatory act would not be unlawful because of any

---

[37] Ibid, regs 5 and 25.
[38] Ibid, reg 27.
[39] Paragraph 4.57.
[40] Cf *O'Neill v Symm and Co Ltd* [1998] IRLR 233, EAT; *Heinz and Co Ltd v Kenrick* [2000] IRLR 144; *London Borough of Hammersmith and Fulham v Farnsworth* [2000] IRLR 691. All three cases were heard in the Employment Appeal Tribunal.
[41] See note 3.
[42] DDA 1995, s 58.
[43] Ibid, s 58(5).
[44] Ibid, s 57.

provision of the DDA 1995, and it must be reasonable to rely upon that statement. That other person will be guilty of a *criminal* offence if they knowingly or recklessly make such a statement, which is false or misleading in a material respect.[45]

These vicarious liability principles also apply, at least in part, to the relationship of principal and agent. Anything done by a person as agent for a principal, and with the principal's express or implied authority, is treated for the purposes of the DDA 1995 as also done by the agent.[46]

Less favourable treatment

To establish *less favourable treatment*, the employment tribunal will apply the 'comparator test'. This means that the applicant must produce an example (real or hypothetical) of another individual *without* their disability being treated *more* favourably than themselves in the employment-related situation.[47] They must be able to relate their less favourable treatment to their disability (for example, a refusal to employ a wheelchair user because of the inconvenience of a wheelchair in the office, or a blind person because of a dislike of guide dogs).

Duty to make reasonable adjustments

The notion of 'reasonable adjustments' is based on a 'difference' model of discrimination. This model recognises that individuals who possess the relevant characteristic are different in a relevant respect from individuals who do not, and that treating them similarly can lead to discrimination. It requires that employers treat some individuals – persons with disabilities who would be qualified if the employer modified the job to enable them to perform it – differently from other individuals. This is an asymmetric notion and requires that some definition or classification of the covered group be included in the legislation.

The EU Framework Directive[48] specifies in Article 5:

> In order to guarantee compliance with the principle of equal treatment in relation to persons with disabilities, 'reasonable accommodation' shall be provided. This means that employers shall take appropriate measures, where needed in a particular case, to enable a person with a disability to have access to, participate in, or advance in employment, or to undergo training, unless such measures would impose a disproportionate burden on the employer. This burden shall not be disproportionate when it is sufficiently remedied by measures existing within the framework of the disability policy of the Member State concerned.

---

[45] Ibid, s 57(4).
[46] Ibid, s 58.
[47] *Clark v Novacold* [1999] ICR 951.
[48] Directive 2000/78/EC.

The Directive states in the Preamble, para 20, that:

> Appropriate measures should be provided, i.e. effective and practical measures to adapt the workplace to the disability, for example, adapting premises and equipment, patterns of working time, the distribution of tasks or the provision of training or integration resources.

The United Kingdom legislation, which predated the Directive, but nevertheless remains compliant with its requirements, adopted the term 'reasonable adjustments' in preference to 'reasonable accommodation'. To all intents and purposes the concept is identical. Under the DDA 1995, the duty to make reasonable adjustments arises whenever any physical feature of the premises, or any arrangements made by or on behalf of an employer, places the disabled person concerned at a substantial disadvantage in comparison to those who are not disabled. In these circumstances, the employer (or potential employer when related to a job application) must take such steps as can be considered *reasonable in all the circumstances*, in order to prevent those features or arrangements having that effect.[49]

In many cases, the adjustments necessary to allow a disabled employee to continue working require more imagination than expense. One employer was, for example, found to have discriminated against an employee who suffered from pain and discomfort associated with a clubfoot by failing to provide her with a suitable chair, which would have been a simple adjustment to the workplace. Modifications to equipment, seating, lighting, rest places, hours of work and work locations are often all that is needed to allow the employee to continue, and the role of the social worker in helping the parties to achieve such a compromise arrangement can be crucial.

However, employers do not have a duty to make reasonable adjustments if they do not know that they are necessary for the employee and could not reasonably be expected to know. It is therefore important that employees realise they must declare their disability, in order to give the employer a chance to make adjustments, before they can establish any discrimination.

Detailed advice on what steps employers might be expected to take by way of reasonable adjustments in order to avoid charges of discrimination has emerged through the Code of Practice, and case law. The DDA 1995 provides some illustrations of typical 'reasonable adjustments' as follows:[50] making physical adjustments to premises; allocating some duties to another employee; being flexible with regard to working hours; being flexible in terms of place of work; being flexible as to absence from

---

[49] DDA 1995, s 6. Note that there will be further tightening regulations relating to 'reasonable adjustments' coming into force in October 2004, as a result of the Disability Discrimination Act 1995 (Amendment) Regulations 2003, SI 2003/1673, reg 5.
[50] DDA 1995, s 6.

work for rehabilitation, treatment and assessment; giving or arranging special training; training; acquiring or modifying equipment; reference manuals; modifying procedures for testing or assessment; providing a reader or interpreter: and providing supervision.

The DDA 1995 provides guidance on what factors should be taken into account in deciding whether a particular proposed adjustment is or is not reasonable in all the circumstances.[51] The factors it lists are the following:

* Consider the preventative effect of the action, i.e. will it achieve its goal?
* Is the proposed adjustment practicable?
* Weigh up the financial and other costs that it would incur.
* Consider any disruption to the employer's activities.
* Consider the employer's financial and other resources.
* Consider the availability of financial or other assistance.

Note however, that employers faced with expensive adaptation bills to carry out reasonable adjustments may well have access to the government-sponsored Access to Work Scheme[52] whereby they can receive an unlimited grant towards the cost of reasonable adjustments to premises over a five-year period.

Case law examples

In one of the earliest cases decided in the United Kingdom under the DDA 1995, in which a failure to provide reasonable adjustments was successfully pleaded[53] (employee recovering from ME asked to be able to work from home, but was simply offered the same redeployment process as non-disabled employees), the Employment Appeal Tribunal made it clear that a person with an identified disability could not simply be treated as a normal redeployment case.

A number of cases taken by the Disability Rights Commission in subsequent years illustrate the implementation of this principle in practice.[54]

Failure to offer alternative employment

Failure to make reasonable adjustments through changes to the job or any offer of suitable alternative employment, for employee with hand injury, culminating in ill-health retirement.[55]

Following an injury sustained whilst at work, the complainant experienced a restriction in the strength of, and ability to move, her hand. Upon

---

[51] Ibid.
[52] See p 146.
[53] *London Borough of Hillingdon v Morgan* EAT/1493/98.
[54] All these, and other similar cases, can be found on the Disability Rights Commission website at www.drc.gb.org.
[55] DRC/00/809.

returning to work she was given light work duties for a number of months, but was then expected to perform full duties thereafter. She did this for a period of two months before being moved to a number of temporary positions, instead of her employer making adjustments to allow her to return to her original job. She was not advised of, or offered any, suitable job vacancies that had arisen during this period. The complainant subsequently had an operation on her hand, but, upon being certified fit to return to work, her employers told her that her original job had changed and now included substantially more lifting tasks and for this reason refused to allow her to return to her original job. The complainant wanted *either* to return to work in her original position (with the provision of reasonable adjustments) *or* to be given a job of similar status and career prospects. Instead, she was offered jobs of lower status, voluntary redundancy or ill-health retirement. She accepted the latter and subsequently commenced a claim of disability discrimination in the employment tribunal against her former employers. Terms of settlement were agreed, which included the former employer paying out the sum of £18,000 in compensation.

Employer's decision to terminate employment for reasons relating to employee's stress-related illness.[56]
The employee's original job as warehouse assistant covered fork-lift truck driving and computer-related tasks. His employer decided to allocate to him other responsibilities such as maintenance, team leader and acting supervisor, the latter for a period of three months. As a result of the amount of work he was required to do, coupled with withdrawal of supervisory duties, the client developed a stress-related illness causing him to take time off work. During the period of absence the employer sought a medical report, but terminated the employee's employment before the report was received on the grounds of urgent operational necessity. The employee issued proceedings for disability discrimination, and the case settled for an undisclosed amount.

Failure to alter work practices

Failure to make reasonable adjustments for a deaf employee during a disciplinary process leading to termination of employment.[57]
The complainant was employed as a sign language tutor. He was alleged to have continued to work with a local organisation teaching sign language after taking sickness absence for reasons not connected to his disability, which, according to his employer, meant that he was in breach of his contract of employment with them. The employer instituted disciplinary

---

[56] DRC/01/1053.
[57] DRC/00/195.

proceedings against him, but failed to provide an independent interpreter at all the disciplinary hearings and did not provide him with clear written transcripts, or minutes, of those hearings. This prevented him from being able to present his case adequately, culminating in his dismissal. The case settled for an undisclosed sum shortly before the hearing was due to take place.

Failure at interview stage

Failure to make reasonable adjustments in respect of the recruitment process led to the failure of a job application submitted by a complainant with learning disabilities.[58]
The complainant was 22 years old and had a learning disability. He had volunteered as a porter and general groundsman for a local NHS Trust in order to gain experience in this field to secure employment. The Trust advertised a vacancy for which he applied. The Trust only informed him verbally of the interview date and time, without providing written confirmation. Consequently, the client missed the interview but, after enquiring about the recruitment process, he was re-interviewed by his manager alone without the opportunity to have some form of support at the actual interview. His job application did not succeed. The case was listed for hearing at the employment tribunal over three consecutive days. Terms of settlement, including the sum of £2,500, were agreed before the hearing took place.

Failure to adapt workplace

Failure of employer to make reasonable adjustments to physical features of premises when employee manager of betting shop became a wheelchair user.[59]
A betting shop manager had worked for over thirty years for the same employer. He developed a mobility impairment due to a back injury and the side effect of a pre-existing medical condition, and he subsequently used a wheelchair to aid mobility. Upon attempting to return to work after a short period of sickness absence, his employer advised him that use of the wheelchair would present them with problems in the work premises, which were not suitably accessible for wheelchair users. The employer proceeded to terminate his employment, only looking into the possibilities of making changes to the premises after he appealed against the decision to dismiss him. A technical access consultant working for the Employment Service prepared a report recommending various reasonable adjustments, the cost of which would be in the region of £7,500. However, the employer still decided to uphold the decision

---

[58] DRC/01/4497.
[59] DRC/02/6151.

to terminate the employment and not make the recommended adjustments to its premises. Employment tribunal proceedings were subsequently commenced. The case settled before hearing for the sum of £100,000.

Defences under the DDA 1995 employment provisions

Once a discriminatory act has been shown on the balance of probabilities to exist, the employer can only avoid a finding of unlawful discrimination if it can be established that the discriminatory act was *justified*. To be *justified*, the reason for the less favourable treatment of the disabled employee must be shown to have been both material to the circumstances of the particular case and substantial.

The Code of Practice stresses that 'substantial' means 'not just trivial or minor' and goes on to provide a series of examples to explain the scope of the defence. Thus, a general assumption that blind people cannot use computers is not a material reason unless it is related to the particular individual in question. Dismissing a clerical worker with a learning disability who cannot sort papers as fast as other colleagues, but with relatively little overall difference in productivity, would not be justifiable as a substantial reason. But rejecting a person for a job modelling cosmetics with psoriasis on a part of their body severely disfigured by the condition would probably be justified as the reason is material to the circumstances of the particular requirement, and is substantial.

The Government's Disability Discrimination Act 1995 (Amendment) Regulations 2003 introduce significant modifications to this defence, from October 2004, in order to bring the DDA 1995 in line with the Framework Directive.[60] The revised s 3A(3) of the DDA 1995 will make clear that less favourable treatment cannot be justified if it occurs *merely* because an individual has a disability, rather than being based on a consideration of that person's abilities, i.e. blanket bans in certain occupations upon persons with a particular disability will generally not be allowed. The Explanatory Notes to the Draft Amendments[61] provided the following examples of this type of less favourable treatment:

- An employer, on learning that a job applicant has diabetes, summarily rejects the application without giving any consideration of the applicant's circumstances or whether the person concerned would be competent to do the job (with or without a reasonable adjustment).
- A disabled employee is refused access to the employer's sports and social club simply on the basis that the club does not allow disabled members, and without any consideration of whether the employee might

---

[60] See note 9.
[61] Available at www.dti.gov.uk/er/equality/index.htm.

benefit from membership, and even though they could access the club with a reasonable adjustment.

- Without any consideration of whether he will be able to work for as many years as other employees, a newly recruited disabled person is required to pay the same contributions to an occupational pension scheme even though he is denied access to ill-health retirement benefits available to other scheme members.

Enforcement provisions

Under Part II of the DDA 1995, any individual experiencing discrimination under the above provisions can apply to an employment tribunal alleging discrimination, as long as they do so within three months of the alleged discriminatory act. As legal aid is not available for representation at employment tribunals (although free or subsidised legal advice and assistance short of representation is), disabled people's action groups have an important role to play in this activity. Applicants can require, under the DDA 1995, that the defendant employer fill out a detailed Statutory Questionnaire,[62] similar to those used in sex and race discrimination cases, in response to the allegation.

If the matter is not resolved informally, it will proceed to an employment tribunal hearing. Applicants should be aware of a number of procedural problems they will have to face. Employment tribunals are quite formal, intimidating settings, overburdened with procedures and often requiring complex argument on points of evidence or law.

The employment tribunal has the following options in the event of a finding in favour of the applicant:

- a declaration that discrimination has occurred;
- recommendations to ensure that there is no future recurrence of such discrimination;
- the power to award to the applicant unlimited compensation, plus interest, such compensation to include, where appropriate, a category of compensation for 'injury to feelings'.

A major study of the first 2,500 cases registered in employment tribunals up to July 1999 showed that 90% related to dismissal and 10% to failure to recruit. The great majority of cases settled, or were withdrawn, before coming to a tribunal. Citizens' Advice Bureaux were the most common source of advice for applicants. Of those applicants attending a tribunal, 34% were legally represented. In only 16% of cases heard was the applicant successful, and in these cases the applicants were normally legally

---

[62] DDA 1995, s 56.

represented. Although the median compensation award was about £2,000, awards ranged widely from £700 to, in one case, around £167,000.

Notion of positive action under current law

There are no quotas in operation in the United Kingdom, the previous quota scheme having been deemed a failure, and abolished by the DDA 1995. Similarly, there are no affirmative action programmes as such for disabled people, so the question of breaches of equal treatment norms does not arise.

There are, however, a number of positive assistance measures to prevent or compensate for disadvantages linked to disability in force in the United Kingdom in the employment sector, in addition to the 'reasonable adjustment' provisions of the DDA 1995, of which the following are some key examples:

- *Job Introduction Scheme*: The Job Introduction Scheme is for disabled people who are suited to a job but need to demonstrate their capabilities to a new employer. The scheme pays a sum of money to the employer for six to thirteen weeks. The employment must be expected to last at least six months after the scheme payments have stopped.
- *Access to Work*: Access to Work, run by Jobcentre Plus for the Department for Work and Pensions, provides practical advice to help overcome work-related obstacles resulting from disability and a grant towards extra employment costs, including: special aids or equipment for employment; adaptations to premises and existing equipment; help with travel to work if public transport is unsuitable; a support worker to provide help in the workplace; a communicator for support at interviews.

  Access to Work defines 'disability' as in the DDA 1995, but extends it to include disabilities that are only apparent in the workplace. The amount of financial support available is quite substantial depending on what is needed, and is granted for a maximum three-year period, after which it may be possible to reapply, depending on any changes to the rules in the interim.

  The scheme, whilst good on paper, has been criticised as being woefully under-publicised, and insufficiently used, with a suspicion that this may be deliberate policy on the part of the Government. Research by the RNID found that one-third of a sample of 300 deaf jobseekers were not aware of Access to Work,[63] and a report published in 2003 by the Joseph Rowntree Foundation found a lack of knowledge amongst Access to Work Advisers on a range of impairments, and a wide variation in the level of service.[64]

---

[63] *Community Care*, 21–27 August 2003, pp 16–17.
[64] JRF *Thriving and Surviving at Work* (Joseph Rowntree Foundation, 2003).

- *Work Preparation*: Jobcentre Plus can provide individually tailored programmes of Work Preparation (also called Employment Rehabilitation) to help a disabled person to get work by addressing the 'employment-related needs' that result from their disability and currently prevent them from being able to enter employment or training of a type that would otherwise be suitable. Employment Rehabilitation Allowance and other expenses assistance are available.
- *New Deal for Disabled People*: This is an entirely voluntary (and slightly controversial) programme, available in selected areas of the country, to anyone on an incapacity-related benefit. The programme is in the course of being restructured, following a series of pilots across the United Kingdom.
- *Disabled Person's Tax Credit*: This scheme is a means-tested payment for working people who have a 'physical or mental disability which puts them at a disadvantage in getting a job'. This test is defined in considerable detail in Regulations.[65] To be eligible a person must be working, or treated as working, 16 hours or more a week.
- *Disability Living Allowance*: This is a non-contributory benefit for disabled people who need help to care for themselves, or have mobility problems, or both. It is tax-free, is not means tested, and can be paid on top of any employment earnings.
- *Disability premiums*: Disabled people receiving income-related benefits may on occasion be entitled to further disability premiums.
- *Industrial Injuries Disablement Benefit*: This benefit is paid to a person who has become disabled by a loss of physical or mental faculty caused by an industrial accident or a prescribed disease. The compensation will be paid, whether or not the person is able to continue in employment, according to a complex 'disablement test'.[66]
- *Residential Training for Disabled Adults*: Whilst most disabled adults are able to access mainstream vocational training, residential training is available to help unemployed disabled adults with more complex needs, where appropriate and high-quality provision is not available locally. This is provided by thirteen providers, of which six cater for all disabilities, five for adults with visual impairments, and two for people with a hearing impairment.
- *WORKSTEP*: This programme provides job support to around 21,500 people with disabilities who face complex barriers to getting a job, but who can work effectively with the right support. It provides opportunities for disabled people to work for 16 hours or more in a supportive environment and, where possible, to progress in mainstream employment. Provision is through a mix of supported factories and placements with mainstream employers.

---

[65] Disability Working Allowance and Income Support (General) Regulations 1995, SI 1995/ 482.
[66] See R(I) 1/81 and the *Disability Rights Handbook* (Disability Alliance).

Treatment of medical examinations under current law

Employers only have a duty to make 'reasonable adjustments' if they know (or could reasonably be expected to know) that an actual or potential employee has a disability. It follows that it is quite legitimate for an employer to request medical reports on a future employee, or actual employee who may be disabled. If the reports reveal a disability, the employee is fully protected by the 'less favourable treatment' clauses of the DDA 1995, in the event that their employer thereafter acts towards them in a discriminatory manner.

The Access to Medical Reports Act 1988 (AMRA 1988) provides a statutory right of access to any medical report relating to an individual which is to be, or has been, supplied by a medical practitioner for employment or insurance purposes, but subject to a number of safeguards. The Act applies to medical reports commissioned both before and during employment. If an employer wishes to obtain such a report, the person's consent must first be obtained; consent can be withheld. In addition, the medical practitioner who wrote the report may refuse to disclose the report, on a number of statutory grounds: e.g. disclosure might cause serious harm to the person concerned, might reveal information about another individual, might reveal the intentions of the practitioner in relation to the individual, or might reveal the identity of another non-medical person who has supplied information to the medical practitioner.

Although the right to withhold consent is absolute, there is nothing to stop employers (actual or potential) from drawing adverse conclusions from such a step being taken. In addition, withholding consent could in certain circumstances discharge an employer from responsibility to make reasonable adjustments to accommodate a disability, on the grounds that they were not made aware of it.

Finally, it should be noted that the medical practitioner carrying out a pre-employment medical assessment owes a duty of care to the employer, not to the employee.[67]

Discrimination in the provision of goods, facilities and services

By virtue of the DDA 1995, Part III, s 19, it is unlawful for a provider of goods, facilities or services to the public to discriminate against a disabled person in any of a number of defined ways.

---

[67] *Kapfunde v Abbey National plc* [1998] IRLR 583.

Who are 'service providers'?

The DRC has provided an extensive (and non-exhaustive) list of potential service providers, as follows:

- hotels, guest houses and hostels
- shops, pubs and restaurants
- estate agents and private landlords
- accommodation agents, councils and housing associations
- property developers, management agencies, investment companies and institutions
- banks and building societies
- mail order or telephone order businesses
- central and local government services
- courts and law firms
- employment agencies
- hospitals and doctors' and dentists' clinics
- churches or other places of worship
- sport and leisure facilities
- bus and railway stations
- amenities and places of interest such as parks and historic buildings
- theatres and cinemas
- libraries and museums
- telecommunications and broadcasting services.

What does 'discriminate against' mean in the provision of goods and services?

Under the DDA 1995, discrimination will occur when for a reason which relates to the disabled person's disability, the service provider treats that person less favourably than they treat others to whom the reason does not, or would not, apply, and that treatment is not justified.[68]

The Code of Practice, Rights of Access, Goods, Facilities, Services and Premises 2002, provides some concrete examples of 'less favourable treatment' as follows:

1. A football club admits visiting supporters to its stadium. However, one visiting supporter is refused entry because he has cerebral palsy and has difficulty co-ordinating his movements. No other visiting supporter is refused entry. This would amount to less favourable treatment for a reason related to disability, and unless the football club can justify its actions it would be an unlawful refusal under the DDA 1995.

2. A party of adults with learning difficulties has exclusively booked a restaurant for a special dinner. The restaurant staff spend most of the evening making fun of the party and provide it with worse service than

[68] DDA 1995, ss 20 and 24.

normal. The fact that there are no other diners in the restaurant that evening does not mean that the disabled people have not been treated less favourably than other people. Other diners would not have been treated in this way.

What are the specific circumstances in which less favourable treatment in the provision of services will amount to discrimination?

There are four sets of circumstances under which discrimination may arise, as follows:[69]

Refusing or deliberately not providing to a disabled person a service provided to the public, without justification

Examples

One case involved the refusal of service to a group of people with learning difficulties, on Boxing Day, at a public house, when the landlady had asked them to leave because she said that she could not cope with them. Each member of the group of 10 was awarded £800 in compensation for injury to their feelings.

The Code of Practice offers other examples of discrimination under this head:

- An assistant in a small shop refuses to serve a disabled person, arguing that a nearby large shop can offer a better service to disabled people.
- A disabled person with Tourette's syndrome (which causes him to utter obscenities involuntarily and compulsively) wishes to book a hotel room. The hotel receptionist pretends that all rooms have been taken in order to refuse his booking because of his disability.

Failing to make a 'reasonable adjustment' to the way in which the services are provided to a disabled person seeking to make use of that service

As this provision requires a service provider to anticipate potential problems before they occur, and if necessary to make pre-emptive 'adjustments', it is the provision that requires the most forward planning. Since October 1999, under the DDA 1995, service providers are required to take all of the following reasonable steps:

- Change practices, policies or procedures that make it impossible, or unreasonably difficult, for disabled people to use a service that is

[69] Ibid, s 19.

provided to other members of the public. For example, reasonable adjustments should be made to premises such as improving access routes and ensuring the routes are free of clutter, or by redecorating dimly lit parts of premises to provide better contrast to someone with a visual impairment. Service providers must ensure that they provide appropriate or additional training for staff who may come into contact with customers with disabilities, to assist them in the provision of services to and for people with different types of disabilities.

- Find a reasonable alternative method of delivering a service, where a physical feature is a barrier to service.
- Service providers also have a duty to take reasonable steps to provide auxiliary aids or services, if such provision would enable, or make it easier for, a disabled user to use the service that is provided to other members of the public. Examples of such changes could include equipment changes, such as acquiring or using modified equipment (e.g. a telephone with text display for use by deaf customers, installing a portable induction loop), making service literature and instructions more accessible (e.g. providing a Braille version for blind customers, or providing information on cassette).

From 1 October 2004[70] providers of goods, facilities or services are obliged to take reasonable steps to remove, alter or to provide a way around a physical feature, such as a step, where the feature makes it impossible or unreasonably difficult for a disabled person to use the service, unless they can provide the service by a reasonable alternative method.

Providing a service to a lesser standard than to a non-disabled person, without justification

One recent case was settled on the basis that a refusal to serve a blind guide dog owner is a *prima facie* example of providing a service on worse terms to a disabled person, although in the particular case the defence of the service provider had been that they (mistakenly) believed the dog to be acting in an unruly manner.

Providing a service to a disabled person on worse terms than to a non-disabled person, without justification

The Code of Practice offers the following examples:

- A person who is deaf-blind is booking a holiday. The travel agent asks her for a larger deposit than it requires from other customers,

---

[70] Disability Discrimination (Providers of Services) (Adjustment of Premises) Regulations 2001, SI 2001/3253. See also Rights of Access Code of Practice 2002.

believing, without good reason, that because of her disability she is more likely to cancel her holiday.
- A disabled customer who is partially sighted applies for a hire-purchase loan from a finance company. The company is willing to lend to the customer, but on the condition that he should have his signature to the loan agreement witnessed by a solicitor. The company would not ask other borrowers to do this.

The DRC has explained how 'less favourable treatment' can often simply be the result of poor communication skills on the part of the service provider, and offers advice on ways of avoiding this pitfall, as follows:

- Talk to a disabled person directly if they are with someone, not to the person with them. This also applies to a deaf person accompanied by a sign language interpreter.
- When talking to a deaf person, find out whether they lip-read, in writing if necessary. If they do, make sure your face is in the light, look directly at the person, speak clearly and naturally, remembering to keep your hands away from your face.
- Introduce yourself when you first meet a blind person. When you are going to move away, tell them. Do not leave them talking to an empty space.
- When you are talking to someone with a speech impediment, concentrate on what is being said, be patient and do not try to guess what they want to say. If you do not understand, do not pretend you do.
- If someone has difficulty understanding you – perhaps because they have a learning disability – be patient and be prepared to explain something more than once. Concentrate on using simple language.
- When talking to a wheelchair user, try to ensure that your eyes are at the same level as theirs, perhaps by sitting down. Do not lean on the wheelchair – it is part of the user's personal space.
- Avoid questions about a person's disability, such as 'Were you born like that?' But you could ask, 'Does your disability affect your ability to use our service?'
- Avoid staring. If someone looks 'different', concentrate on what they are saying, not on the way they look.
- If you are talking to an adult, treat them like an adult.
- Offer assistance if someone looks as if they need it, but wait for them to accept before you help.
- When guiding a blind person do not push or pull them. Ask if they would like to take hold of your arm. If there are steps, tell them whether the steps go up or down.
- Remember that guide dogs for blind people, hearing dogs for deaf people and other assistance dogs are working animals, not pets. They should not be fed, patted or distracted when they are working.

• As a final point, put yourself in the disabled person's place. Most of the above points are just good manners.

What does 'justification' mean in the provision of goods and services?

The DDA 1995 provides a list of six situations in which discrimination in the provision of services may be legally 'justified'.[71] The Code of Practice provides some examples of treatment that might be (a) unlikely to be justified, and (b) justified, under each head.

The treatment is necessary in order not to endanger the health or safety of any person, which may include the disabled person

This is a key area of genuine difficulty for both providers and disabled users of services. It is the form of 'justification' most commonly put forward by providers.

Unlikely to be justified

Although there are adequate means of escape, a cinema manager turns away a wheelchair user because she unreasonably assumes, without checking, that he could be in danger in the event of a fire.

Likely to be justified

An amusement park operator refuses to allow a person with muscular dystrophy onto a physically demanding, high-speed ride. Due to her disability, the disabled person uses walking sticks and cannot stand unaided. The ride requires users to brace themselves using their legs. The refusal is based on genuine concerns for the health or safety of the disabled person and other users of the ride.

The disabled person is incapable of entering into an enforceable agreement or of giving an informed consent, and for that reason the treatment is reasonable in that case

Unlikely to be justified

A jeweller refuses to sell a pair of earrings to a person with a learning disability. It is claimed that she does not understand the nature of the

---

[71] DDA 1995, s 20(4)(a)–(f).

transaction, even though her order is clear and she is able to pay for the earrings.

Likely to be justified

A person with senile dementia applies for a mortgage loan from a building society. Although he has the means of keeping up with the mortgage loan repayments, the building society has sound reasons for believing that the applicant does not understand the nature of the legal agreement and obligations involved.

In a case where a refusal of service is alleged, the treatment is necessary because the provider of the service would otherwise be unable to provide the service to members of the public

Unlikely to be justified

A disabled customer with a speech impairment or learning disability has difficulty explaining to the bank cashier what his service requirements are, and she asks him to go to the back of the queue, so as not to delay other customers waiting in the queue.

Likely to be justified

A tour guide refuses to allow a person with a severe mobility impairment on a tour of old city walls because he has well-founded reasons to believe that the extra help the guide would have to give her would prevent the party from completing the tour.

Where service of a different standard or terms is alleged, the treatment is necessary for the service provider to be able to provide the service to the disabled person, or other members of the public

Unlikely to be justified

A public fitness centre restricts the times a customer with AIDS is allowed to use its facilities. The other users have objected to his presence and use of the centre's facilities because of a groundless fear that they might become infected with HIV by normal contact with him. Despite his reassurances, the centre has bowed to the pressure of the other customers.

Likely to be justified

A hotel restricts a wheelchair user's choice of bedrooms to those with level access to the lifts. Those rooms tend to be noisier and have restricted views. The disabled person would otherwise be unable to use the hotel.

Where service on different terms is alleged, the difference in the terms on which the service is provided to the disabled person and those on which it is provided to other members of the public reflects the greater costs to the provider of services in providing the service to the disabled person (this justification is not applicable where the greater cost is as a result of making 'reasonable adjustments')

Unlikely to be justified

A guest house has installed an audio-visual fire alarm in one of its guest bedrooms in order to accommodate visitors with a sensory impairment. In order to recover the cost of this installation (which was in effect a 'reasonable adjustment'), the owner charges disabled guests using this room a higher daily rate, although the room is otherwise identical to the other bedrooms.

Likely to be justified

A furniture shop charges more for an orthopaedic bed, made to the disabled customer's specification, than it does for a standard bed.

Where the steps necessary to provide the service to the disabled person would fundamentally alter the nature of the service

For example, a night club with low level lighting would not be obliged to turn up the lighting to accommodate partially sighted customers, nor would a hairdressing business be obliged to provide a home appointment service to a housebound customer, if home services did not form a part of their business.

Any action claiming discrimination in the provision of goods, facilities or services must be brought in the county court, not the employment tribunal, within six months of the alleged discriminatory act. Compensation, including for injury to feelings, can be awarded in an unlimited sum.

Finally, note that there are special rules affecting the provision of insurance, guarantees, and deposits in respect of goods and facilities, which are outside the scope of this chapter.

Helpful clarification on each of the above descriptions, and many other aspects of this complex part of the legislation, are contained in the revised Code of Practice – Rights of Access, Goods, Facilities, Services and Premises 2002.

Discrimination in public transport provision

The above provisions in connection with goods, facilities and services do not apply to any service 'so far as it consists in the use of any means of transport'.[72] The emphasis upon the word 'use' means that activities of transport providers ancillary to the actual use of the transport will be caught by the DDA 1995. Thus timetables, ticketing arrangements, booking facilities, waiting rooms, platforms, toilets and other areas in the vicinity of transport facilities are all covered by the DDA 1995 anti-discriminatory provisions. In addition, taxi drivers have certain statutory responsibilities towards passengers using guide dogs,[73] and the relevant Secretary of State has power to make new 'taxi accessibility regulations'[74] (not yet used); the Public Service Vehicle (PSV) Accessibility Regulations 2000[75] have established a rolling programme of responsibilities for PSV manufacturers and service providers to secure that disabled passengers can get on and off regulated PSVs in safety and without difficulty. The programme is partial, ongoing and of patchy effect. The Department for Transport has produced detailed guidance on the long-term implementation of this programme.[76] In addition the Government promises further legislative changes in the November 2003 Queen's Speech.

Finally, note that the Rail Vehicle Accessibility Regulations 1998[77] came into force on 1 November 1998, setting out a series of measures to be taken by the rail authorities to improve access to trains, taking particular account of people with disabilities.

Discrimination in education

The Special Educational Needs and Disability Act 2001 (SENDA 2001) introduced important new protection against discrimination on grounds of disability for pupils and students at all levels within the education system. The legislative changes are supplemented by two Codes of Practice.[78] Prior to the introduction of this legislation, the education system was largely outside the protections afforded by the anti-disability discrimination regime of the DDA 1995. The protections afforded by SENDA 2001 can be divided into two groups: those concerning *schools and education*

---

[72] Ibid, ss 19–21.
[73] Ibid, s 37 and Disability Discrimination Act 1995 (Taxis) (Carrying of Guide Dogs etc.) (England and Wales) Regulations 2000, SI 2000/2990.
[74] DDA 1995, s 32(1).
[75] Public Service Vehicle Accessibility Regulations 2000, SI 2000/1970, as amended by the Public Service Vehicle Accessibility (Amendment) Regulations 2000, SI 2000/3318.
[76] *The Public Service Vehicles Accessibility Regulations 2000 Guidance* (Department of Transport, 2000).
[77] SI 1998/2456.
[78] See note 3.

authorities, and those concerning *institutions providing further and higher education*. The protections take legal effect as amendments to the DDA 1995.

Schools and education authorities

SENDA 2001 has created three sources of support for disabled pupils in school, as follows:

- a set of anti-disability discrimination duties
- planning duties
- an amended and expanded Special Educational Needs (SEN) regime (outside the scope of this chapter).

Anti-disability discrimination duties

Admission

It is unlawful for the 'body responsible for a school'[79] to discriminate against a disabled person *either* in the arrangements it makes for determining admission to the school as a pupil *or* in the terms on which it offers to admit a person to the school as a pupil *or* by refusing or by deliberately omitting to accept an application for admission to the school as a pupil.[80]

Post admission

It is unlawful for the 'body responsible for a school' to discriminate against a disabled pupil in the education or associated services provided for (or offered to) pupils at the school by that body, or by excluding them from the school.[81]

The definition of what constitutes discrimination within a school context is essentially the same as for the other contexts that are covered by the DDA 1995,[82] with 'less favourable treatment' and a 'failure to make reasonable adjustments' as the two core principles. The duty to make reasonable adjustments applies both at the admissions stage and thereafter throughout the educational experience of the pupil. The latter duty is essentially that of ensuring that a disabled pupil is not placed at a substantial disadvantage in comparison with pupils who do not have a disability.[83] There

---

[79] The body will vary according to the nature of the school: DDA 1995, ss 28A(5), 28Q(6) and Sch 4A.
[80] DDA 1995, s 28A(1).
[81] Ibid, s 28A(2), (4).
[82] See pp 135–6.
[83] DDA 1995, s 28C(1)(b).

are also special rules concerning the effect of a 'confidentiality request' in connection with concealing the pupil's disability,[84] and the relevance of the school's prior knowledge of the disability. A 'discriminatory act' against a disabled pupil will not amount to unfavourable treatment if at the time the responsible authority did not know, and could not reasonably have been expected to know, that the person in question was disabled.

Planning duties

By virtue of SENDA 2001, schools and LEAs are under a new duty to develop accessibility strategies or plans for disabled pupils.[85] An accessibility strategy (LEA schools) or plan (all other schools) should be designed to:

- increase the participation of disabled pupils in the school's range of curricula;
- improve the school's physical environment to widen the disabled pupil's capacity to engage in all school activities;
- improve delivery of written information such that it does not disadvantage disabled pupils.

The strategy or plan must be in writing and kept under regular review.

Institutions providing further and higher education (F/HEI)

It is unlawful[86] for the 'body responsible for [an F/HEI]' to discriminate against a disabled person, without justification, by treating them less favourably for a reason related to their disability in *either* the application, admissions and enrolment process, *or* the offer and provision of 'student services' (defined as 'services of any description that are provided wholly or mainly for students'), *or* by failing to make reasonable adjustments, in circumstances where a disabled student is likely to be placed at a substantial disadvantage in comparison to a non-disabled person.

What constitutes discrimination and less favourable treatment in an F/HEI is essentially the same as for schools.[87] The Code of Practice provides detailed assistance on what might constitute a reasonable adjustment in an F/HEI setting. It suggests that the factors to consider should include: the need to maintain academic and other prescribed standards; the financial resources available to the responsible body; special student loans/grants that might be available in addition to a disabled student; the cost and practicality of taking a particular step; health and safety requirements; and the relevant interests of other parties, including the effect upon other

---

[84] Ibid, s 28C(5).
[85] Ibid, ss 28D–28E.
[86] Ibid, s 28R(1).
[87] See p 157.

students. As for school pupils, special rules cover both confidentiality requests,[88] and the relevance of a lack of prior knowledge of the disability.[89]

Defence of justification

Discrimination can be legally 'justified' in an F/HEI setting if it is required in order to maintain academic standards, or standards of any other prescribed kind, in prescribed circumstances – for example, as a requirement of a professional course.[90] The defence might be raised, therefore, in a sport and leisure management course where a lifeguard certificate is deemed to be a necessary and essential requirement to follow the course; or in a fine arts course where sufficient vision is required to identify examples of art history; or in a law course where the ability to advocate is essential; or in a medical training where the physical capacity to change drips, and administer emergency resuscitation, is deemed essential. The reason for the discrimination must, however, in such circumstances be both material to the circumstances of the particular case and substantial. Note that the full weight of the anti-discrimination provisions will apply to 'qualifications bodies' and 'practical work experience' from October 2004, which will inevitably impact upon this defence, and render it far more limited.[91]

Examples of areas in F/HEI where disability discrimination might become an issue are set out in the following list, which is illustrative, and is not intended to be exhaustive:

- not providing publicity materials in accessible format
- requiring handwritten application forms
- offering inaccessible interviews
- confusing health and disability issues
- exclusion of a student following a mental health incident
- providing discriminatory course materials (either in format or in content)
- poor access to teaching rooms
- tight turnarounds between classes
- inaccessible canteen or student bar facilities
- limited range of social and recreational activities
- discriminatory assessment procedures
- offering inaccessible field trips, exchanges, placements
- discriminatory job shop arrangements
- discriminatory careers advice

---

[88] DDA 1995, s 28T(3).
[89] Ibid, s 28S(3).
[90] Ibid, s 28S(5)–(9).
[91] Disability Discrimination Act 1995 (Amendment) Regulations 2003, SI 2003/1673, reg 13.

- inadequate residential accommodation
- poor inter-campus transport
- inaccessible graduation ceremonies
- inadequate distance learning opportunities
- discriminatory welfare and financial advice services.

A number of imaginative approaches to teaching, learning and assessment are currently being developed in some F/HEIs as anticipatory rather than reactive responses to the anti-discrimination philosophy infused by SENDA 2001.[92] Examples include making greater and more sensitive use of electronic materials, audio visual aids, case studies, recording lectures, coloured backgrounds for presentations, computer-based assessments, critical diaries or learning journals, design tasks, electronic presentations, exhibitions, portfolios, simulation exercises, and vivas.[93]

Reform proposals

Early in 2003 the Disability Rights Commission published its first full review of the impact of the DDA 1995 and made a number of suggestions for reform, of which the key proposals were as follows:[94]

Changes in the definitions sections

- People with HIV should be deemed to be disabled from the point of diagnosis.
- People with cancer should be deemed to be disabled from the point at which the cancer is diagnosed as likely to require substantial treatment.
- All progressive conditions should be covered from the point of diagnosis.
- Receipt of specified state disability benefits should automatically allow applicants to be deemed to be disabled.
- The list of normal day-to-day activities should be revised to include 'the ability to communicate with others' and to ensure that those acting out self-harming behaviour are covered.

---

[92] For examples consult LINK, Learning and Teaching Support Network, 'Considering Students with Disabilities', Issue 3, 2002, at www.brookes.ac.uk/ltsn. The HEFCE website also contains information about a number of ongoing learning and teaching initiatives in response to SENDA 2001. See also *Into Higher Education (2003): the Higher Education Guide for People with Disabilities* (Skill, 2003).
[93] For examples of imaginative strategies being used in other jurisdictions, see Cooper 'From Exclusion to Inclusion: Some Lessons from Abroad', in Powell (ed) *Special Teaching in Higher Education* (Routledge Falmer, 2003).
[94] Disability Rights Commission *Legislative Review – A First Review of the Disability Discrimination Act 1995* (Disability Rights Commission, 2003).

- The requirement that a mental illness be 'clinically well recognised' should be removed.
- For individuals whose day-to-day activities are substantially affected as a result of depression, the requirement that the effects last twelve months should be reduced to six months.
- Discrimination because of an association with a disabled person (for example, against carers), or because a person is mistakenly treated as a disabled person, should be made unlawful.

Changes in the employment provisions

- Volunteers should be covered by the DDA 1995.
- Tribunals should be able to order reinstatement or re-engagement.
- Disability-related enquiries before a job is offered should be permitted only in very limited circumstances.
- The armed services should be covered by the DDA 1995.
- Employers should be required to anticipate the access needs of potential disabled employees and applicants, and to take reasonable action to remove barriers in advance.
- Less favourable treatment should be justifiable only where a person is shown not to be competent, capable or available to perform the essential functions of the job, even after allowing for reasonable adjustments.

Changes in the access to goods, facilities and services provisions

- The DDA 1995 should apply to all the functions of public authorities.
- The public sector should be under a duty to promote equalisation of opportunities for disabled people in the provision of services and in employment, to mirror Race Relations (Amendment) Act 2000 provisions. The latter Act sets out a number of steps that public authorities should take to audit and monitor equal opportunities and equal treatment for people from minority ethnic communities within their workforce and client group, as a response to the phenomenon of 'institutional racism'.
- Rather than requiring reasonable adjustments where it is 'impossible or unreasonably difficult' to access a service, the DDA 1995 should be altered to require these where a disabled customer is 'at a substantial disadvantage' in accessing a service.
- The law should be clear that all landlords of commercial premises have reasonable adjustment duties for the common areas of their buildings.
- Goods and services cases should be heard by a tribunal, rather than by the county or sheriff court, so that disabled people find it easier to get redress.
- A Questionnaire procedure should be introduced into the goods, facilities and services enforcement system, as with employment cases.

The Government has announced its intention of implementing some of these proposals in the near future.[95] Note that, for general updating on the UK Government initiatives in the field of disability, the reader should consult *http://www.disability.gov.uk/*.

Further reading

Blackburn, J and Libson, J *Disability Discrimination* (Industrial Society, 2001)

Brading, J and Curtis, J *Disability Discrimination: a Practical Guide to the New Law* (2nd edn, Routledge Falmer, 2000)

Casserly, C and Gor, B *Disability Discrimination Claims: an Adviser's Handbook* (Jordans, 2001)

Cooper, J (ed) *Law, Rights and Disability* (Jessica Kingsley Publishers, 2000)

Disability Rights Commission *Definitions of Disability* (Disability Rights Commission, 2003)

Disability Rights Commission *Disability Equality: Making It Happen – A First Review of the Disability Discrimination Act 1995* (Disability Rights Commission, 2003)

Disability Rights Commission *50 Key Cases for the DRC* (Disability Rights Commission, 2003)

Doyle, B *Disability Discrimination: Law and Practice* (4th edn, Jordans, 2003)

[95] Queen's Speech, November 2003.

Chapter 7

Discrimination and the family

Erica Neustadt

Introduction

Discrimination and the family. The very subject area begs fundamental questions. What exactly is a family, in the twenty-first century? Who is being protected from discrimination? If it is, say, people with children, is this not positive discrimination? Do people without a partner, or without offspring, suffer discrimination, in fact, by being outside such protection? What about people who have other major family commitments, such as caring for an elderly relative? Do they not deserve protection from discrimination or the option of taking extra, unpaid leave?

Surely people who make a conscious choice, as usually happens, when they marry or reproduce, should take responsibility for that choice, rather than expecting concessions from the state, society at large, and people who have decided not to take such a course?

There is no legislation equivalent to, say, the Sex Discrimination Act 1975 or Race Relations Act 1976 which directly protects the family from discrimination. So, if an employer wishes to recruit childfree workers, for instance, there is nothing specifically to prevent it from doing so. However, there is a great deal of legislation, mostly emanating from the European Union, that has as its focus the wellbeing of working families.

This chapter will look at family-orientated legislation and consider whether it protects against discrimination (and how successfully it does so), or whether it goes further and provides positive discrimination.

The Government's paper 'Balancing work and family life: enhancing choice and support for parents' goes some way to explaining the policies behind the plethora of family-friendly legislation which has hit the statute book since the Labour party came to office.

> . . . in today's fast changing economy . . . families need security and support. Our starting point is . . . [to ensure that] parents are well placed to face the challenges of combining work and family . . .

> Today, there are more dual-income couples, more single parent households, and many more women in employment. Some of the greatest pressures that parents face today [are] . . . the loss of income when one parent ceases employment or moves to part-time work after the birth of a child; or the costs of childcare when both parents go to work.
>
> We are providing parents with more choice and support than ever before to balance family and work in ways that benefit everyone – employers, employees and their children . . .
>
> Together these initiatives . . . [tackle] poverty and [invest] in the potential of every single child in our country . . .[1]

Apart from taking legislative measures, the Government is also trying to achieve these aims through the tax system and investing in childcare. Arguably, this is positive discrimination in favour of the family.

The Government considers that these policies will benefit business as well as families. For example, they may encourage women, after having children, to bring their experience back to the jobs that they were previously doing, thereby saving employers the management time and money of recruiting and training someone new. However, such policies have been labelled by, for example, the Institute of Directors, somewhat derisively, as female-friendly policies, and seen as wholly negative both for employers and the economy.

It is clear from this that, for such policies to be politically acceptable, the legislators must constantly strive to strike a balance between the interests of the family, by protecting women particularly, and parents generally, from discrimination in the workplace, and those of the employer. Thus, many policies remain just that, and stop short of becoming rights. Others do give new rights, but through lack of flexibility, or non-payment, exclude many from taking advantage of them.

As well as women caring for children, one particularly large pool of potential labour is that of lone parents. Obviously, these two groups overlap to a significant extent. Lone parents are the single poorest group of adults in the United Kingdom. A Labour party manifesto pledge for the 2001 election was to help children in poverty. A large proportion of such children are members of one parent families. Therefore, getting such parents into work is both a way of increasing the workforce and a major part of the policy of reducing or attempting to eradicate child poverty in this country.

So protection from discrimination and positive rights for families are increasing because of political or social imperatives. Is the change also driven by a higher morality, such as human rights? In fact, the Human Rights Act 1998 is a good place to start. This incorporates the European Convention on Human Rights into the law of England and Wales. Article 8 of the Convention sets out the right to respect for private and family

---

[1] Published by HM Treasury and DTI, 14 January 2003.

life: 'Everyone has the right to respect for his private and family life, his home and his correspondence'.

Respect for family life must surely include the right to be protected from discrimination. Therefore, a further motivating factor for legislative protection may well be human rights.

Sex discrimination

This subject is dealt with fully in Chapter 4 and therefore the discussion here will be limited to the family.

Under the Sex Discrimination Act 1975 (SDA 1975), there is direct and indirect discrimination on the basis of sex or marital status. Whilst the SDA 1975 extends its protection to both men and women, it anticipates that women will need its protection more than men. This is clear from its reference to an employee as 'she'. The use of the feminine pronoun is unusual in legislation, and is typically reserved for legislation which cannot apply to men, namely maternity protection. Whilst this use may merely reflect the period, nearly 30 years ago, when the SDA 1975 hit the statute book, it now seems inappropriate, and counterproductive, to identify women as the primary victims of the dominant male employer.

> A person discriminates against a woman . . . if
> (a) on the ground of her sex he treats her less favourably than he treats or would treat a man . . .[2]

This also presupposes, and therefore perpetuates, the idea that the way that men are treated is the norm, and thus places men at the centre of the legislation, rather like the sun is at the centre of the solar system. Again, this seems anachronistic and it is odd that legislation aiming at equality between the sexes subsists in this form. That said, it is clear that this legislation is still intended to protect women. Since women are typically the primary carers of children, this must protect the family from discrimination. So action may be taken, for example, where an employer fails to promote a woman who has a family. This may protect her status as an important breadwinner for the family.

The SDA 1975, together with anti-discrimination law at European level, has been extremely important as a basis for protection of women against discrimination in employment and has driven the development of the law in other areas, such as the protection of part-time workers (see below).

[2] SDA 1975, s 1.

Direct discrimination

Direct discrimination occurs in the employment field, where there is less favourable treatment of an employee by the employer, on the grounds of the employee's sex or marital status.[3] Therefore, to analyse whether direct discrimination on the basis of sex has occurred, a comparison of the treatment of the complainant with that of a person of the opposite sex, in a similar position, is made. In cases of alleged differential treatment because of marital status, the comparator will be a single person of the same sex. There is no general defence to claims for direct discrimination, and the employer's motive or intention is not relevant. There is, however, an exception where sex is a genuine occupational qualification.[4]

The SDA 1975, sets out protection relating to employment.[5] It covers the recruitment period, as well as the time after the employment relationship has been entered. Prior to employment, discrimination may be found in the arrangements that an employer makes for determining who should be recruited, the terms on which employment is offered or by refusal or deliberate omission to offer employment. Once employed, there is protection from discrimination in the way access to opportunities for promotion, training, benefits, facilities or services is offered, and against refusal or deliberate omission to provide such access.

Indirect discrimination

Pursuant to the SDA 1975, indirect discrimination may be caused where the employer applies a requirement or condition to its workforce. The requirement or condition might apply equally to members of both sexes, but is discriminatory if it is harder for one sex than the other to comply, or if it has a greater detrimental effect on one sex than the other.[6] Statistical evidence showing disparate effect should usually be provided to a tribunal to back up an allegation of indirect discrimination.

Unlike direct discrimination, there is a defence to claims of indirect discrimination – that of objective justification. An employer will use this defence successfully only if able to show that the requirement or condition was justifiable, irrespective of sex, in terms of the needs of its business, and was an appropriate measure to achieve the desired end.

The definition of indirect discrimination has been changed by the Burden of Proof Directive,[7] implemented in this jurisdiction by the Sex Discrimination (Indirect Discrimination and Burden of Proof) Regulations 2001.[8] These state that indirect discrimination results from:

---

[3] Ibid, s 1.
[4] Ibid, s 7.
[5] Ibid, s 6.
[6] See, e.g., *London Underground v Edwards (No 2)* [1997] IRLR 157, EAT.
[7] 1997/80 EEC.
[8] SI 2001/2660.

an apparently neutral provision . . . [which] disproportionately disadvantages
the members of one sex, by reference inter alia to marital or family status,
unless [it] . . . meets a necessary aim of the social policy of the member
state . . . and as such is objectively justified . . .[9]

It follows that the level of proof to be shown by an employee alleging
indirect discrimination under the SDA 1975 is now less stringent, and
does not relate purely to contractual matters. So the employee no longer
needs to show any requirement or condition that has been imposed by
the employer. All that now needs to be shown is a discriminatory practice. The employer may still successfully withstand such a claim, if it is
able to argue in its defence that the provision, criterion or practice is
appropriate and necessary to its business and that it may be justified by
objective factors unrelated to sex.

This recent legislation has had an impact on the protection from discrimination available primarily to women and, effectively, to the family.
Women may argue that failure to agree to a change to part-time work,
having to work a shift system or even nights may be found to be indirectly
discriminatory. Although such arguments have been made successfully
by women, such a course is unavailable for men. Therefore, these rights
do not necessarily increase equality between the sexes in the workplace,
and may disadvantage men (and their families) who are trying to combine the demands of work with caring responsibilities. Also, there may
well be resentment where one section of the workforce is seen to be treated
better, or at least more carefully, than another.

Discrimination on the basis of marital status

The SDA 1975 protects against discrimination on the basis of marital status:

A person discriminates against a married person of either sex . . . if
(a) on the ground of his or her marital status he treats that person less
    favourably than he treats . . . an unmarried person of the same sex,
    or
(b) he applies to that person a requirement or condition which he
    applies . . . equally to a married person but –
    (i)   which is such that the proportion of married persons who
          can comply . . . is considerably smaller than the proportion
          of unmarried persons of the same sex who can comply . . . and
    (ii) which he cannot show to be justifiable irrespective of the marital
          status of the person to whom it is applied, and
    (iii) which is to that person's detriment because he cannot comply
          with it.[10]

This in fact only gives protection to the married employee. A single person
complaining of discrimination on the basis of their singlehood has no

[9] Ibid, Article 2.2, reg 3.1.
[10] SDA 1975, s 3.

redress. Thus, it is perfectly legitimate for a company to have a policy to give first choice to married employees when to take holidays, on the basis that they are more likely to have children.

This is a very old, and a very clear, example of positive discrimination in favour of the family. Furthermore, it is specific protection for the archetypal family – in other words, one which is headed up by a married couple. Thus, if a person, straight or gay, has a long-term and stable relationship, financial interdependence and children with a partner, but has not legally tied the knot, or is divorced (or, presumably, widowed) with or without children from the marriage, he or she is not accorded the same legal status or protection under the SDA 1975 as a married person. This clearly detracts, for instance, from rights available for single parent families.

It can only be concluded that there is legal hierarchy applying to families, giving some types of family higher status in terms of better protection than others. Whilst this might simply be because the law has not kept pace with demographic and social change, it may also reflect an underlying value system.

Is there any remedy available for non-archetypal families at a supranational level?

European legislation

The Equal Treatment Directive is wider than the SDA 1975, covering discrimination 'by reference . . . to marital or family status'.[11] However, as noted by Townshend-Smith,[12] there are no court rulings on the ambit of this provision. In any event, it is not directly effective and may only be used in actions against emanations of the state, and therefore does not cover the majority of private employers.

It also appears that there is a hierarchy in anti-discrimination legislation protecting the family at European level. This is shown, for example, in the area of freedom of movement.[13] Whilst the spouse of a migrant worker may accompany that worker to the state providing employment, as Nielsen and Szyszczak[14] note, 'The [ECJ] has not been persuaded to expand the categories of family members . . . to include cohabitees'.[15]

Looking at legislation more widely, it is clear that this value system is present as, across the board, members of a conventional married couple family are afforded more rights and protection by the law.

---

[11] Article 2.
[12] RJ Townshend-Smith *Discrimination Law: Text, Cases and Materials* (Cavendish, 1998), p 129.
[13] Regulation 1612/68/EEC, Article 10(1)(a).
[14] R Nielsen and E Szyszczak *The Social Dimension of the European Union* (Handelshojskolens Forlag, 1997), p 74.
[15] Case 59/85 *Netherlands v Reed* [1986] ECR 1283.

All pension schemes are subject to Inland Revenue rules which provide that pensions may be paid to widows or widowers as of right, but in other cases can only be made where the beneficiary is 'financially dependent' on the member.[16]

This clearly gives cohabiting heterosexuals and homosexuals lower legal status than married people, and effectively is positive discrimination in favour of the traditional family.

There is a shout for universal protection pursuant to Article 14 of the European Convention on Human Rights.

> The enjoyment of the rights and freedoms set forth in this Convention shall be secured without discrimination on any ground such as sex, race, colour, language, religion, political or other opinion, national or social origin, association with a national minority, property, birth or other status.

Whilst a superficial look may suggest that the phrase 'other status' hints at a free-standing right of equality, Fredman points out: 'The equality guarantee in Article 14 requires the equal enjoyment of the Convention rights rather than providing a free-standing right'.[17]

In conclusion, the sex discrimination legislation sets out to provide equality between the sexes and, in so doing, it enhances any protection from discrimination against the family. However, it does so through a narrow definition of the shape of the family. As greater numbers of families no longer conform to this norm, its protective effect is reduced.

Maternity rights

Some of the most fundamental protections from discrimination available for families are those which apply to a woman's pregnancy and the maternity leave which follows. The rights that will be discussed here are protection from discrimination on the basis of pregnancy or having borne a child, various types of maternity leave and maternity pay. The following sources of protection will be reviewed: those outlined in the Employment Rights Act 1996 (ERA 1996), the Maternity and Parental Leave etc Regulations 1999[18] (MPL Regulations) and the Employment Act 2002 (EA 2002), which adds new rights as well as modifying and simplifying previously existing protection.

Whilst these rights are available in principle to all women, no matter what their marital status, it is worth noting that many such rights are available only to employees, and not to all workers.

[16] 'Equality for lesbians and gay men in the workplace' (1997) 74 *Equal Opportunities Review* 20, pp 25–26, as cited in Townshend-Smith (Cavendish, 1998). The article notes that 'financial dependence' has been replaced with 'interdependence'.
[17] Sandra Fredman 'Equality: A New Generation?' (2000) 30(2) *Industrial Law Journal* 150.
[18] SI 1999/3312. See also the Maternity and Parental Leave (Amendment) Regulations 2001 (SI 2001/4010) and those of 2002 (SI 2002/2789).

Leave

Childbirth is defined as the birth of a living child, or the birth of a child, whether living or dead, after 24 weeks of pregnancy. In other words, if a woman suffers a stillbirth before 24 weeks, then legally this does not amount to childbirth and the woman will not be covered by the maternity leave legislation. (This is also demonstrated by the fact that if a pregnancy ends in a stillbirth before 24 weeks, the parents will not be able to obtain a birth certificate.) In these circumstances, a woman's absence will be treated as caused by illness.

While a woman is pregnant, she has the right to paid time off work, during normal working hours, for the purpose of attending antenatal checks.[19] Her employer may not require her to rearrange her working hours, nor to make up the time. If her employer unreasonably denies a woman such time off, or forces her to take the time off without payment, she has a right to complain to an employment tribunal within three months of the date of the relevant antenatal appointment.[20] If the tribunal finds in her favour, it may:

- make a declaration that her rights have been infringed;
- where the infringement is failure to pay, order the employer to pay her the appropriate amount;
- where the employer has failed to allow time off, order the employer to pay the employee however much she would have been entitled to had she been allowed to take the time off.

It may be concluded that these remedies hardly preserve the right to paid time off for antenatal care; they simply provide a low level of compensation. It may well be that an employee, particularly a pregnant one, will be unwilling to go to the trouble of seeking such weak remedies from a tribunal, particularly when the remedy is likely to be given somewhat after the event.

Further, where the complaint is of unreasonable refusal of time off, the remedy available is not drafted clearly: '. . . the tribunal shall also order the employer to pay to the employee an amount equal to the remuneration to which she would have been entitled . . . if the employer had not refused.'[21] Since the woman, having been refused time off, presumably worked during the relevant time, she would have been paid as normal. It is unclear whether or not the above provision takes this into account, i.e. whether the woman should be paid an additional amount, as a penalty on the employer. Where rights are unclear, it is even more unlikely that employees will complain to employment tribunals.

---

[19] ERA 1996, ss 55–57.
[20] Ibid, s 57.
[21] Ibid.

Apart from this, there are three types of maternity leave: ordinary, compulsory and additional.

Ordinary maternity leave (OML)

A woman is entitled to OML as soon as she is employed. A woman may choose when her OML is to start, although the earliest that it may do so is the beginning of the eleventh week before the expected week of the birth. A woman may work right up to the birth of her child. If, after the beginning of the fourth week before the baby is born, a woman is absent from work, wholly or partly because of the pregnancy, this may trigger OML. OML now lasts for a maximum of 26 weeks, having recently been increased from 18 weeks.[22]

Compulsory maternity leave (CML)

A woman may not return to work within the two weeks following the birth of her child, but must take maternity leave to cover this period. This is reinforced by the fact that it is an offence for an employer to allow a woman to work at this time.[23]

Additional maternity leave (AML)

The right to AML is earned by a qualification period. A woman qualifies for AML if she both is entitled to OML and has, at the beginning of the fourteenth week before the expected week of the birth, been continuously employed by her current employer for 26 weeks.[24]

This qualification period was shortened from one year to 26 weeks by the Employment Act 2002, so that many more women qualified for the right to AML. This development is interesting to consider in the context of discrimination and the family. First, why is there a qualification period at all? Why should some women be entitled to more protection than others? Why should some babies be entitled to have their mothers with them for longer than others? AML is not driven by health concerns, otherwise all women would be entitled to the same period. Secondly, why has it now been shortened? Surely this will increase the impact on employers of women having children. It is also argued in some quarters that it will discourage the employment of women.

Taken together with the increase in the period of OML, part of the answer to these questions must be that this is a further example of discrimination in favour of the family. But is it as simple as this? Again, there

---

[22] Social Security Contributions and Benefits Act 1992, s 35(2), as amended by the Employment Act 2002, s 18.

[23] ERA 1996, s 72 and MPL Regulations, reg 8.

[24] ERA 1996, s 73, MPL Regulations, regs 5 and 7, as amended by the Maternity and Parental Leave (Amendment) Regulations 2002, SI 2002/2789.

is clearly a hierarchy of rights in this area of the law. Women who are employed have greater rights than those who are self-employed and those who have been employed for a longer period have greater rights than those who have recently started a job. The whole answer must therefore be more complex.

One possible part of the explanation is that the Government's policies were influenced by the need to increase the workforce, and legislation has been used to make it more attractive to women to continue to work after having a child. Take OML for example: in recent times, this has been increased from 14 weeks to 18 weeks, and then to 26 weeks. Say, when it was fourteen weeks, a woman went on leave six weeks before the expected week of the birth. If the child was born on time, she would have just eight weeks with it, before having to leave it, possibly wean it, and return to work. Bearing in mind the most recent Government guidelines, announced on 13 May 2003, that babies should be exclusively breastfed for the first six months of life, this period was clearly too short, and many women would have left work, or decided to take a career break, rather than detract from the care given to their child.

Possibly, therefore, the legislators balanced the needs of women, in order to make the workplace more attractive, with the impact on, and perception of, employers, and the result was an extension of the period of OML, plus the retention of a shorter period of qualification for additional leave rights: in other words, a compromise. The shortening in the qualification period for AML may also be influenced by the fact that women typically do not have as much continuous employment as men. Therefore, to impose a long qualification period for an employment right may be seen as effectively discriminatory even though there is no comparable situation for men. This is because the European Court of Justice has held that women during the maternity period are in an exceptional position and do not require comparison with men in order to find discrimination.[25]

Status of the contract of employment during maternity leave

When a woman is on maternity leave, the contract of employment continues to subsist. During OML, a woman is entitled to the terms and conditions of employment, except for remuneration, which would have applied had she not been on maternity leave. 'Remuneration' is narrowly defined to include only wages and salary.[26] Therefore, a woman is entitled to all other benefits during this period, such as a company car or access to a bonus scheme. Rights go with responsibilities, so that a woman is bound, while on OML, to honour any obligations arising out of her contract, which are not inconsistent with being on maternity leave.

[25] Case C-342/93 *Gillespie v Northern Health and Social Services Board* [1996] ECR I-475.
[26] ERA 1996, s 71 and MPL Regulations, reg 9.

During AML, a woman is entitled only to the benefit of the employer's implied duty of trust and confidence, together with basic contractual terms such as the notice period, disciplinary and grievance procedures, and compensation for redundancy. She is bound by reciprocal duties such as the implied obligation of good faith, terms relating to notice of termination of contract and confidential information.

Maternity pay

Employees are entitled to statutory maternity pay (SMP), and workers, who have worked and paid national insurance contributions for at least 26 weeks of the 66 weeks before the expected week of the childbirth are entitled to maternity allowance. Both payments last a maximum of 26 weeks. SMP has always been somewhat modest. Maternity allowance is set at the same level as SMP. Both are flat-rate payments; they now stand at £100 per week. As a result, in the past when payment was even lower, women typically returned to work without using their full entitlement to leave, as they could not afford to take it. It is unlikely that the recent increase will perceptibly ameliorate the position.

The level of SMP and maternity allowance will particularly impact on lower paid workers and families where the woman is the sole or primary breadwinner. It will also affect a woman's lifetime earnings and possibly the accrual of her pension provision. To this extent, the state does not go far enough to provide a structure to support and enhance family life at this time and, in fact, accepts a level of discrimination against women in this way.

The case of *Gillespie v Northern Health and Social Services Board*[27] took the issue of maternity pay to the European Court of Justice. The ECJ refused to prohibit discrimination against women while on maternity leave where it related to pay. It held that women on maternity leave are not comparable to either men or women at work. Therefore women on maternity leave could not argue an entitlement to full pay.

This is a major source of damage to women's financial wellbeing. In terms of discrimination and the family, this is a retrograde step as it is highly detrimental to sexual equality, causing a high percentage of the female population to become financially dependent on men, during women's working life and also in older age. It also provides a model of inequality to be passed on to the next generation.

Protection from detriment

A woman is protected from being subjected to detriment by any act or deliberate failure to act by her employer, by reason of being pregnant,

---

[27] Case C-342/93 *Gillespie v Northern Health and Social Services Board* [1996] ECR I-475.

having given birth, having been suspended from work on the grounds of maternity or having taken or attempted to take maternity leave.[28] This provision has been shown to be wide. It covers contractual and non-contractual matters that are connected with her employment, with the exception of remuneration.

Termination of the contract during pregnancy and maternity leave

A woman has the right to return from maternity leave to the job she was employed to do before her absence. Following OML, she should go back to work with the seniority, pension and other rights she would have had had she not been absent.[29] Thus, if the employer awards the woman's colleagues a pay rise while she is on leave, the woman should be awarded a comparable rise. Following AML, a woman is entitled to the seniority etc. that she would have had if her employment before taking AML had been continuous with her employment following her return to work.

A woman may not be dismissed for being pregnant. However, she is not protected from being dismissed, merely because she is pregnant or on leave. She may, of course, decide to resign during this period. The following outlines the extent of protection from dismissal.

Unfair dismissal

It is automatically unfair to dismiss a woman because of, or for a reason connected with her pregnancy. ERA 1996, s 99 includes in this dismissal for pregnancy, childbirth or maternity, and ordinary, compulsory or additional maternity leave. Employers who have fewer than five employees before the end of the employee's AML or dismissal, who find that it is not reasonably practicable to allow the woman to return to a suitable and appropriate job, are excepted from this rule.[30]

Women dismissed from employment for reasons connected with pregnancy, birth, maternity leave or suspension from work on maternity grounds may also have a claim under sex discrimination legislation. Typically, this is on the basis that they have been treated less favourably on the ground of their sex, i.e. having suffered direct discrimination. In one case, although not a claim for unfair dismissal, the power of this protection is demonstrated. An employment tribunal held that a pregnant employee who needed to take regular breaks to eat was unreasonably disciplined for failure to comply with instructions over notification of breaks, and that her treatment amounted to sex discrimination.[31]

---

[28] ERA 1996, s 47C.
[29] Ibid, s 71.
[30] MPL Regulations, reg 20.
[31] Case 14020778/01 *Bosworth v Memorandum Ltd* (2002) 113 *Equal Opportunities Review* 30.

It is direct discrimination to dismiss a woman during her pregnancy for being absent from work because of a pregnancy-related illness. As mentioned above, since pregnancy is unique to women, there is no need to establish this by showing that another employee was treated differently, as an applicant would have to do in other areas of anti-discrimination law.[32]

Note that a woman who is unable to return to work, through illness, at the end of the maternity leave period is no longer treated as such a special case, but as any other sick employee, even if it is clear that her illness is related to her pregnancy.[33] In this case it will clearly be a fiction that her illness is no longer to be treated in the context of pregnancy. This artificial limitation on the protection that women have during maternity is another example of balancing the interests of the employee with those of the employer.

Paternity leave

This entitlement is inserted into the ERA 1996 by the Employment Act 2002.[34] The specific rights are set out in the Paternity and Adoption Leave Regulations 2002.[35]

Paternity leave of up to two consecutive weeks is available to employees only who have at least 26 weeks' continuous employment with their employer, ending with the fifteenth week before the baby is due. Leave must be taken within 56 days of the child's birth. It may not be taken before the child is born. The purpose of taking leave must be to care for the child and/or to support the mother. Partners taking advantage of this right are entitled to statutory paternity pay of £100 per week.

An employee is eligible for paternity leave if he or she has or expects to have responsibility for the baby's upbringing and is the child's biological father or the mother's husband or partner. The DTI guidance specifically addresses the case of same-sex couples, so that a female partner may qualify for paternity leave.[36]

Where a child is born prematurely, this will not affect entitlement to leave, where the partner would have been entitled had the child been born when due. This is also the case where a child is stillborn after 24 weeks. The employee must tell the employer of the intention to take paternity leave, saying when the child is expected, how much leave the

---

[32] *Brown v Rentokil Ltd* [1998] IRLR 445.

[33] Case 179/88 *Handels- og Kontorfunktionaerernes Forbund i Danmark v Dansk Arbejdsgiverforening* [1991] IRLR 31.

[34] Employment Act 2002, s 1 and ERA 1996, ss 80A ff.

[35] SI 2002/2788.

[36] 'Working fathers – rights to paternity leave and pay' (PL 517).

employee would like to take and when the employee would like to take the leave.

During paternity leave, the employee is entitled to the benefit of all terms and conditions of employment which would have applied if he or she had not been absent, and is bound by any obligations arising under the contract. As with OML, 'terms and conditions of employment' excludes remuneration.

An employee has the right to return from leave to the same job that he or she did before the absence, with the same seniority, pension and similar rights. An employee is protected from receiving detrimental treatment for taking paternity leave. Dismissal for taking or seeking to take paternity leave is automatically unfair.

Again, this right is extremely helpful to some families, but why a qualification period? If this were truly a policy with families at its heart, it would be a right available across the board. It seems harsh and illogical that some new parents are not entitled to leave, and that their partners are not entitled to this support at such a time.

Parental leave

The very title of this right defines it as a type of positive discrimination in favour of a family with children. This leave is available only to parents, not grandparents, nor someone who has a dependent elderly relative, or a menagerie in the back garden, or any other responsibility or interest for which the right to time off from work would be extremely useful and socially beneficial.

Part III of the MPL Regulations brought the Directive on the Framework Agreement on Parental Leave into force in the United Kingdom. There have been two sets of amendments: the Maternity and Parental Leave (Amendment) Regulations of 2001[37] and 2002.[38]

In the majority of Member States in the European Union, the concept of parental leave was nothing new, but long established at national level, typically (as, for example, in Sweden and Germany) as a measure to reverse falling birth rates. Therefore, the European legislation did not present a culture shock, and in fact drew on schemes already in place around the Union. This was not the case in the United Kingdom: parental leave was unprecedented and has met with resistance from the state and employers' representatives. Historically, the accepted view has been that employees give priority either to career or family, but not both. It is submitted that for this reason, and in sectors of the economy where long hours are worked, parental leave is culturally dissonant.

---

[37] SI 2001/4010; in force 10 January 2002.
[38] SI 2002/2789.

Since the MPL Regulations represent such a shift towards additional rights for families before the law, they and their genesis will be considered closely.

The framework agreement

The preamble to the framework agreement states that parental leave and time off from work is 'an important means of reconciling work and family life and promoting equal opportunities and treatment between men and women'. The general considerations recognise 'that an effective policy of equal opportunities presupposes . . . [a] strategy for better organisation of working hours and greater flexibility, and for an easier return to working life'.

Thus, while sexual equality is one motivation, the framework agreement is also driven by the desire to increase the workforce by enabling or attracting people of working age, not currently economically active, to join the workforce. This approach is clearly at one with the stated aims of the UK Government. The emphasis making working time more compatible with other commitments is recognition of what will encourage women with children (constituting the largest single group of potential workers) to consider it possible to combine domestic responsibilities with paid work. Legislation driven by this aim should, at least in theory, result in positive discrimination in favour of the family.

The framework agreement reflected the changing shape of the family and asserted that it should influence the drafting and enactment of legislation: 'measures to reconcile work and family life should encourage the introduction of new flexible ways of organising work and time which are better suited to the changing needs of society and . . . family policy must be looked at in the context of demographic changes . . .' However, the agreement also refers to 'promoting women's participation in the labour force' and states that 'men should be encouraged to assume an equal share of family responsibilities'.

In themselves, these aims are positive and forward looking, but it is clear that, to take full advantage of the legislation, a family must have two parents. The reference to encouraging men to 'share' domestic responsibilities presupposes that there is someone else currently taking the bulk of that responsibility and therefore only includes partnered men. This is juxtaposed with getting women back to work, as a result of the sharing of domestic responsibility and clearly indicates a woman in a partnership. The partnerships are clearly heterosexual. Thus, despite explicitly recognising the current changing structure of the family, the framework agreement looks back to the traditional family model as a basis for drafting. This marginalises all other family forms, including, for example, the lone parent family, and to a large extent limits positive discrimination to the heterosexual dual parent family. If the legislation was not modelled on the dual parent family, it is likely that leave would have been allocated per child, rather than per parent.

The drafters, in this case the social partners, must have made a choice, conscious or not, between this approach and one which would have been more inclusive, possibly more liberal and certainly a better reflection of demographic reality. The result of their choice is that, again, we see that there is a hierarchy amongst families, with the more traditional ones qualifying for greater protection.

The framework agreement required leave to be non-transferable. The purpose of non-transferability was to provide an incentive for men to share domestic responsibility by taking parental leave because if they do not, they lose it. According to government statistics, partnered men are far less likely to take parental leave than partnered women. They would be inclined, if able, to transfer leave to their partner. This is an interesting aspect of the framework agreement. Where women stand to benefit from legislation, one can always conclude that it is as a result of an economic policy such as increasing the available pool of labour. Here, though, men are clearly targeted, and are unable to pass on the benefit that they gain from the legislation. The most obvious conclusion to be drawn from this is that it is a genuine move towards equality between the sexes, and that the motivation for this policy is to break down, admittedly in a fairly small way, gender barriers as it provides as strong a persuasion as is possible (considering there is no pay structure for parental leave) for men to spend more time with their children.

Member States were given a wide discretion on implementation. They could decide whether parental leave was granted on a full or part-time basis, piecemeal or on a time-credit system. It could be made subject to a qualification period not exceeding one year. It could be postponed by the employer for justifiable reasons related to the operation of the under-taking, examples of which are given.

The agreement provided for workers to be protected from dismissal for applying for, or taking, parental leave. Following leave, workers were to be given the right to return to the same, equivalent or similar job. The framework agreement dictated that employment rights would not accrue during the period of parental leave, but would be maintained as they stood. Each Member State was entitled to define the status of the employment contract or relationship during the period of parental leave.

The agreement did not deal with payment for leave. It merely stated that 'all matters relating to social security . . . are for . . . determination by member states'. In addition to parental leave, the framework agreement dealt with the right of employees to be absent from work to deal with a crisis at home. This leave is known as time off for dependants or 'force majeure'. Time off on grounds of force majeure covers 'urgent family reasons in cases of sickness or accident making the immediate presence of the worker indispensable'. The framework agreement allows Member States to put a limit on the number of times or the length of each time this right is exercised. The agreement also sets out minimum requirements for implementation by Member States on parental leave and time off work on the grounds of force majeure. It does not call for payment for either type of leave. Obviously, Member States may adopt more favourable provisions than these minimum requirements.

The Maternity and Parental Leave etc Regulations 1999[39]

The framework agreement was adopted by the Council of Ministers, without amendment, as a Directive on 3 June 1996. Since the United Kingdom, under the Conservative administration, excluded itself from the social chapter, it was only after the election of the Labour Government in 1997, when the United Kingdom opted into the social chapter, that the Directive was extended to include the United Kingdom. As a result, the MPL Regulations came into force in the United Kingdom on 15 December 1999.[40]

As noted, in many other Member States parental leave was an established concept. By contrast, in the United Kingdom it was a completely novel statutory development, although some employers provided such a scheme before being obliged to do so. As McColgan noted, 'this issue has become an ever-greater lacuna in the legal protection of employees as the traditional pattern of a working father and homemaker mother has been replaced increasingly by dual-earner couples and lone parents'.[41]

Importantly, the MPL Regulations provide a default position for employees who have no or less favourable rights under their employment contracts or are covered by collective or workforce agreements incorporated into their contracts. Thus, the MPL Regulations provide a 'bottom line' for parental leave rights.

It is old ground that the Parental Leave Directive was implemented in a minimalist way in this jurisdiction. The MPL Regulations apply only to employees (someone entering into or working under a contract of employment), and not workers. There is a qualification period of one year's continuous employment, the maximum allowed by the framework agreement. Parental leave may generally only be taken in minimum units of one week. It is unpaid.

Leave must normally be taken before the child's fifth birthday. A worker with responsibility for a child is entitled to 13 weeks' leave over this period, and a maximum of 4 weeks per year.

The employer may refuse to allow leave to be taken at the requested time if it considers that such leave would unduly disrupt its business. It may decide unilaterally when, within the following six months, the employee should take the leave. There is a duty to consult with the employee regarding the provision of substitute leave. There is no requirement for

[39] SI 1999/3312.
[40] Council Directive 97/75/EC of 15 December 1997; MPL Regulations passed pursuant to Employment Relations Act 1999, s 76.
[41] A McColgan 'Family Friendly Frolics? The Maternity and Parental Leave etc. Regulations 1999' (2000) 29(2) *Industrial Law Journal* 125.

agreement between the parties, or any duty on the employer to act reasonably. If an employer does decide on a substitute period which the employee does not want, is the employee obliged to take leave then? In effect it would seem not, as this might be viewed as detriment, particularly in view of the non-payment of parental leave. However, the fact that there is a need only for consultation and not agreement muddies the waters.

Most controversially, the rights were initially available only to employees with parental responsibility for children born or adopted on or after 15 December 1999, when it appeared that there was no such limitation in the Directive. This has since been amended to include all parents who had a child under the age of five years at the time of implementation, after being challenged by the TUC by way of judicial review[42] and referred to the ECJ for a preliminary ruling under Article 234 (ex Article 177).

This would indicate that, although the new Labour Government had swiftly opted into the social chapter and appeared to be increasing families' rights, this would indicate that it was doing so grudgingly. This is shown both by adopting the most minimal implementation possible, and by withholding rights from what was agreed at the judicial review hearing to be approximately 2.7 million parents.

During the period of parental leave, the contract of employment continues, but rights do not accrue.

Only employees with parental responsibility are entitled to parental leave, as defined by the Children Act 1989, s 3. This particularly benefits children of married couples. As Sargeant[43] notes, this again presupposes the traditional family model with a parent of each sex and throws up difficulties for other models.

As noted above, the framework agreement allows Member States '[to] apply or introduce more favourable provisions than those set out in this agreement'. The MPL Regulations do not do so. Since the ERA 1996, ss 76–79 provide the Secretary of State with wide powers on the implementation of parental leave, this narrow approach must be a conscious choice.

As McColgan notes, 'the government has refused to mitigate the impact of non-payment with provision for flexibility . . .'[44]

It is a widely held view that a minimum unit of one week's leave is deeply unhelpful to parents. It is frequently unnecessary and unaffordable to take a whole week as parental leave. The effect on children is patent, as a parent is likely not to take parental leave rather than lose a whole week's pay. The obvious suggestion is that leave may be taken in smaller

---

[42] *R v Secretary of State for Trade and Industry, ex parte Trades Union Congress* [2000] IRLR 565, HL.

[43] M Sargeant 'Maternity and parental leave' (2000) 1 *New Employment Law Review*.

[44] McColgan 'Family friendly frolics? The Maternity and Parental Leave etc Regulations 1999' (2000) 29(2) *Industrial Law Journal* 125 at p 143.

units of, say, one day. At the time of implementation, Britain was one of only six Member States in which parental leave is unpaid and one of four providing the minimum leave entitlement. It was one of only three combining non-payment with minimum leave. The other two were Greece and Ireland.

The qualification period is the maximum allowed by the framework agreement, and the effect of its imposition is to exclude one-fifth of parents, and one-quarter of women otherwise eligible.[45]

It is interesting to note that, while Britain prefers to present itself as one of the most advanced and politically important of the Member States, on a par, say, with France and Germany, the drafting of such social policies does not reflect this. Further, the MPL Regulations tend to show that, while the Government recognises the social importance of parents being protected from discrimination for trying to run both a family and a working life, it is somewhat uncomfortable about providing the necessary rights to do so.

Force majeure

The entitlement of workers to time off work is narrowly drafted by the framework agreement. Time off is permitted 'for urgent family reasons in cases of sickness or accident making the immediate presence of the worker indispensable'. Member States may 'limit this entitlement to a certain amount of time per year and/or per case'.

Thus, not only may States control this right very tightly in terms of how often and for how long leave may be taken, but the wording (the vagueness of 'family reasons', and the narrowness of 'urgent . . . sickness or accident . . . immediate presence . . . indispensable') allows minimalist implementation. Again, these are minimum standards and cannot be ousted by less favourable provisions in a collective or workplace agreement.

The force majeure clause is enacted by the ERA 1996, s 57A. This gives employees the right to leave to take necessary action for a range of domestic demands, with the emphasis on looking after the care needs of a dependant. The leave available is limited to dealing with unforeseen circumstances, so if a dependant was known to suffer regular lapses needing attention, then the time off for dealing with these emergencies may not come within the terms of s 57A of the ERA.[46] 'Dependant' includes, in addition to immediate family members,

> a person who lives in the same household as the employee, otherwise
> than by reason of being his employee, tenant, lodger or boarder [and]
> any person who reasonably relies on the employee
> (a) for assistance . . . when the person falls ill or is injured or assaulted, or

---

[45] TUC's Memorandum to the Select Committee on Social Security (Ninth report, HC 543, October 1999).
[46] See *Qua v John Ford Morrison Solicitors* [2003] IRLR 184.

(b) to make arrangements for the provision of care in the event of illness or injury [and]

any person who reasonably relies on the employee to make arrangements for the provision of care.

In section 57A, 'dependent' is framed widely, even including cohabitees of either sex, who in the traditional sense of the word are not family members. Unlike the MPL Regulations then, the opportunity for minimalism has not been taken here.

Further, 'dependent' is clearly a less stringent relationship to show than that of 'parental responsibility'. Thus, it is clear that a grandparent could reasonably take emergency leave.

The categories of incident qualifying for emergency leave under section 57A are also more generous than those in the framework agreement. The notice provisions are realistic, as the employee is obliged to inform the employer as soon as reasonably practicable. The amount of leave must be reasonable and there is no qualification period. However, there is no provision for paid leave under this provision.

In contrast to the provisions of the MPL Regulations, this aspect of the framework agreement has been transposed into national law much more inclusively, in a way that more closely reflects the changing nature of the family.

As a result, it is clear that section 57A is generally successful in protecting the family from discrimination.

Why is there such a difference in implementation between the MPL Regulations' minimalism and the provision for force majeure? It is possible, as Sargeant points out,[47] that the majority of employers already respond to employees' needs for time off to respond to family crises. Therefore, employers may not see it as an additional burdensome right and the Government might not have been worried about a backlash. Possibly, therefore, there was less need for legislation in this area.

Protection of parental leave

The ERA 1996 provides three protective mechanisms for parental leave rights.

(1) Employees are protected from detriment by reference to s 47C of the ERA 1996 for either taking or seeking to take parental leave under the MPL Regulations or time off under s 57A of the ERA 1996.
(2) Section 57B allows complaint of the employer's refusal to allow leave under s 57A.
(3) Section 80 allows complaint of unreasonable postponement or prevention of parental leave.

---

[47] At p 49.

Where a complaint is upheld, a tribunal may make a declaration to that effect and compensate the employee. Schedule 2 para 6(b) to the MPL Regulations allows an employer to postpone parental leave where 'the employer considers that the operation of his business would be unduly disrupted if the employee took leave during the period identified'. To pursue the remedy under s 80 of the ERA 1996, 'an employee may present a complaint to an employment tribunal that his employer has unreasonably postponed a period of parental leave requested by the employee'. Note that Schedule 2 para 6 allows the employer to make a subjective evaluation of effect on business needs. There is no obligation to make such an evaluation, nor is there an obligation for reasonableness in considering whether to postpone leave. Nevertheless, the remedy at section 80 is for unreasonable postponement. Section 80 places the burden of showing unreasonableness on the employee. It also provides the employer with the strong defence that, in its subjective assessment, its business would have been unduly disrupted. It remains to be seen whether an employment tribunal would be prepared or able to substitute its own objective assessment of the decision to postpone. In the meantime, it is likely that the absence of a need for objective justification from Schedule 2 para 6 will make it difficult for an employee to use this protection effectively.

The only tangible remedy for complaints under sections 80, 47C or 57B is compensation. There are no interim measures available which would preserve the employee's right to the period of leave originally requested. Furthermore, the main financial loss suffered by an employee by working when parental leave has been postponed is likely to be childcare costs. However, the employee will be paid for working during this period, whereas had parental leave not been postponed, but taken, it would have been unpaid. Where a court is assessing loss, it is open to the paying party – in this case, the employer – to argue that any loss suffered by the employee flowing from the refusal of parental leave was fully mitigated by the income earned by the employee during the relevant period. Frequently, therefore, the employee will be entitled only to simple compensation.

It may therefore be concluded that the level of protective and effective remedies is confused and poor, and must detract from the right. People in work may hesitate to ask for parental leave if they feel that this might put their family's income at risk. Also, the lack of real protection may well act as a barrier to those trying to join the workforce, as the right to reconcile family life with working responsibilities may be seen as unavailable in practice.

According to the TUC, both job security and protection from discrimination are factors affecting take up of parental leave.[48] Thus, the

---

[48] Memorandum to Select Committee on Social Security (Ninth report, HC 543, October 1999), p 2.

half-heartedness of these remedies strikes at the very core of the rights brought in by the MPL Regulations.

Finally, if this legislation is aimed at helping parents to balance the demands of work with the needs of their children, why is it available only until children reach school age? While children are physically attending school, their childcare needs are met, but this is not so after school hours, or during holidays. Young children are clearly not able to take care of themselves during these periods, and it is arguably poor social engineering to leave older children to their own devices for days at a time. It may therefore be concluded that, whilst the MPL Regulations go some way in helping parents to meet the various demands on their time, and to facilitate their entry to or continuing presence in the workforce, they are at their very best a half-measure.

Part-time workers

The number of people engaged in 'atypical' working practices, such as working from home, short-term contracts and part-time work, has dramatically increased in recent years. In 2001, for example, approximately one-quarter of the labour force, or seven million workers, worked part-time.[49]

The drive for protection for part-time workers has been closely related to the fact that the majority of such workers are women, who work atypically in order to fit in with the demands of raising children. According to government statistics, the rate of female part-time work in the United Kingdom is the second highest in Europe, standing at 44.4%, compared with an average across the Union of 33.8%. In the United Kingdom, 79% of part-time workers are women.[50] Therefore, initial steps in reaching equality, not only in treatment, but also before the law, were taken on the basis of application under sex discrimination legislation. However, there was no free-standing right of protection for part-time workers, nor was this approach open to male part-timers. Historically, not only were part-time workers often side-lined in terms of career advancement, and more vulnerable to redundancy in times of recession, they were also excluded from some statutory protection to which full-time workers were entitled. For example, many had a five- as opposed to two-year qualification period for employment protection. This discrepancy was held to be in breach of Article 141 (ex Article 119) of the EC treaty,[51] and part-time

---

[49] Labour Force statistics for June to August 2001, quoted in *The Law at Work* (Spiro, 2003), p 23.

[50] 'Balancing work and family life: enhancing choice and support for parents' (HM Treasury and DTI, 14 January 2003).

[51] *R v Secretary of State for Employment, ex parte Equal Opportunities Commission* [1994] ICR 317.

workers now have the same qualification period for employment protection as their full-time colleagues.

Increasing protection in this area and rendering discrimination unacceptable clearly helps part-timers and therefore primarily women to balance their working lives with their family lives. As such, it is clearly an aspect of the law relating to discrimination and the family. The governing legislation in this area is the Part-time Workers (Prevention of Less Favourable Treatment) Regulations 2000,[52] as amended from 1 October 2002 by the Part-time Workers (Prevention of Less Favourable Treatment) Regulations 2000 (Amendment) Regulations 2002.[53]

The definition of a part-time worker in the Regulations is not transparent:

> A worker is a part-time worker for the purposes of these regulations if he is paid wholly or in part by reference to the time he works and, having regard to the custom and practice of the employer in relation to workers employed by the worker's employer under the same type of contract, is not identifiable as a full-time worker.[54]

Elsewhere, it is apparent that a part-time worker is one whose contract requires him or her to work for a number of weekly hours that is less than the contractual hours of a comparable full-time worker (i.e. one working in the same establishment doing the same or similar work, under the same or a similar contract).

Various points may be gleaned from this. First, the Regulations apply to workers, not just employees, and as such they are more inclusive than much legislation. The reason for this is somewhat obscure. On the DTI's website, it is 'explained' as follows:

> Why do the regulations cover workers as well as employees?
>   The Government has decided in this particular case to extend coverage to workers. Coverage of workers will ensure that all part-timers are protected against less-favourable treatment.

Secondly, the full-time worker is 'the norm' at the centre of the legislation as the appropriate comparator, which, as with men being at the centre of sex discrimination legislation, may be seen as discriminatory in itself, and hardly a basis upon which to build equality. Thirdly, in order to establish a comparator, a part-time worker has to find a full-time employee on the same type of contract.

Originally, this provision demanded strict compliance, so that a part-time worker on, say, a permanent contract could not compare himself or herself with a full-time worker on a fixed-term contract. The Fixed-term Employees (Prevention of Less Favourable Treatment) Regulations 2002[55]

---

[52] SI 2000/1551.
[53] SI 2002/2035.
[54] Part-time Workers (Prevention of Less Favourable Treatment) Regulations 2000, reg 2.
[55] SI 2002/2034.

came into force on 1 October 2002. It was felt that demanding such compliance once the fixed-term regulations were in force would amount to less favourable treatment of fixed-term part-timers on the grounds that they were fixed-term. This would be contrary to the fixed-term regulations and therefore had to be changed. The DTI acknowledges that:

> the legal arguments are not quite the same for allowing part-timers on permanent contracts to compare themselves with full-timers on fixed-term contracts. However, we believed that it would be excessively complicated for all concerned to continue to prohibit this one form of comparison.

As a result, the Part-time Workers (Prevention of Less Favourable Treatment) Regulations 2000 (Amendment) Regulations 2002 came into force on 1 October 2002, at the same time as the Fixed-term Work Regulations. Now, therefore, a part-time worker may compare him or herself to a comparable full-time colleague who is working either on a permanent or fixed-term contract. Where an individual has changed from full-time to part-time work, he or she has the option of comparing him or herself either with a current full-time colleague or may compare the new contract or treatment with his or her own contract or treatment received while previously working full-time.[56]

So, what protection is provided? The primary protection is against receiving less favourable treatment because the worker is employed on a part-time contract. The worker should not have less favourable contractual terms, nor should he or she suffer any detriment by any act, or failure to act, by the employer.

Practically, the first step for a part-time worker who believes that the employer has infringed his or her rights is to request a written statement from the employer of the reasons for the less favourable treatment. The employer must provide these reasons within 21 days of the request. If the employer fails to provide a written statement, or where the statement provided is evasive or equivocal, a tribunal may draw any inference that is just and equitable to draw, including that the employer has treated the individual less favourably on the basis of being a part-time worker.

Complaint is to an employment tribunal within three months of the date of the less favourable treatment or detriment. The onus is on the employer to identify the ground for the less favourable treatment. As ever, the employer may successfully defend itself if able to show objective justification for any discrepancy in contractual terms or for detrimental treatment.

When making a comparison with a full-time worker, in order to show less favourable treatment, the part-time worker should apply the 'pro rata principle'. The pro rata principle is defined as an entitlement by the part-time worker to receive not less than the appropriate proportion of pay or other benefits that the full-time worker receives. It is clear that, when

---

[56] SI 2002/2035, reg 3.

comparing the part-timer's lot with that of the comparable full-timer, the global 'package' being received will be assessed, rather than the contract being analysed on a term-by-term basis. For instance, if the part-time worker complains that his or her contract of employment provides for, pro-rata, less holiday than the comparable full-timer, but it is clear that he or she also receives, pro-rata, a higher salary, the conclusion may well be that, globally, this does not show less favourable treatment.

Note that the Regulations do not give workers the legal right to change from a full-time to a part-time contract. This is particularly relevant to women who, having been on maternity leave, wish to continue working for the same employer, but for fewer hours each week. Currently, a woman only has the right to return to work on the same terms and conditions as she had before her maternity leave. However, a refusal of such a request from a woman may well expose the employer to a claim of indirect discrimination under sex discrimination legislation. This is because the employer's refusal may be seen as a requirement or condition that the employee must work full-time. If the employee is able to establish that less women than men are able to comply with this requirement or condition, she has built the basis of her claim. Further, under the Sex Discrimination (Indirect Discrimination and Burden of Proof) Regulations 2001, referred to above, the requirement to work full time is likely to be an apparently neutral provision which disproportionately disadvantages the members of one sex. The employer should therefore take such a request very seriously, and, it is submitted, try to accommodate the request, for example, by considering a job share. If it wishes to refuse, it should be able to show that the refusal may be objectively justified. A tribunal is unlikely to accept the discriminatory impact of such a refusal unless the employer is able to make strong business arguments. It would not be enough to show that it would just be less convenient, or not accepted practice.[57]

Various cases are cited by the DTI which, whilst they pre-date the Regulations, show the attitude of the courts when assessing the grounds put forward by an employer for refusing a request to change to part-time work. In the case of *Bilka-Kaufhaus v Weber von Hartz*,[58] the ECJ held that the requirement for an employee to work full-time 'must correspond to a real need on the part of the employer and must be appropriate and necessary to achieve the objective in question'.[59] In other words, the employer will have to show that it specifically needs a full-time worker to carry out the job – for instance, for commercial reasons. The mechanism to request a change from a full-time to a part-time contract is in fact dealt with in the Employment Act 2002, rather than the part-time workers' legislation. This is discussed under 'flexible working' below.

---

[57] See *British Telecommunications plc v Roberts and Longstaffe* [1996] ICR 625.
[58] [1987] ICR 110.
[59] *Work and Parents, Competitiveness and Choice* (DTI), Annex E.

Note that an exception to the protection provided is overtime working by part-time workers. Where a part-time worker works overtime, up to the amount of hours that a comparable full-time worker would normally work, that worker may be paid a lower overtime rate than the full-timer, without it amounting to less favourable treatment. This may result from fears that there would be bad feeling within the workforce if full-timers were effectively paid a lower hourly rate than part-timers doing overtime (although presumably this would not amount to discrimination before the law) or, less likely, that some workers would request a part-time contract, and then claim overtime rates for doing the same hours as before.

Flexible working

The Employment Act 2002 brought in another controversial right for working parents. This is the statutory right to request a variation to an existing contract of employment.[60] The Flexible Working (Procedural Requirements) Regulations 2002[61] and the Flexible Working (Eligibility, Complaints and Remedies) Regulations 2002,[62] both made under the Employment Act 2002, came into force on 6 April 2003, at the same time as the Employment Act 2002. These regulations flesh out the rights, responsibilities and remedies provided by the Employment Act 2002.

The basic right is that an employee with at least 26 weeks' continuous employment, with a child or children under the age of six, or a disabled child under 18, may request a change to his or her contract of employment. Note that agency workers have no right to request flexible working. Interestingly, a much wider class of employee qualifies for this right than for parental leave. With parental leave, it is only people with 'parental responsibility', as defined by s 3 of the Children Act 1989 (mentioned above), who may be entitled.[63] To apply for flexible working, the employee may be the parent, adopter, guardian or foster parent of the child, or may be married or the partner of the parent, adopter, etc. This right therefore may extend, for example, to homosexual couples. As drafted, this is a right which applies to wider family forms than just the traditional one.

A request may relate to the hours or times of work, whether the work is carried out at the employer's premises or the employee's house, and 'such other aspects of . . . terms and conditions of employment as the Secretary of State may specify in regulations . . .' An employee may therefore request either the same hours, but in a different pattern (for example,

---

[60] Employment Act 2002, s 47. This amends the ERA 1996, by inserting Part 8A after Part 8 of that Act.
[61] SI 2002/3207.
[62] SI 2002/3236.
[63] Flexible Working (Eligibility, Complaints and Remedies) Regulations 2002, reg 3.

a change from five days working eight hours each day to four days working ten hours each day), or a reduction in the number of hours worked. The employee's reason for making such a request should be to enable him or her to care for his or her child.

The statutory procedure for applying is detailed and specific, and is the subject of a detailed guide produced by the DTI.[64] The DTI has also produced various forms which, whilst their use is not mandatory, would ensure strict compliance with the procedure. The request should be dated, in writing and contain the following points: it should state that it is an application under s 80F of the ERA 1996 and specify the contractual change requested, and when it should start. It should explain as clearly as possible what effect, if any, the employee perceives that such a change will have on the employer, and how the employee feels that effect may be dealt with. The request should also explain the employee's eligibility to make such an application, by confirming that the employee has responsibility for bringing up a child, and his or her relationship to that child. The application must also state if and when a previous application has been made to the same employer.

The employer is under no obligation to agree to the employee's request. However, there is a formal mechanism, including a timetable, by which the employer must consider the request, meet with the employee and, if it intends to refuse, put the reasons for the refusal in writing. The timetable is triggered when the employer receives an application for flexible working. Within 28 days, the employer must hold a meeting with the employee to discuss the application. Within 14 days of that meeting, the employer must tell the employee whether or not the request has been successful.

Where an employer agrees to the variation sought by the employee, it must provide the employee with the agreed variation in writing, and the date upon which it is to take effect. There will be no trial period (unless otherwise agreed with the employer) and the change to the contract will be permanent; the employee will have no right to return to his or her previous contractual hours, but may make a fresh application at least one year later (see below).

An employer should only refuse an application if it considers that it will result in an additional costs burden, have a detrimental effect on its performance, quality or ability to meet customer demand, be impossible to re-organise the work amongst existing staff or to recruit additional staff, or interfere with planned structural changes. It may also refuse if it believes that there will be insufficient work during the hours that the employee proposes working, or upon such other grounds as the Secretary of State may specify by regulations.[65]

[64] 'Flexible working: The right to request and the duty to consider' (DTI Booklet PL 520).
[65] ERA 1996, s 80G.

Where the employer refuses, the employee has 14 days in which to appeal. If the employee decides to do so, he or she must notify the employer in writing, and the notice must contain the grounds for the appeal. The employer and employee should then meet within 14 days to discuss the appeal. Within 14 days of that meeting, the employer must give the employee the result of the appeal, again in writing. If the appeal is rejected, the employee may then make an application to a tribunal, or may opt for binding arbitration.

An employee who makes an application under this provision may complain to a tribunal, within three months, that the employer has failed to comply with its duties in relation to the application, insofar as it has not complied with the statutory procedure or reasons for rejection of the application, as set out in the ERA 1996, s 80G. An employee may also complain that the employer's decision to reject the application was based on incorrect facts.

A tribunal may declare that the complaint is well founded, order the employer to reconsider the application and/or make an award of up to eight weeks' pay,[66] by way of compensation, payable by the employer to the employee.

Further, an employee has the right not to be subjected to any detriment for exercising any of the rights given in connection with flexible working, including making or proposing to make an application to vary the contract.[67] Where the detriment suffered is dismissal, this will amount to unfair dismissal.[68]

An employee has a right to be accompanied to the meetings with the employer to discuss the application and, if applicable, to discuss the employee's appeal.[69] The employee's request to be accompanied must be reasonable, and may extend to one companion. This companion must be a worker employed by the same employer as the employee making the application. He or she may address the meeting, may confer with the applicant during the meeting but should not answer questions on the applicant's behalf. An employer must allow the companion to take time off during working hours to accompany the applicant. If the companion is unavailable at the time that the employer has scheduled the meeting, the employer must postpone the meeting to a mutually convenient time within the next seven days.

An employee may complain to an employment tribunal, within three months, that the employer has either failed or threatened to fail to allow the applicant to be accompanied, or the companion to speak or confer during the meeting.[70] He or she may also complain should the employer

---

[66] Flexible Working (Eligibility, Complaints and Remedies) Regulations 2002, reg 7.
[67] ERA 1996, s 47E.
[68] Ibid, s 104C.
[69] Flexible Working (Procedural Requirements) Regulations 2002, reg 14.
[70] Ibid, reg 15.

refuse or threaten to refuse to postpone the meeting. Where the complaint is upheld, a tribunal may order the employer to pay compensation of up to two weeks' pay[71] to the employee. This appears to be by way of a penalty on the employer, rather than a reflection of actual loss.

An employee is protected from suffering detriment or dismissal by the employer for exercising the right to request a companion at meetings with the employer. Companions are similarly protected.[72]

An employee may not make a further application to the same employer within 12 months of the first application.[73] Whilst this is easy to understand in the event that an employer has refused the application, it may lead to problems where the application has been accepted, the change has gone ahead, and the employee finds that it does not work as well as anticipated, or his or her childcare responsibilities suddenly change. Employees therefore need to use this right with caution.

Employers may also find that, having agreed a change, it does not work as well as anticipated. The employer has no right under the legislation to force the employee to revert to former working patterns.

How useful and available are the rights to flexible working? There is anecdotal evidence that employers will be unwilling to consider employees' requests to change their hours. Although there are statutory remedies, employees will be aware that the antagonism inevitably resulting from seeking such a remedy is going to damage the relationship with their employer, and may well hesitate to assert these rights. Ultimately, many workers with children, particularly if the sole or major breadwinner, will be unwilling to take action that may undermine their job security or prospects.

It is also interesting to consider why there is such a specific procedure. Is it to make applications as administratively free as possible for employers? It may be that in fact it increases this burden. Is it to elevate the request as near as possible to the status of a right? This is more persuasive. It may well be that, again, the interests of employers are being balanced with those of employees. So, whilst employees may perceive that a simple right to request is an apology for a real right, it has been given a formal procedure, with a limitation on the reasons for which a request may be rejected. From an employer's point of view, the sop is that the legislation does not force it to change an employee's contract of employment. Interestingly, the DTI guidance is full of persuasion aimed at the employer: how this new right will lead to a happier, more productive workforce, for example, and that business needs will still be fully met. The Government has committed to review how this right is working after three years.

Arguably, this is another right aimed primarily at women, who are frequently the second breadwinner and main child carer in a family with

---

[71] As limited by ERA 1996, s 227(1).
[72] Flexible Working (Procedural Requirements) Regulations 2002, reg 16.
[73] ERA 1996, s 80F(4), inserted by Employment Act 2002, s 47.

two parents. Again, this may be perceived as positive discrimination in favour of women, or the family, as having young children is the criterion which qualifies an employee for this right. In contrast, a person such as a man with a disabled wife who goes to a day centre every day until 4pm, but is then cared for in the home, is not entitled to flexible working, or the attached protections. If he tries, for example, to broker some contractual changes with his employer, but fails, and the employer then refuses to promote him, or subjects him to other detriment, he has no legal recourse under this legislation. This may be a source of understandable resentment.

It is also strange that the right applies only to parents with children under the age of six. The most obvious situation in which parents would apply for a change to their working hours is where they want to be home for their children after school. Under the legislation as drafted, provided one child is currently under six, a parent can set up working hours in order to provide childcare that is compatible with school hours for as long as is necessary. If the child is older, the need may be just as great, but a parent will have no right to apply for a contractual variation. This may impact negatively on women and the family. First, there are great numbers of parents with children older than six who are excluded from these rights and, therefore, for whom access to the working world remains unchanged. Secondly, where an employee has adapted his or her working hours with one employer to fit in with school hours while the child is younger than six, once the child is older than six the employee will hesitate about changing employer, having lost the right to request a change. This may inhibit women's mobility, promotion and earning prospects substantially.

If the policy was truly trying to help parents combine the imperatives of looking after a family with work, and in particular get women out of the home and into the workforce, surely the right would extend to a realistic age, when children are more able to look after themselves, and less dependent on their parents? Again, this may be part of the legislators' balancing act between the rights of parents, the policy of increasing the available workforce, and employers' actual or perceived commercial needs. It may well be that in practice, with many employees being excluded from these rights, the ability of the employer to refuse and the perceived risks attached to applying for a variation, the balance is tipped towards the employer in this instance.

Conclusion

In conclusion, legislation is clearly developing with the aim of facilitating working for parents and increasing the number of families who are able to engage in economic activity. Frequently, however, its approach is conservative, as legislators perform a constant balancing act between conflicting interests.

It also appears that, to some extent, legislation is beginning to reflect demographic changes to the family, and is evolving to take more account of more modern family shapes.

It is interesting to consider that anti-discrimination legislation started with the aim of outlawing discrimination and pursuing equality. It seems now to have crossed the rubric, so that it actually gives additional rights to people on the basis of their 'family' status. Whilst this may currently be a novel development, much argued about, welcomed or resisted, it is likely that here, as already in other parts of the European Union, it will quickly be subsumed into our day-to-day lives, and future generations will hardly raise an eyebrow.

Further reading

Sargeant, M 'Maternity and parental leave' (2000) 1 *New Employment Law Review*
Sargeant, M *The Law at Work. A Practical Guide to Key Issues in Employment Law* (Spiro Press, 2003)
Wilkinson, H, Ridley, S, Christie, I, Lawson, G and Sainsbury, J (1997) *Time Out. The Costs and Benefits of Paid Parental Leave* (Demos, 1997)

Chapter 8

Discrimination and religion or belief

Susan Mayne

Background

Until the Employment Equality (Religion or Belief) Regulations 2003[1] ('the EERB Regulations') were published there was no explicit protection against religious discrimination in the United Kingdom other than in Northern Ireland, which has long had its own religious troubles to tackle, principally between the divided Roman Catholic and Protestant communities.

Within the United Kingdom, there is a large amount of religious diversity. There are inevitably cultural differences within groups and distinctions based on a number of factors, including age, sex and social status. To address issues of equal treatment, it is essential that the UK courts and tribunals are aware of the nature of different religions within the United Kingdom.

There have been early attempts to introduce legislation to protect against religious discrimination elsewhere in the United Kingdom. In 1998 John Austin MP introduced a Private Member's Bill in the House of Commons to prohibit religious discrimination in employment and in the provision of goods, services and facilities, but the Bill did not proceed due to lack of time. Lord Ahmed also initiated a debate on religious discrimination in the House of Lords and a Race Relations (Religious Discrimination) Bill was introduced by him and given a second reading in the House of Lords in June 2000.[2]

European Directives

The most immediate impetus for introducing legislation against religious discrimination came from the European Union. Prior to the Treaty of

---

[1] SI 2003/1660.
[2] HL Deb, 7 June 2000, cols 1189–1209.

Amsterdam there was no express power for the Community to deal with racial or religious discrimination. Article 13 of the EC Treaty, as introduced by the Treaty of Amsterdam, provides a legal basis for the Council, acting unanimously, on a proposal from the Commission and after consultation with the European Parliament, to take 'appropriate action' to combat discrimination based on 'sex, racial or ethnic origin, *religion or belief*, disability, age or sexual orientation' (emphasis added).

On 29 June 2000 the Council adopted Directive 2000/43/EC implementing the principle of equal treatment between persons irrespective of race or ethnic origin ('the Race Directive'). On 27 November 2000 Directive 2000/78/EC was adopted establishing a general framework for equal treatment in employment and occupation without discrimination 'on grounds of *religion or belief*, disability, age or sexual orientation' (emphasis added) ('the Framework Directive'). The Race Directive is wider in scope than the Framework Directive because, in addition to employment, it covers social protection, social advantages, goods and services. The Race Directive needed to be implemented in the United Kingdom by 19 July 2003 and the Framework Directive by 2 December 2003 in respect of religion or belief. The Council has also adopted a Community action programme to combat discrimination in the period 2001 to 2006.

The Race and the Framework Directives apply to both the public and the private sectors, regardless of size. 'Pay' is likely to include all remuneration and fringe benefits such as performance-related pay, health insurance and so on. All state benefits (including state pensions) are excluded. Discrimination is identified in the Framework Directive as follows:

Article 1   Purpose
The purpose of this Directive is to lay down a general framework for combating discrimination on the grounds of religion or belief, disability, age or sexual orientation as regards employment and occupation, with a view to putting into effect in the Member States the principle of equal treatment.

Article 2   Concept of discrimination
1. For the purposes of this Directive, the 'principle of equal treatment' shall mean that there shall be no direct or indirect discrimination whatsoever on any of the grounds referred to in Article 1.
2. For the purposes of paragraph 1:
    (a) direct discrimination shall be taken to occur when one person is treated less favourably than another is, has been or would be treated in a comparable situation, on any of the grounds referred to in Article 1;
    (b) indirect discrimination shall be taken to occur where an apparently neutral provision, criterion or practice would put persons having a particular religion or belief . . . at a particular disadvantage compared with other persons unless:
        (i) that provision, criterion or practice is objectively justified by a legitimate aim and the means of achieving that aim are appropriate and necessary, . . .

3. Harassment shall be deemed to be a form of discrimination within the meaning of paragraph 1, when unwanted conduct related to any of the grounds referred to in Article 1 takes place with the purpose or effect of violating the dignity of a person and of creating an intimidating, hostile, degrading, humiliating or offensive environment. In this context, the concept of harassment may be defined in accordance with the national laws and practice of the Member States.

Difficult questions arise – for example, the definition of genuine occupational qualification in Article 4 permits discrimination in certain cases but only where the objective is legitimate and the requirement is proportionate. There is also a wide definition of harassment, which may cause problems in the workplace. For example, the belief held by some strict Christians that homosexuality is a sin – does that create an intimidating environment for a homosexual employee?

Home Office research studies

The Home Office accordingly commissioned a paper[3] to identify and examine the main options available to policymakers and legislators for tackling religious discrimination in Great Britain. The paper took into consideration the implications of the recent anti-discrimination Directives under Article 13 of the EC Treaty, the Human Rights Act 1998 and relevant UK legislation and practice. The report reviewed the main options but did not make any specific recommendations.

A separate report was also commissioned to assess the evidence of religious discrimination in England and Wales, both actual and perceived; to describe the patterns shown by this evidence, including its overall scale, the main victims, the main perpetrators and the main way in which discrimination is manifested; to indicate the extent to which religious discrimination overlaps with racial discrimination and to identify the broad range of policy options available for dealing with religious discrimination. This report was published in February 2001.[4] One interviewee commented:

> ... you need to make people aware, to have access to information but you also need a way of making such things not optional – establishing these as responsibilities is key; that's possibly where the law comes in.

Interviewees noted the significant demographic changes that have taken place in the United Kingdom in recent years. Local interviews suggested that a complementary approach based on measures from 'within' communities and measures from 'outside' will be necessary. Generally, interviewees felt a general scepticism about relying on the law and that it was

---

[3] 'Tackling Religious Discrimination: practical implications for policy makers and legislators', published 12 January 2001.
[4] 'Religious Discrimination in England and Wales' (Home Office, 2003).

inappropriate or unwise to rely on legislation alone. A holistic approach was preferred in which education, training and an effort to teach comparative religion in schools were recommended.

'Towards Equality and Diversity' consultation

'Towards Equality and Diversity'[5] was the consultation document issued by the Government as a first step towards implementing legislation on discrimination including religion and belief. This document set out the Government's position that in the longer term 'there are good arguments to move ... towards a single Equality Commission' but that 'a major change of this nature cannot be achieved effectively in the short term'. It is unlikely that a single Equality Commission will be established before 2006 but the consultation document refers to 'transitional arrangements that will enable us to move towards a single commission in the longer term'.

The consultation document addresses the derogation in the Framework Directive which permits difference in treatment based on a person's religion or belief in respect of employment by churches and similar bodies where this is a 'genuine legitimate and justified occupational requirement having regard to the organisation's ethos' (see below). The consultation document stated:

> a religious organisation may be able to demonstrate that it is a genuine requirement that all staff – not just senior staff or people with a proselytising function – should belong to the religion concerned, so as to ensure the preservation of the organisation's particular ethos. Alternatively, depending on the circumstances, the exemption might apply only to a number of key posts.

'Equality and Diversity: The Way Ahead'

Over 950 responses to the consultation document were received by the closing date of March 2002. In October 2002, the Government published 'Equality and Diversity: The Way Ahead', together with draft implementing regulations in relation to the sexual orientation, religion or belief, and disability strands of the Framework Directive.

The Government stated that its approach to implementing the Directives was guided by three main principles:

- to develop practical, workable and effective legislation which fully meets the standards required by the Framework Directive and will have a real impact in removing unfair discrimination and improving people's lives – but without stifling business with unnecessary burdens

---

[5] See the DTI website at www.dti.gov.uk/er/equality.

- to seek greater coherence where possible between strands (e.g. race, religion, age, etc.) so that rights and obligations are easier for individuals and employers to understand; wherever sensible and practical, aiming to ensure that requirements in new and existing legislation contain the same or similar concepts and wording
- to ensure that sufficient time is given to employers, employees and other interested parties to consider proposals for implementing the Directives; to respond to consultation at each stage; and to prepare for their implementation.

The Government laid the EERB Regulations before Parliament on 8 May 2003, the general format being broadly similar to the existing anti-discrimination legislation for sex and race. The Government's Regulatory Impact Assessment (produced for each set of new regulations) has estimated about 1,000 employment claims per year under the EERB Regulations. It states:

> in total, small employers, those with less than 50 employees, may be expected to spend about 30 minutes in total reading and understanding the guidance on religion or belief. Medium to large employers, those with 50 or more employees, will be expected take more time, about an hour, in reading and considering the guidance, as some of them may produce and disseminate guidance for personnel department and other staff.

Statutory protection pre-EERB Regulations

Race discrimination

Employees who have felt that they have suffered detrimental treatment, even dismissal, at the hands of their employer by reason of their religion or belief have therefore had to shoehorn their complaint into the ambit of the pre-existing race discrimination legislation. The Race Relations Act 1976 (RRA 1976) prohibits discrimination on 'racial grounds', which is defined for the purposes of the RRA 1976 at section 3(1) as any of the following grounds: colour, race, nationality or ethnic or national origins. 'Racial group' means a group of people defined by reference to the same matters. There is no reference to protection on religious grounds but some limited protection has been afforded over the years by case law stretching the boundaries of the wording of the statute.

For example, in *Mandla v Lee*[6] the House of Lords considered the question of whether a Sikh boy (who was refused entry to an independent school because he wore a turban) was treated in a discriminatory way on grounds of race as defined in the RRA 1976. The House of Lords

---

[6] [1983] ICR 385.

considered the ethnic origins of Sikhs and applied the New Zealand Court of Appeal decision in *King-Ansell v The Police*.[7] They accepted that ethnic origin was wider than race and construed it widely in a broad cultural and historical sense. To establish itself as an ethnic group, the House of Lords held that a group had to show that it regarded itself and was regarded by others as a distinct community with a long shared history and a cultural tradition of its own. Other characteristics were also identified as relevant (although not essential):

- either a common geographical origin or descent from a small number of common ancestors
- a common language, not necessarily peculiar to the group
- a common religion different from that of neighbouring groups or from the general community around it
- being a minority or being an oppressed or dominant group within a larger community.

The House of Lords accordingly found that, on applying these tests, the Sikhs were a distinct racial group. The tests have since been applied in a number of cases finding gypsies (*CRE v Dutton*[8]) and Jews (*Seide v Gillette Industries Ltd*[9]) to fall within the definition of race, although Muslims (*Tariq v Young*[10]), Rastafarians (*Crown Suppliers v Dawkins*[11]) and Jehovah's Witnesses (*Lovell-Badge v Norwich City College*[12]) did not.

It has also traditionally been possible to find protection against religious discrimination by using the indirect discrimination provisions of the RRA 1976. Indirect race discrimination occurs when a requirement or condition is applied irrespective of race but a considerably smaller proportion of people of a particular racial group can comply with it than a proportion of people not of that racial group and the discrimination is not justifiable. The complainant must show that he has suffered a detriment. So, for example, it is possible that an action taken by an employer which causes a detriment to a particular group (e.g. refusing to allow time off for religious festivals) may constitute indirect race discrimination against those from a particular ethnic or national origin (*JH Walker v Hussain*[13] but see *Safouane & Bouterfas*[14]).

The amended RRA 1976 provides a new statutory duty on public authorities to promote racial equality. This includes providing fair and

[7] [1979] 2 NZLR 531.
[8] [1989] IRLR 8.
[9] [1980] IRLR 427.
[10] Case no 247738/88, EOR Discrimination Case Law Digest No 2.
[11] [1993] ICR 517.
[12] Case no 12506/95/LS and 12569/95 cited in a paper for the Commission of British Muslims, Seminar on Religious Discrimination (December 1999).
[13] [1996] IRLR 11.
[14] Case no 12506/95/LS & 12568/95 *Safouane & Bouterfas v Joseph Ltd and Hannah* (decision entered on register 17 July 1996).

accessible services as well as improving equal opportunities in employment. Since 3 December 2001, public authorities have been required to prepare and publish a race equality scheme. In doing so, organisations must:

- assess whether their functions and policies are relevant to race equality;
- monitor policies to see how they affect race equality;
- assess and consult on policies they propose to introduce;
- publish the results of consultations, monitoring and assessments;
- make sure that the public have access to the information and services they provide;
- train staff in their new duties.

A race equality scheme is a statement of how a public authority plans to meet both its general and specific duties to promote equality. It is meant to help organisations make sure that they address their general duty at a corporate level.

Sex discrimination

It has also been possible to successfully claim under the existing sex discrimination legislation where a religious right has been infringed. The Sex Discrimination Act 1975 (SDA 1975) makes it unlawful to discriminate on the grounds of sex in employment, education and the provision of housing, goods and services. In *Sardar v McDonalds*[15] a Muslim successfully claimed against her employer who had refused to allow her to wear a scarf to cover her hair.

Human rights, European and international law

The Human Rights Act 1998 (HRA 1998) – implemented under the European Convention for the Protection of Human Rights and Fundamental Freedoms ('the Convention') – may also afford some limited protection for employees from religious discrimination in the United Kingdom outside Northern Ireland. The HRA 1998 incorporates the operative parts of the Convention into UK domestic law and makes it unlawful for any public body to act in a way that is incompatible with the Convention.[16] This duty extends to the legislature and the judiciary. When applying legislation, UK courts and tribunals must interpret it so far as possible to be compatible with Convention rights (so-called 'Convention rights'). Section 2 of the HRA 1998 requires courts and tribunals to have regard to the case law of the ECHR.[17]

---

[15] (1998) cited in seminar, note 12 above.
[16] HRA 1998, s 6(1).
[17] See also the not legally binding EC Charter of Fundamental Rights.

So far as is possible, primary legislation and subordinate legislation must be read and given effect to in a way that is compatible with Convention rights. If a court determines that it is impossible to interpret an Act of Parliament in a way that is compatible with Convention rights, a formal declaration of incompatibility may be made and the Government and Parliament must decide whether or not to amend the domestic legislation. The courts, however, may strike down or set aside secondary legislation that is incompatible with Convention rights.

Articles 9 and 14 of the Convention and Article 2 of Protocol 1 are most relevant to religious discrimination. Article 9 establishes two rights: the first is a right to freedom of thought, conscience and religion including the freedom to change one's religion or belief. There is no qualification on this right. The second right is the freedom, alone or in community with others and in public or in private, to manifest one's religion or belief. This is limited to acts of worship, teaching, practice and observance and must be 'prescribed by law' and 'necessary in a democratic society, in the interests of public safety, for the protection of public order, health or morals, or for the protection of the rights and freedoms of others'. Case law has interpreted this to cover the right to worship with others, to teach and practise a religion and to disseminate hostile beliefs and doctrines. The right extends to non-religious beliefs such as pacifism and to proselytising (trying to persuade others to change their beliefs). It was noted in *Kokkinakis v Greece*[18] that this right is a 'precious asset for atheists, agnostics, sceptics and the unconcerned'. In *Kokkinakis* the European Court of Human Rights considered activities by a Jehovah's witness, which were described by the Greek court as an attempt to 'intrude on the religious beliefs of orthodox Christians with the intention of undermining them'. Despite this, it was held to be within 'the practice' of the complainant's religion. However, in *Arrowsmith v United Kingdom*[19] the applicant (a pacifist), who attempted to persuade soldiers to go AWOL rather than serve in Northern Ireland, was held to have been lawfully prevented by the United Kingdom because she had committed an offence, 'incitement to disaffection', rather than having been prevented because of her pacifist beliefs.

In *Serif v Greece*[20] the ECHR considered that even an unofficial representative of a particular religion was entitled to the protection of Article 9: 'the State did not need to take measures to ensure that religious communities remained or were brought under a unified leadership'.

Article 9 does not deal with non-discrimination; that is addressed in Article 14 of the European Convention on Human Rights. This states that the exercise of the rights and freedoms in the Convention must be secured without discrimination on any ground including religion, political or other opinion. It is not a free-standing right and can be exercised only

---

[18] (1994) 17 EHRR 397.
[19] (1978) 19 DR 5.
[20] [2001] Application no 38178/97, ECHR, 14 December 1999.

with another Convention right. The European Convention allows for a 'margin of appreciation' – in other words, a discretion as to whether the right may be limited or restricted in the light of prevailing social conditions, subject to the principle of proportionality.

Section 13 of the HRA 1998 provides for the right to freedom of religion and requires that any court or tribunal determining any question under the HRA 1998 which might affect the exercise by a religious organisation of the Convention right to freedom of thought, conscience or religion must have 'particular regard to the importance of that right'. The term 'religious organisation' is not defined.

All employees may be able to secure protection under the HRA 1998 from their employers in tribunals or courts that are obliged to give effect to the fundamental rights contained in the European Convention on Human Rights; UK law must be construed in accordance with the European Convention and decisions must be based on human rights principles. Further, under Article 6 a litigant has the right to a fair trial. This right applies only to civil rights and obligations, which probably include employment rights. It may therefore be possible to use Article 6 to judge the fairness of court or tribunal procedures.

International human rights law also creates an obligation on the United Kingdom to provide protection against religious discrimination. The United Kingdom has ratified the International Covenant on Civil and Political Rights (ICCPR), which contains two articles prohibiting religious discrimination: Articles 2(1) and 26. Article 2(1) provides:

> Each State Party . . . undertakes to respect and to ensure to all individuals within its territory and subject to its jurisdiction the rights recognised in the present Covenant, without distinction of any kind, such as race, colour, sex, language, religion, political or other opinion, national or social origin, property, birth or other status.

State parties must 'take the necessary steps . . . to adopt such laws or other measures as may be necessary to give effect to the rights recognised' in the Covenant. This includes measures to secure enjoyment of Covenant rights without discrimination.

Article 26 of the ICCPR provides:

> All persons are equal before the law and are entitled without any discrimination to the equal protection of the law. In this respect, the law shall prohibit any discrimination and guarantee to all persons equal and effective protection against discrimination on any ground such as race, colour, sex, language, religion, political or other opinion, national or social origin, property, birth or other status.

The International Covenant on Economic, Social and Cultural Rights addresses economic, social and cultural rights and provides that the Covenant rights must be guaranteed 'without any discrimination of any kind as to religion'.

The UK Government in 1999 ratified the 1958 ILO Convention dealing with discrimination in employment and occupation. This requires each Member State to 'declare and pursue a national policy designed to promote . . . equality of opportunity and treatment in respect of employment and occupation, with a view to eliminating any discrimination in respect thereof'.

Finally, the 1981 UN General Assembly (Resolution 36/55) has made a declaration on religious discrimination, requiring Member States to take 'effective measures to prevent and eliminate discrimination on the grounds of religion or belief in the recognition, exercise and enjoyment of human rights and fundamental freedoms in all fields of civil, economic, political, social and cultural life'.

Northern Ireland

As mentioned above, previously only Northern Ireland within the United Kingdom has an established domestic legal framework to tackle religious discrimination. Understandably, the legislation there was put in place to deal with the sectarian issues that arose – and continue to arise – between the Roman Catholic and Protestant communities. For example, support for Glasgow Rangers and Celtic football clubs divides along sectarian lines. It is accepted widely that the display of football emblems in the workplace may create a hostile and offensive working environment. In *Brennan v Short Brothers*[21] [1995] the fair employment tribunal stated:

> Regalia and apparel, such as Glasgow Rangers and Glasgow Celtic shirts and scarves, give clear sectarian messages in Northern Ireland. If football shirts have a sectarian significance, they are not simply football shirts, regardless of the intention with which they are worn. It has to be emphasised as often as is necessary that anything which identifies community allegiance needs justification in the workplace.

The Northern Ireland Act 1998 (NIA 1998) makes it unlawful for a public authority to 'discriminate, or to aid or incite another person, on the grounds of religious belief or political opinion'.

The Fair Employment and Treatment (Northern Ireland) Order 1998 (FETO 1998) prohibits discrimination on grounds of religious belief or political opinion and extends cover to goods, services and facilities. It may be that individuals believe that they are less favourably treated than others because they are Catholic or Protestant or because they are presumed to come from either of these communities; or because they are presumed to be nationalist, republican, loyalist or unionist. The FETO

---

[21] Case ref 63/92 FET.

1998 applies to all employers including subcontractors and franchises, regardless of size. It is unlawful for an employer to discriminate:

- in recruitment and selection
- in terms and conditions of employment
- in relation to access to benefits
- by dismissing or subjecting an employee to a detriment.

The FETO 1998 defines three types of unlawful discrimination:

- direct discrimination
- indirect discrimination
- victimisation.

An individual may also suffer sectarian harassment in the workplace, which is a form of direct discrimination. A complaint of sectarian harassment may be made against the employer as well as the harasser. In certain circumstances, individual employees can be held personally liable to pay awards of compensation.

Employees can bring claims before an independent tribunal, the Fair Employment tribunal or a court.

Under section 75 of the NIA 1998 there is additionally a duty on public authorities to promote equality of opportunity:

1. A public authority shall in carrying out its functions relating to Northern Ireland have due regard to the need to promote equality of opportunity –
   (a) between persons of different religious belief, political opinion, racial group, age, marital status or sexual orientation;
   . . .
2. Without prejudice to its obligations under subsection (1), a public authority shall in carrying out its functions relating to Northern Ireland have regard to the desirability of promoting good relations between persons of different religious belief, political opinion or racial group.

Private sector employers with more than ten full-time employees in Northern Ireland are required under article 48 of the FETO 1998 to register with the Equality Commission, which has responsibility for enforcing the FETO 1998 and working for the elimination of unlawful discrimination. It also has general duties with regard to promoting equality of opportunity, and affirmative action, as well as a duty to keep under review the operation of the Order. There is an obligation on employers to provide an annual return to check the composition of the workforce to establish the breakdown of Catholic and Protestant staff.

The FETO 1998 also requires affirmative action policies to be followed in relation to access to training, selecting staff for redundancy and encouraging applicants from under-represented communities. 'Affirmative action' is defined in article 4(1) of the FETO 1998 as:

action designed to secure fair participation in employment by members of the Protestant, or members of the Roman Catholic, community, in Northern Ireland by means including –
(a) the adoption of practices encouraging such participation; and
(b) the modification of practices that have or may have the effect of restricting or discouraging such participation.

Article 5(5) of the FETO 1998 states that any reference to the promotion of equality of opportunity includes a reference to affirmative actions and accordingly any reference to action for promoting equality of opportunity includes a reference to affirmative action. Article 7 of the FETO 1998 places a duty on the Equality Commission to promote affirmative action.

In 1999 the House of Commons Northern Ireland Affairs Committee reported as follows:

> the extent to which employers have complied with the regulatory requirements of the legislation appears to be impressive . . . The [Fair Employment Commission] reported a high level of compliance by employers with their statutory duties of monitoring, submitting monitoring returns, and periodically reviewing their employment practices. It also reported that there have been considerable improvements in equality based employment practices in recent years.[22]

The Committee also reported that there had been a reduction in employment segregation, in the under-representation of the Catholic community overall and of Protestant and Roman Catholic communities in specific areas, and in the unemployment differentials between the communities.

The Employment Equality (Religion or Belief) Regulations 2003

The Framework Directive establishes a general framework for equal treatment in employment and vocational training and these have been translated into domestic law by the EERB Regulations. These do not apply to Northern Ireland nor to occupational pensions – there are separate regulations for these. The EERB Regulations extend to England, Wales and Scotland and are broadly similar in structure and form to the SDA 1975 and RRA 1976. Some provisions are also similar to those in the Disability Discrimination Act 1995. However, unlike these Acts, the EERB Regulations apply only to discrimination in employment and vocational training as the Directive does not extend beyond those fields.

The EERB Regulations should be read together with the Employment Equality (Sexual Orientation) Regulations 2003, which were published at

<hr>

[22] House of Commons Northern Ireland Affairs Committee, Fourth Report (1999).

the same time. The framework for the regulations is broadly similar to the sex and race discrimination legislation. The Government has issued an explanatory memorandum with the Regulations. ACAS has published helpful draft guidance on both sets of regulations, on which it currently seeks feedback, and the Regulatory Impact Assessment produced by the Government sets out further advice. The Assessment states:

> Under the new legislation, and in line with best practice, employers may need to accommodate a wide variety of religious and cultural needs of workers, such as different dietary requirements and prayer room facilities. Employers may also need to be flexible in order to accommodate cultural or religious holidays and restrictions on hours of work. People should not be discriminated against in recruitment decisions if they cannot work on particular days of the week; particular times of the day; or in particular areas of a business (for example, the meat and alcohol sections of supermarkets) [unless this can be objectively justified].

Regulation 2 defines religion or belief as 'any religion, religious belief, or similar philosophical belief'. This definition is narrower than in the Framework Directive, which simply makes unlawful discrimination based on 'religion or belief'. The terms 'religion' and 'belief' are not defined and it is left to tribunals to develop principles for determining the scope of these terms. Tribunals will need to consider whether any particular activity is a manifestation of a religion or similar philosophical belief. Political beliefs are not covered. The Regulations probably do not cover single-issue beliefs such as being anti-abortion unless these form part of a wider belief system. The Government's explanatory notes to the Regulations state that courts and tribunals may consider a number of factors when deciding what is a 'religion or belief' (e.g. collective worship, clear belief system, profound belief affecting way of life or view of the world). Insofar as case law of the European Court of Human Rights will be used, there will be a wide interpretation (see *X v UK*[23] for veganism and *X and Church of Scientology v Sweden*[24] for scientology). However, the wider the definition used, the more problematic it will be to reconcile the law in this context with the right to freedom of expression. In respect of religion and belief, the Government has not tried to define 'religion' but has said that it will make clear that belief does not extend to 'political belief': 'In our view belief extends only to religious beliefs and profound philosophical convictions similar to religious beliefs which deserve society's respect.' This is not intended to include political opinions, unlike Northern Ireland. But what about an absence of belief, e.g. humanism, agnosticism or atheism? In the House of Lords debate on the EERB Regulations, Lord Sainsbury stated: 'it is clearly the intention that where people have strongly held views which include humanism, or atheism or

---

[23] (Commission) Appeal 18187/91, 10 February 1993.
[24] (1979) 16 DR 68.

agnosticism, they would be covered under the phrase "or similar philo-sophical belief".' But what about non-believers who do not fall into any of the prescribed camps?

Clearly, all the major religions will be covered by the EERB Regulations but some religious groups may be more difficult for tribunals. Employers will doubtless face practical difficulties in establishing what religions are protected – there is no justification defence for direct discrimination on grounds of religion or belief. Guidance may be obtained from case law on charities in domestic cases and case law on Article 9 of the European Convention on Human Rights.

Direct discrimination

Regulation 3 defines direct discrimination as less favourable treatment on 'grounds of religion or belief', which covers less favourable treatment on the grounds of a person's actual religion or belief and also treatment based on the discriminator's perception of a person's religion (which may be mistaken). The explanatory memorandum states: 'this means that people will be able to bring a claim even if the discrimination was based on (incorrect) assumptions about their religion or belief. Nor will they be required to disclose their religion or belief in bringing a claim – it will be sufficient that they have suffered a disadvantage because of the assumptions made about their religion or belief.'[25] Thus, the explanatory memorandum states that direct discrimination on grounds of religion . . . may include discrimination based on A's perception of B's religion ('this means that people will be able to bring a claim even if the discrimination was based on (incorrect) assumptions'). It will also cover discrimination based on a person's association with people of a particular religion or discrimination based on a refusal to comply with a discriminatory instruc-tion.[26] It does not cover discrimination based on the discriminator's religion or belief.[27] The main point to note is that direct discrimination cannot be justified by an employer (contrast the Part-time Workers (Pre-vention of Less Favourable Treatment) Regulations 2000[28] and the Fixed-term Employees (Prevention of Less Favourable Treatment) Regulations 2003[29]). If an employer discriminates against an employee on grounds of his religion that will be automatically unlawful (unless it falls within the narrow exception of genuine occupational requirements). This reflects the law on race and sex discrimination.

An example of direct discrimination given in the ACAS guidance (see below) is where, at interview, it is clear that the applicant is a Hindu: he

---

[25] Paragraph 9.
[26] *Showboat Entertainment Centre v Owens* [1984] 1 WLR 384.
[27] The Government has inserted a new sub-clause into regulation 3 to provide that '(2) The reference in para (i)(a) to religion or belief does not include A's religion or belief.'
[28] SI 2000/1551.
[29] SI 2003/2034.

possesses all the skills for the job but is not offered it because he is a Hindu. This is direct discrimination.

Indirect discrimination

Regulation 3 defines indirect discrimination as occurring where:

> A applies to B a provision, criterion or practice which he applies or would apply equally to persons not of the same religion or belief as B, but –
> (i)   which puts or would put persons of the same religion or belief as B at a particular disadvantage when compared with other persons,
> (ii) which puts B at that disadvantage, and
> (iii) which A cannot show to be a proportionate means of achieving a legitimate aim.

A comparison of B's case with that of another employee must be such that the relevant circumstances in the one case are the same or not materially different in the other. This wording reflects that in the new s 1(2)(b) of the SDA 1975, as inserted by the Sex Discrimination (Indirect Discrimination and Burden of Proof) Regulations 2001[30] and in the Race Relations Act 1976 (Amendment) Regulations 2003.[31] A 'provision, criterion or practice' can be challenged. It is much broader than a 'requirement or condition', as is presently contained in the definition of indirect discrimination in s 1(1)(b) of the RRA 1976.

The clause refers to 'puts' or 'would put', which indicates that it will not always be necessary to produce detailed statistics to show the effect of the practice, provision or criterion. It must still be shown that the practice etc. would have an adverse impact on the group to which the applicant belongs. However, the applicant must still show that he suffered a detriment as a result of the practice etc., so hypothetical cases cannot be brought. There will be obvious issues for employers to address such as dress codes, days of rest for religious reasons, and so on. It is inevitable that employers will need to demonstrate flexibility and tolerance.

An example of indirect discrimination is given in the ACAS guidance: 'dress codes which do not allow Sikh men to wear a turban, or Muslim women to wear a Hijab – such codes disadvantage people because of their religion and are indirectly discriminatory unless the organisation can sufficiently justify their decision'. A good example of sufficient justification is given in the ACAS guidance:[32]

> Example: A small finance company needs its staff to work late on a Friday afternoon to analyse stock prices in the American Finance market. The figures arrive late on Friday because of the global time differences. Because of their religious beliefs some staff would like to be released for a short

---

[30] SI 2001/2660.
[31] SI 2003/1626.
[32] Paragraph 1.3.

period on Friday afternoon for prayers and to make the time up later. The company is not able to agree to this request because the American figures are necessary to the business, they need to be worked on immediately and the company is too small to have anyone else able to do the work. The need to work on Friday afternoon may therefore not be discriminatory as it is a legitimate business aim and because the company is not able to reorganise the work.

The traditional employer's defence of 'justification' is now replaced by the concept of 'proportionality'. A tribunal will need to consider whether an indirectly discriminatory practice is 'a proportionate means of achieving a legitimate aim'. It should be noted that this wording does not reflect the wording in the Framework Directive. The explanatory memorandum states:[33]

the definition of indirect discrimination . . . does not copy out the reference to Article 2(2)(b) of the [Framework] Directive to the provision, criterion or practice being 'objectively justified' by the legitimate aim. The addition of those words would not add anything to the requirement . . . for the discriminator to demonstrate the existence of a legitimate aim (to which he must then show the provision, criterion or practice to be proportionate).

The definition of indirect discrimination also requires the means to be 'proportionate' rather than 'appropriate' and 'necessary', the term used in Article 2(2)(b) of the Directive. The Directive appears to use the two terms 'proportionate' and 'appropriate and necessary' interchangeably – compare Articles 2(2)(b) and 6(1) with Article 4(1). Similarly, the European Court of Justice (ECJ) has used the two terms interchangeably, explaining that proportionality requires that the means used to achieve an aim must not exceed the limits of what is appropriate and necessary to achieve that aim – (see, for example, *R v MAFF* ex parte Lay[34], *R v MAFF* ex parte NFU[35] . . . and *Johnston v Chief Constable of the RUC*[36] . . .). Since the two terms have the same meaning in light of the case law, the Regulations use the same term ('proportionate') for the sake of consistency throughout.

The explanatory memorandum continues:[37]

The term 'proportionate' is considered to be clearer than 'appropriate and necessary' in implementing the Directive in that it sets the requirement of necessity in its proper context. Were the Directive's formulation to be simply copied out, there might be a risk that this would be interpreted as a very strict requirement (for example, that the legitimate aim pursued was essential to the employer's business), in accordance with the usual English law approach to the concept of necessity. But, as the ECJ case law set out above demonstrates, the term 'appropriate and necessary' in the European

---

[33] Paragraphs 12 and 13.
[34] Case 156/95 [1997] ECR 1-5543.
[35] Case 157/96 [1998] ECR 1-2211.
[36] Case 222/84 [1986] ECR 1651.
[37] Paragraph 14.

context does not set out an absolute test but, rather, one of proportionality involving balancing between the discriminatory effects of a measure and the importance of the aim pursued.

Victimisation

Regulation 4 deals with discrimination by way of victimisation: in other words, if A discriminates against B less favourably than others because he has brought or given evidence in proceedings under the EERB Regulations, or because B has alleged that A or another person has contravened the EERB Regulations. So, for example, A victimises B if he sacks him because he gave evidence on behalf of C in proceedings in which C alleged that A had discriminated against her because she was a Christian. However, regulation 4 does not apply if B makes allegations, which he knows to be false and which are not made in good faith. The ACAS guidance gives the example of a worker who has given evidence at a tribunal for a colleague who claimed discrimination on the grounds of religion or belief. The worker applies unsuccessfully for promotion even though her skills are exemplary. Her manager says she is not being promoted because she is a troublemaker for giving evidence against the company: this is victimisation.

Harassment

Harassment is defined in regulation 5 as occurring where, on the grounds of religion or belief, A engages in 'unwanted conduct' which 'violates B's dignity' or creates 'an intimidating, hostile, degrading, humiliating or offensive environment for B'. These are broad terms that use the wording of the Framework Directive and are broadly unchanged from the consultation document. Harassment also occurs if, taking into account all the circumstances, A's conduct 'should reasonably be considered' as having violated B's dignity or created such an environment for him.[38] There are two parts – the conduct must be unwanted by the recipient (see the European Commission Code of Practice on measures to combat sexual harassment at work) and such conduct can be unlawful where it violates the complainant's dignity or creates the intimidating etc. atmosphere. The Framework Directive provided that the complainant's dignity must be affected *and* the working environment must be intimidating etc., so this definition is rather broader. The explanatory memorandum states that, although 'or' has been used instead of 'and', 'it is difficult to see how the two concepts differ in practice . . . and that it is difficult to envisage a practical example of harassment which involves one but not the other'.[39] Quaere however, a lone incident – this may not create an intimidating etc. environment although it may be of such magnitude to fall within the definition of violating the complainant's dignity.

[38] See the EAT decision in *Driskel v Peninsula Business Services Ltd* [2000] IRLR 151.
[39] Paragraph 19.

Regulation 5(2) provides:

> Conduct shall be regarded as having the effect specified in paragraph 1(a)
> or (b) only if, having regard to all the circumstances, including in particular
> the perception of B, it should reasonably be considered as having that effect.

The explanatory memorandum states[40] that 'an over sensitive complainant
who takes offence unreasonably at a perfectly innocent comment would
probably not be considered as having been harassed'. There is a degree of
objectivity here. However this may be problematic and lead to arguments
by the alleged harasser that he did not mean the intended effect and was
only joking. The law on sex and race discrimination docs not contain
this qualification – innocent motives are irrelevant. Further, the EERB
Regulations distinguish between discrimination and harassment and the
definitions section states that 'detriment' does not include harassment.

Discrimination in employment

Part 2 of the EERB Regulations deals with discrimination in the employment field. Regulation 6 provides that it is unlawful for an employer to
discriminate against a person:

- in the arrangements he makes for the purpose of determining to whom
  he should offer employment
- in the terms on which he offers employment
- by refusing to offer, or deliberately not offering, employment.

Further, an employer must not discriminate against an employee:

- in terms of employment
- in opportunities for promotion, transfer, training or benefit
- by refusing any opportunity
- by dismissing or subjecting the employee to any detriment.

All this is in line with other anti-discrimination legislation, and case law
in those areas will be useful. So, for example, a refusal to write a fair
reference would be covered.

GOR exception

Regulation 7(2) follows the wording of Article 4.1 and 4.2 of the Framework Directive. It allows an employer to treat job applicants differently
on grounds of religion or belief if being of a particular religion or belief
is a 'genuine and determining occupational requirement' (GOR) for the
job and it is proportionate to apply that requirement in the particular

---

[40] Paragraph 20.

case. The nature of the job and the context in which it is carried out will need to be considered – and reviewed over time. Guidance is given in Appendix 1 to the ACAS draft guidance. The ACAS example given is of a hospital wishing to appoint a Chaplain to minister to the spiritual needs of patients and staff. The hospital is not a religious organisation but decides that a Chaplin should have a religion or similar belief. The hospital may be able to show that it is a GOR for the successful applicant to have a religion or similar belief.

This GOR exception applies whether or not the employer has an ethos based on religion or belief.

There is an additional exception in regulation 7(3) (the 'religious organisations' GOR') available to an employer who does have such an ethos (e.g. denominational schools). In this case, however, the religious organisations' GOR does not have to be a determining occupational requirement. The religious organisations' GOR is slightly broader than the general GOR because the employer is not required to show that religion or belief is a determining (ie decisive) factor in selection for the post. The employer must still show that religion or belief is a requirement and not just one of many relevant factors. There is no equivalent provision in other discrimination legislation. There is still the requirement of proportionality but regard should be had to the religious ethos of the organisation and the context of the employment. It suggests a less rigorous approach. Under this regulation, employers who wish to create a religiously homogenous workplace will be able to do so. For example, if the employer is a religious employer he may argue that the workplace is Muslim because all employees are Muslim and it operates according to a religious ethos. The employer may require that all employees share the religion even where the nature of the job (cleaning, for instance) does not make religion a determining requirement. However, religion will still need to be a GOR, so there is some fetter on the provision.

The ACAS guidance gives the example of a Christian school, which may be able to show that being Christian is a requirement of its teachers whatever subject they teach. Teachers may be required to promote the Christian ethos, e.g. counselling, saying grace before meals, etc. They may not, however, be able to justify a similar requirement for other staff, e.g. maintenance.

The onus is on the employer to show that it has an ethos based on religion or belief and that, having regard to that ethos, being of a particular religion or belief is a GOR for the job.

In both regulation 7(2) and (3) the onus is on the employer to establish that applying a GOR is 'proportionate' as regards a particular job.

The EERB Regulations were amended to enable the GOR exception to apply to the dismissal of an employee who no longer fulfilled the genuine occupational requirements of the job. However, the exception does not apply to the terms on which someone is employed. If an employee is taken on, he is entitled to the same pay and benefits.

Regulation 8 covers contract workers whose employer contracts to supply their services to another person or business ('the principal'). It is unlawful to discriminate against, or harass, a contract worker. However, a principal may treat contract workers differently on grounds of religion or belief if they are required to do work for which a particular religion or belief is a GOR.

Employment in Great Britain

Regulation 9(1) provides that for the purposes of the EERB Regulations employment is to be regarded as being at an establishment in Great Britain if the employee:

(a) does his work wholly or partly in Great Britain; or
(b) does his work wholly outside Great Britain and paragraph (2) applies.

Paragraph (2) applies if:

(a) the employer has a place of business at an establishment in Great Britain;
(b) the work is for the purposes of the business carried on at that establishment; and
(c) the employee is ordinarily resident in Great Britain –
  (i)   at the time when he applies for or is offered the employment, or
  (ii) at any time during the course of the employment.

This has a wider ambit than currently under the SDA 1975 and RRA 1976, where employees are protected unless they do their work wholly outside Great Britain.

Other areas

The EERB Regulations have a number of supplementary provisions which mirror those in other discrimination legislation making discrimination on religious grounds unlawful in the context of office holders, post holders, police forces, barristers, advocates, partnerships, trade organisations, qualifications bodies, pension schemes, insurance providers and providers of vocational training.

In respect of vocational training, training is defined to include facilities for training and practical work experience provided by an employer to a person he does not employ. It does not include higher and further educational establishments, which are covered by regulation 20. The Government has taken the view that the meaning of 'vocational training' would include most higher and many further education courses. In *Gravier v the City of Liège*,[41] the ECJ held that vocational training included 'any

[41] [1985] ECR 593.

form of education which prepares for a qualification for a particular profession, trade or employment'.

With respect to office holders, the explanatory memorandum states that this includes 'company directors (where they have no contract of employment), the chairs/members of some non-departmental public bodies, judges and members of tribunals, members of the clergy and other ministers of religion'.[42]

Regulation 18 also makes it unlawful for an employment agency to discriminate against a person in the way it provides (or refuses to provide) its services to that person. It also makes it unlawful for an agency to harass such a person.

Post employment discrimination

Regulation 21 covers relationships that have come to an end. For the purposes of this regulation, a 'relevant relationship' is one during the course of which an act of discrimination against, or harassment of, one party to the relationship (B) by the other party (A) is unlawful under the EERB Regulations. Where such a relevant relationship has come to an end, it is unlawful for A to discriminate against B by subjecting him to a detriment or to harass B where the discrimination or harassment arises out of and is closely connected to that relationship. The Race and Framework Directives make clear that Member States must ensure that individuals have legal recourse 'even after the relationship in which the discrimination is alleged to have occurred has ended'. This is presently not available under domestic race and sex discrimination legislation. In *Coote v Granada Hospitality Ltd*[43] the ECJ decided that the Equal Treatment Directive protects former employees who have brought sex discrimination complaints – however, this decision has so far been narrowly construed by the UK courts. The key area where this provision will be relevant is in the context of references – for example, the former employer who refuses to provide a reference to an ex-employee who brought proceedings under the Regulations against him. The wording in this regulation does not contain a time-limit on the obligation not to discriminate and the real question is that of causation. The explanatory memorandum states: 'The further removed the alleged act of discrimination is from the former working relationship, in both time and context, the less likely it is that a person will be able to establish the necessary close connection back to the relationship.'

Two helpful examples are given in the ACAS guidance:

Example: A manager is approached by someone from another organisation saying that Mr Z has applied for a job and asks for a reference.

---

[42] Paragraph 32.
[43] Case 185/97 [1998] ECR 1-5199.

The manager says that he cannot recommend the worker on the grounds that he did not 'fit in' because he refused to socialise in the pub with his colleagues (his religion forbade alcohol). This worker may have been discriminated against on the grounds of his religion after his working relationship with the organisation has ended.[44]

Example: Some time after resigning from employment with an organisation, a man meets his ex-colleagues at a football match. They ask him if he is now a terrorist, alluding to current world events. He is distressed by the name calling as the harassment is not connected with nor arises out of his previous working relationship with the company.

Vicarious liability

In line with other anti-discrimination legislation, any act done by a person in the course of his employment shall be treated as done by his employer as well as by the person himself, whether or not it was done with the employer's knowledge or approval (regulation 22). A person who knowingly aids another person to do an unlawful act shall be treated as doing the unlawful act himself (regulation 23). There is an exception if the person acts in reliance on a statement made to him by that other person that, by reason of any provision of the EERB Regulations, the act which he aids would not be unlawful and it is reasonable for him to rely on that statement. The person who makes such a statement knowingly or recklessly commits an offence if the statement is materially false or misleading.

General exceptions

Part IV of the EERB Regulations contains the general exceptions, which include: safeguarding national security (regulation 24); positive action (regulation 25 – mirroring the limited positive action requirements in the SDA 1975 and RRA 1976); and the protection of Sikhs from discrimination in connection with requirements to wear safety helmets (regulation 26). Positive action is lawful insofar as it is permissible to give those of a particular religion or belief access to facilities for training which would equip them for particular work, or which encourage them to take advantage of opportunities for doing particular work, where it reasonably appears that such actions will prevent or compensate for disadvantages linked to religion or belief suffered by persons of that religion or belief.

Enforcement of rights

Part V of the EERB Regulations deals with enforcement of the rights contained in the Regulations. Regulation 28 confirms the jurisdiction of employment tribunals to hear complaints. A complaint must be brought

---

[44] Paragraph 1.5.

before an employment tribunal within three months beginning with when the act complained of was done (regulation 34) (the period is extended to six months where the claim is brought to a county or sheriff court). Where an employment tribunal considers that a complaint is well founded it can make any of the following that it considers to be just and equitable:

- an order declaring the rights of the complainant and the respondent in relation to the act to which the complaint relates;
- an order that the respondent pay to the complainant compensation equivalent to damages he could have been ordered by a county court (unlimited);
- a recommendation that the respondent take within a specified time action appearing to the tribunal to be practicable for the purpose of obviating or reducing the adverse effect on the complainant of any act of discrimination or harassment to which the complaint relates (regulation 30).

If without reasonable justification the respondent to a complaint fails to comply with a recommendation made by a tribunal, the tribunal may increase the amount of compensation if it thinks it just and equitable to do so.

Regulation 29 implements the burden of proof provisions in the Framework Directive. It states that where the complainant proves facts from which the tribunal could, apart from this regulation, conclude in the absence of an adequate explanation that the respondent had committed an act of discrimination or harassment (or vicariously done so as employer), the tribunal shall uphold the complaint unless the respondent proves that he did not commit (or is not to be treated as having committed) that act. In other words, once a *prima facie* case is made out it is for the respondent to prove that he did not commit the act of discrimination or harassment.

This moves quite radically from the present position under the RRA 1976 but in *Barton v Investec Henderson Crosthwaite Securities Ltd*[45] the EAT reviewed the SDA 1975 after the Burden of Proof Directive had been implemented and commented:

> it is necessary for the respondent to prove, on the balance of probabilities, that the treatment was in no sense whatsoever on the grounds of sex, since 'no discrimination whatsoever' is compatible with the Burden of Proof Directive . . . That requires a tribunal to assess not merely whether the respondent has proved an explanation for the facts from which such inferences can be drawn, but further that it is adequate to discharge the burden of proof on the balance of probabilities that sex was not any part of the reasons for the treatment in question.[46]

---

[45] [2003] IRLR 332.
[46] Ibid at 337.

Questionnaire

Again, in line with the SDA 1975 and RRA 1976, the Regulations afford help in obtaining information in the form of a prescribed questionnaire (Regulation 33 and Schedule 2). The questionnaire must be served within three months of the act complained of or within twenty-one days of presentation of a claim to an employment tribunal. Answers to such questions are admissible as evidence in the proceedings. If it appears to the court or tribunal that the respondent deliberately, and without reasonable excuse, omitted to reply within eight weeks of service of the questions, or that his reply is evasive or equivocal, the court or tribunal may draw any inference from that fact that it considers just and equitable to draw, including the inference that an unlawful act was committed.

ACAS Guide

ACAS has now published draft guidance (on which it seeks feedback) on the new legislation (with regard to religion and belief and sexual orientation). It is likely that a Code of Practice will follow. The draft guidance sets out useful guidelines for employers with regard to recruitment, retention of staff and how to deal with religious observance in the workplace. Section 7 sets out a list of some 'frequently asked questions', which provide answers to common problems faced by employers. Appendix 1 sets out a list of points to be borne in mind by employers wishing to rely on GOR as a defence. Appendix 2 of the draft guidance provides a short summary of the salient points of the most commonly practised religions and beliefs in Britain, based on the recent census. The aim is to help employers plan and implement policies and systems.

Clashes of rights

A key issue is what happens when a right arising under the EERB Regulations clashes with a right protected by other legislation. For example, what if a strict Christian organisation refuses to employ a homosexual prospective employee on the ground of his sexual orientation? Reference should be made to other legislation as the EERB Regulations are silent on this point. Furthermore, it should always be remembered that the underlying aim of the Framework Directive is that all employees should have the right to work with dignity. Under the Employment Equality (Sexual Orientation) Regulations 2003,[47] an employer who refused to employ a gay applicant on the ground of religion would be liable for direct discrimination on grounds of sexual orientation. The fact that an act may be legal under the EERB Regulations does not make it legal under the Sexual Orientation Regulations. There is one exception in the Sexual Orientation Regulations 2003 – regulation 7(3) provides:

[47] SI 2003/1661.

This paragraph applies where –

(a) the employment is for purposes of an organised religion;
(b) the employer applies a requirement related to sexual orientation –
    (i) so as to comply with the doctrines of the religion, or
    (ii) because of the nature of the employment and the context in which
         it is carried out, so as to avoid conflicting with the strongly held
         religious convictions of a significant number of the religion's
         followers; and
(c) either –
    (i) the person to whom that requirement is applied does not meet it,
         or
    (ii) the person is not satisfied, and in all the circumstances it is
         reasonable for him not to be satisfied, that the person meets it.

This regulation applies only to the employment of religious employees
for the purposes of an organised religion, e.g. the appointment of priests
etc. Discrimination by any other employer on the ground of sexual orientation will continue to be unlawful even if it is for the purpose of trying to create a religiously homogeneous workforce.

The way forward

Raising awareness will be the keynote for the future. Clearly training will
form a very important part of best practice employers' strategy for the
future but employers should be careful not to make this seem too heavy
handed. A report for the Home Office[48] refers to a large public organisation that had held a diversity conference attended by 3,500 employees
over two days. While most were happy, 'there were people who didn't
want to be there, who wouldn't sit down, who talked through the whole
session. One comment said that the person couldn't comment on the
session because she or he couldn't hear it for all of the racist and sexist
comments of the group sitting in front of him or her'.

The report also highlighted the value of employees' support for colleagues, for example with respect to religious days of rest: 'in my organisation, Christian employees are supported on Christian holidays and vice
versa. If there are two people wanting Boxing Day off, the priority goes
to the Christian . . . non-Muslim employees hold down the fort during
[Ramadan], and Muslim employees have done so at other times'.

Dress codes are another difficult issue. Uniforms may infringe the religious codes of certain faiths. Some employers have already considered
this: Boots, Halifax, Lloyds TSB and Barclays have incorporated religious
requirements into their dress regulations.

B&Q's cultural diversity strategy has been in force since September 2001
and has addressed the issue of religious harmony in a holistic way. The
company appointed an independent consultant to run focus groups with

---

[48] 'Religious Discrimination in England and Wales' (Home Office Research Study 220).

employees and customers. The diversity team then set up a steering group to decide what action should be taken. It sent out a calendar of religious festivals, with a briefing paper explaining the relevance of the different festivals and how requests for holiday should be treated. The team also set up a staff group from the diverse backgrounds and wrote an in-house booklet on faiths and cultures and how these translated to the United Kingdom.

Further reading

Hepple, B 'Tackling religious discrimination: practical implications for policy-makers and legislators' (Home Office Research Study, 2001)

Weller, P, Feldman, A and Pudam, K 'Religious discrimination in England and Wales' (Home Office Research Study 220, 2001)

Chapter 9

Age Discrimination

Malcolm Sargeant

Introduction

People of all ages can suffer from age discrimination, but it manifests itself mostly in discrimination against older people and young people. Although this chapter considers both extremes, it does concentrate on older people. It also concentrates on age discrimination in employment, because this is the area in which the new regulations take effect in October 2006.

Article 1 of the Equal Treatment in Employment and Occupation Directive[1] provides that the Directive's purpose is to lay down a general framework for combating discrimination in relation to a number of grounds including that of age. This is to be, according to Article 3, in relation to conditions for access to employment, access to vocational training, employment and working conditions and membership of employers' or workers' organisations.

The Directive, of course, covers a number of other areas besides age. The justification for the Directive, contained in the Preamble, does not refer to any demographic need, but is in terms of fundamental rights and freedoms. The Preamble refers to the principle of equal treatment and the rights of persons to equality before the law and protection against discrimination, as recognised by various UN and ILO declarations.

The approach is the same as other measures in relation to disability, sexual orientation, religion or belief. The Directive aims to introduce the 'principle of equal treatment' into all these areas. This means that there shall be no direct or indirect discrimination (Article 2.2). Harassment is also deemed to be a form of discrimination.

Article 4 provides for the possibility that a difference of treatment may be justified where there is 'a genuine and determining occupational

---

[1] Council Directive 2000/78/EC establishing a general framework for equal treatment in employment and occupation, [2000] OJ L303/16.

requirement, provided that the objective is legitimate and the requirement is proportionate'.

Article 6 refers to the justification of differences of treatment on the grounds of age. Differences in treatment on the basis of age may be justified if 'they are objectively and reasonably justified by a legitimate aim including legitimate employment policy, labour market and vocational treatment'. Examples given of such differences are:

- the setting of special conditions for access to employment and training, including dismissal and remuneration for young people, older workers and persons with caring responsibilities in order to promote their integration into the workforce;
- the fixing of minimum conditions of age, professional experience or seniority for access to employment or certain advantages linked to employment;
- the fixing of a maximum age for recruitment which is based either on the training needs of a post, or the need for a reasonable period before retirement.

It is interesting that it was felt necessary to spell out these exceptions to age discrimination in the Directive. It is perhaps symptomatic of the way that age discrimination is treated differently from other forms of discrimination. These provisions effectively state that some age discrimination is benign. There appears to be an economic or business imperative that suggests that more harm will be done if discrimination does not take place, rather than an imperative that states that age discrimination is wrong and can only be justified in exceptional circumstances. Effectively, widespread discrimination is to be allowed to continue except those forms which are held not to be for the economic good of business.

Profesor Bob Hepple QC[2] criticised the Directive generally on a number of grounds. These criticisms were:

- the Directive is limited to a miscellaneous set of grounds of unfair discrimination; the Council has missed the opportunity to adopt a single unified Directive;
- it is limited to employment and occupation;
- it is based only on negative prohibitions against direct and indirect discrimination, rather than a positive duty to promote equality.

Most of all, however, it is a qualified Directive. As Professor Hepple states, it is limited to employment and occupation and it takes a negative and retrospective approach to discrimination (in line with the other areas of discrimination protection).

---

[2] B Hepple, 'Age Discrimination in Employment: Implementing the Framework Directive' (paper presented to the IPPR seminar, 11 December 2001).

The Directive was due to be transposed into national law by December 2003, but there was a provision, in Article 18, for Member States to have an additional period of three years. Not surprisingly, the United Kingdom took advantage of this flexibility and plans to transpose the Directive by 2006.

The ageing population

Over the 25-year period between 1996 and 2021 the proportion of people, in the United Kingdom, over the age of 44 years will increase from 38% to 46%; the 45 to 59 age group will increase by almost one-quarter; the 60 to 74 age group will increase by over one-third and the 75 years and over group will increase by 28%. In contrast, the 16 to 29 years age group will fall by 5.7%.[3] This process is a Europe-wide one, although the speed of the process is variable.[4] The number of people in the European Union aged between 50 and 64 years is projected to increase by 6.5 million during the next ten years.[5]

The relevance of these statistics here is that, whilst the population is ageing and the proportion of older workers is increasing, there is also a decrease in the proportion of people who are economically active in the older age groups. 'Economically active' here is used to describe those in work and those seeking work. Between 1966 and 1990 the labour force participation rate for workers aged 55 years and over declined from 53.8% to 36.5%.[6] Table 9.1 illustrates some characteristics of older people.[7]

Table 9.1 Characteristics of older people

Background	All aged between 16–59/64	16–24	25–49	50–59/64	Over SPA
Total population (000s)	36 064	6 441	20 916	8 708	10 124
Of all 16+ (%)	78	14	45	19	22
Ethnic minorities (%)	8	12	9	4	3
Women (%)	47	49	49	42	63
With no qualifications (%)	14	9	12	24	32

---

[3] The immediate source was 'Tackling age bias: code or law?' (1998) 80 *Equal Opportunities Review* 32, although the ultimate source was ONS Monitor, 10 March 1998.

[4] See 'Ageing and the Labour Market: Policies and initiatives within the European Union' (report of a European conference at the University of Twente, Netherlands) (Eurolink Age, 1998).

[5] These and other statistics are available from Demographic Report (European Commission Office for Official Publications, Luxembourg, September 1997).

[6] See Age and Employment (Institute of Personnel Management, 1993).

[7] ONS Labour Force Survey, Autumn 2002.

Table 9.2 shows the same groups divided into their working habits.[8]

Table 9.2   Older people in employment

Background	All aged between 16–59/64	16–24	25–49	50–59/64	Over SPA
Total (000s)	27 112	4 052	17 053	6 007	865
% in age band	75	63	82	69	9
% of all in employment who are:					
• self-employed	11	3	11	16	24
• working part-time	24	33	20	26	72
• in a permanent job	94	87	95	95	86
Average time in current job (yrs)	7.4	1.6	7.0	12.6	14.6

Thus, some 69% of those aged between 50 years and State Retirement Age (SRA) and 9% of those over SRA are in employment. This compares with an employment rate of 82% for those aged between 15 and 49 years. Older workers are more likely to work part-time than the 25 to 49 age group, but less likely than the 16 to 25 years group. They are also more likely to be self-employed than any other age group.

One UK Government consultation report also confirmed that 'the average time spent unemployed was substantially longer for those over 50 than all ages. For example, those aged between 55 and 59 spent an average of 44 weeks unemployed as opposed to 23 weeks for all ages'. Two of the issues that are raised by these figures are, first, that older workers are likely to find it more difficult to obtain new employment and, secondly, that the proportion of economically active people declines the greater the age.

The Government consultation document on its code of practice on Age Diversity in Employment[9] concluded that 'it is clear that age discrimination against older workers does exist'. The possible reasons for this are discussed below. It is interesting to speculate at what age a person becomes an older worker. One study asked this question of organisations.[10] Five companies put 40 years as the starting point, four suggested 45 and five said 50 years. One company stated that anyone over 30 years was in the category of older worker. Further information suggested that these generalisations were qualified by consideration of occupation and gender.

[8] Ibid.
[9] First published in 1999 and subsequently updated.
[10] H Metcalf and M Thompson *Older workers: Employers' attitudes and practices* (Institute of Manpower Studies, Report no 194, 1990).

Forty-something was not necessarily old for a management position, but might be for another occupation. Similarly, women seemed to become 'older' at an earlier age. One respondent suggested that when women returned to work after children in their mid-thirties they might be classified as an older worker.

Definitions of age discrimination

The Government's consultation document failed adequately to define age discrimination, it merely stated, at para 2.10:

> It is hard to define age discrimination succinctly. The consultation made it clear that there can be both direct and indirect forms of age discrimination in employment. The most obvious forms are where people held strong, stereotypical views about a person's capabilities to do a job or to be developed because of their age.

There is a problem with arriving at a satisfactory definition. This is partly because 'everybody has some age'[11] and perhaps the concept of discrimination implies that there is a discrete group who are being discriminated against. To define age discrimination as discrimination on the basis of age does not give it meaning, because it defines the discrete group as the whole population. To give the term meaning one needs to define the group, or, perhaps in the case of age discrimination, a number of groups.

The Government's consultation document does not try to identify discrete groups. Rather it talks about the manifestations of discrimination as they affect large numbers of workers. The fault with this approach is that it fails to identify solutions which might be age specific. The solutions to discrimination against workers under the age of 21 years might be different to discrimination against workers over 65 years of age. In a comparative analysis of age discrimination in the European Community,[12] the following definitions are offered:

> Direct discrimination: measures targeted at older workers based solely on grounds of age, and on no other factors, such as abilities or health. These measures use specific age limits to exclude older workers from, for example, training and employment schemes, or from applying for jobs.
>
> Indirect discrimination: measures which are not directly age-specific, but which have a disproportionately negative impact on older workers, compared with other age groups. This hidden discrimination usually has the most widespread negative impact on older workers in employment.

---

[11] LM Friedman *Your time will come: the law of age discrimination and mandatory retirement* (Russel Sage Foundation, New York, 1984).
[12] E Drury *Age Discrimination against Older Workers in the European Community* (Eurolink Age, 1993).

Older workers are defined as those of 50 years and over. There is, according to this definition, a minority of people who may face difficulties because of age-specific measures or prejudice. In this there appears to be a similarity with other recognised and unlawful forms of discrimination in employment. There is an identifiable group against whom discrimination takes place. They are not, in some circumstances, allowed to compete for opportunities on equal terms with workers outside the group.

One should bear in mind that age discrimination does not just take place in relation to older workers, but it also takes place in relation to younger workers. It is interesting to replace the word 'older' in these definitions with the word 'younger'. A study by the Department for Work and Pensions[13] revealed the following forms of age-related behaviour experienced by young people at work:

- age limits on job applications;
- younger people being treated differently from other (older) staff;
- talking (down) to younger people in a patronising fashion and tone of voice;
- not appointing younger people because they are too young;
- not appointing younger people because they are too old;
- not promoting younger people because they are too young;
- refusing access to training on grounds of age;
- making junior staff do all the menial tasks;
- 'rites of passage' involving teasing, bullying;
- paying younger staff less than others who are doing equivalent work;
- excluding young people from pension arrangements;
- restricting redundancy payments to years of employment after the age of 18.

Voluntarism or regulation

It may be unfortunate that the debate about age discrimination has become confused with debates about other issues, such as the cost of defined benefits pension schemes and the demographic change that is taking place within the European Union. The discussion is not only about whether discriminating on the grounds of chronological age is right or wrong; it also about whether the present arrangements can cope with an ageing population. This is perhaps unfortunate because there is a debate to be had about age discrimination in the abstract and whether such discrimination is really the same as that based upon, for example, disability, race or sex.

[13] 'Ageism: Attitudes and Experiences of Young People' (Department for Work and Pensions, 2001).

Table 9.3 Age at which someone was too old to employ[14]

Age	Percentage of respondents
40	12
50	25
55	43
60	60

A survey of 500 companies asked those companies to consider their most common job and estimate at what age, on average, they would consider someone too old to employ[15] – the results are shown in Table 9.3.

The effect of excluding an individual through retirement, redundancy or some other form of dismissal from work is to make it very difficult for them to re-enter the workforce at all. Nevertheless, for those in favour of age discrimination legislation there is comfort to be taken from the demographic and economic imperatives that are driving the arguments for legislation.

A demographic argument for change suggests two outcomes:

(1) that the argument is really about raising the retirement age in order to stop people becoming an economic burden on a reducing workforce;

(2) that there will be a need to retain older workers in the workforce, because there will be a reduction in the number of young people entering it.

This latter point is one of the business benefits that the Government claims will come from a more age diverse workforce.

Prior to the 1997 general election the Labour Party was committed to legislation on age discrimination. In 1995, Ian McCartney MP stated: 'The next labour Government will introduce legislation to make age discrimination illegal, just as discrimination on the grounds of race and sex are today.' After the general election, they changed their minds and decided that a non-statutory route was the correct one. After a consultation, the Government issued a Code of Practice on Age Diversity in Employment in 1999, rather than one on age discrimination. This approach was a failure and one report on the impact of the Code[16] stated: 'Very few people who took part in the research (either employers, employees or others) could offer knowledgeable or spontaneous comments on the Government's position.' Only 9% of employers and less than 1% of employees had seen the Code. At its beginning the Code points out that estimates

---

[14] Ibid.
[15] P Taylor and A Walker 'The ageing workforce: employers' attitudes towards older people' (1994) 8(4) *Work, Employment and Society* 569.
[16] See 'Evaluation of the Code of Practice' (Department of Work and Pensions, 2001).

of the cost to the economy of ageism in employment range from £16 billion to £31 billion each year.

The voluntarist approach was in contrast to the approach of a number of other countries who have adopted legislation to stop age discrimination in employment: these include Australia, the USA and Ireland. The US Age Discrimination in Employment Act (ADEA) 1967, for example, grew out of the Civil Rights legislation. During the passage of the 1964 Civil Rights Act a clause was added requesting the Secretary of Labor to carry out an investigation into the issue. That report to Congress concluded, first, that many employers adopted age-specific limitations, although some American States had their own legislation where employers still operated successfully; secondly, that the setting of such age limits had a marked effect on older workers; thirdly, that age discrimination was rarely based on the same reasons used for sex and race discrimination, but was still based upon stereotypes unsupported by objective fact; fourthly, that available empirical evidence was that arbitrary age limits were unfounded and the performance of older workers was as good as younger ones; finally, that age discrimination was harmful because it deprived the economy of the productive labour of millions whilst it inflicted economic and psychological injury to the affected workers.[17] All these statements could still be applied to the United Kingdom today.

The protection offered by the Act has been gradually expanded as new issues have arisen from employers' practices and litigation. It now covers all employees over 40 years, with no maximum age. Section 4 of the Act states:

> It shall be unlawful for an employer –
> (1) to fail or refuse to hire or to discharge any individual or otherwise discriminate against any individual with respect to his compensation, terms, conditions, or privileges of employment, because of such individual's age;
> (2) to limit, segregate, or classify his employees in any way which would deprive or tend to deprive any individual of employment opportunities or otherwise adversely affect his status as an employee, because of such individual's age; . . .

The Government's consultation document, prior to introducing the Code of Practice, decided that 'on balance, there was no consensus of opinion on legislation and a strong case for legislation was not made during the consultation'.[18] Yet earlier[19] it had stated that 'research findings indicated that managers and employees favoured legislation'.

One journal[20] conducted a survey of 1,200 of its subscribers. There was a response from 319 (27%), who replied as shown in Table 9.4.

---

[17] J Kalet *Age discrimination in employment law* (Bureau of National Affairs, New York, 1990).
[18] At para 2.31.
[19] At para 2.26.
[20] (1998) 80 *Equal Opportunities Review*.

Table 9.4 Survey on preference for a voluntarist or statutory approach to age discrimination in employment

Type of respondent	Voluntary (%)	Statutory (%)	No preference (%)
Public sector	9.4	90.0	0.6
Private sector	24.6	75.0	0.4
All respondents	13.0	86.0	1.0

The Code of Practice

The Government, in the Code of Practice, identified six stages in the employment process in which good practice is required to create an age-diverse workforce and reduce discrimination: recruitment; selection; promotion; training and development; redundancy; and retirement.

Recruitment

Good practice in recruitment is concerned with recruiting on the basis of the skills and abilities to do a job. Specifically, this means avoiding the use of age limits or ranges in job advertisements, specifying skills and abilities required to do a job, thinking carefully about the language used in the advertisement to avoid using phrases which imply an age restriction and ensuring that application forms ask only for job-related information.

Selection

This is about selecting the best candidate on the basis of merit, by focusing on the skills, abilities and potential of the candidates when deciding on whom to interview. It is also about the need to ensure that the interviewers are aware of the need to ask job-related questions, have a good knowledge of the employer's equal opportunities policies, plan the interviews to make sure standards and techniques are fair and consistent, record assessment of candidates against agreed selection conditions; and, where possible, ensuring that the interviewing panel consists of a mixed age group.

These are, perhaps, important measures. It must be questionable, however, whether a voluntary code will achieve them. In one survey of managers, for example, 55% of the respondents admitted to the use of age as a criterion in recruitment and selection.[21]

---

[21] 'Breaking the Barriers: a survey of managers' attitudes to age discrimination and employment', reported in *Labour Market Trends*, May 1996 (HMSO) p 195.

Promotion

This concerns the promotion of people based upon their ability or demon-strated potential. The principles put forward here are also those that apply to measures to stop all forms of discrimination. The same recommenda-tions apply to those making decisions on promotion as those involved in selection. There is the need to select on merit and ensure that promotion opportunities are made available to all staff, using the same approach for promotion interviews as for selection interviews, and making sure that interviewers avoid basing decisions on prejudices and stereotypes.

Training and development

This category concerns the encouragement of all employees to take advantage of relevant and suitable training opportunities. The specific recommendations are about ensuring that the training and development needs of all staff are regularly reviewed and that age is not a barrier to training, making sure that all staff are aware of opportunities available and are encouraged to use them, and ensuring that the different ways that individuals learn is taken into account.

The Government-sponsored report, 'Characteristics of Older Workers', stated that the likelihood of employees receiving employer-paid training peaked for those in their 30s and 40s, and then declined. This might, of course, be as a result of older workers having received their job training at an earlier age and that training was concentrated on newer or less experienced employees, but it may also be a result of employer attitudes towards age. A survey of 500 companies employing 500 employees or more tested some stereotypical attitudes towards age:[22] 43% of respondents agreed that older workers were hard to train, with another 11% not being sure; 40% of the respondents also stated that older workers could not adapt to new technology, with another 14% not being sure.

Redundancy

This looks at removing age as a criterion for making decisions on redund-ancy. Using age as a condition for redundancy can lead to the unnecessary loss of vital corporate skills. Employers are encouraged to make unbiased decisions based upon factors such as performance and skills. There is also a recommendation that alternative options, such as part-time working, job-share, career breaks, short-term contracts, or re-training should be considered as an alternative to redundancy.

Early retirement has been used as a measure to reduce the size of workforces by employers and has been encouraged by governments as a

---

[22] See note 9.

means of reducing the working population at times of high unemployment, as an alternative to redundancy.

One study concluded that there were a number of reasons given by employers for the use of voluntary redundancy schemes as a means of reducing the size of the workforce. These reasons were:

- the policy was in accord with the wishes of employees and trade union members
- it was fairer to reduce the number of older workers, rather than young people
- changes in trade union influence has led to the collaboration of unions
- costs factors lead to the perception that older workers are more expensive than younger ones
- the growth in prosperity of pension funds mean that surplus amounts have been used to fund such schemes
- it is a method of avoiding compulsory redundancies.[23]

What such policies encourage, with Government acceptance, is the view that it is acceptable to discriminate against older employees. It is acceptable to select for a reduction in the labour force on the basis of age.

Retirement

The Code states that 'cliff-edge' retirement schemes which allow people to go from full-time employment to full-time retirement are a problem for both employers and employees. Retirement schemes should be fairly applied and individual and business needs taken into account.

Specific recommendations are that retirement policy should be agreed with employees, mentoring schemes to transfer key skills and knowledge from employees approaching retirement age should be set up and flexible or extended retirement schemes should be considered – for example, part-time working, job sharing and volunteering. It is difficult to understand what much of this has to do with age discrimination policies. They are all examples of good practice when dealing with retirement at normal retirement age or as a result of early-retirement policies.

The Age Discrimination in Employment Regulations

In 2003 the Government consulted on the likely content of future Regulations, which were to be adopted in 2004 and to come into effect on 1 October 2006. The Regulations will provide protection for a number of different categories. These include:

---

[23] R Worsley *Age and Employment* (Age Concern, 1996).

- people who are working (this includes those who are employees as well as those who are agency workers and some self-employed workers);
- applicants for work;
- people undertaking or applying for employment training;
- those undertaking or applying for further education or higher education courses;
- members, or applicants for membership, of trade unions or a trade or professional bodies.

Those covered will be protected against direct and indirect discrimination, as well as victimisation and harassment. It is very much the same approach as for those who receive protection from discrimination on the grounds of sexual orientation or religion or belief.

Article 6 of the Directive (see above) is interpreted as allowing Member States to justify direct discrimination where it can be objectively justified by reference to specific aims which are appropriate and necessary. The sort of specific aims which might justify differences in treatment are likely to be:

- *health and safety matters*: an example of this might be the particular protection given to young people at work, which is included in the Working Time Regulations 1998[24] (e.g. the limiting of young workers' ability to do night work and ensuring that they have the necessary breaks and supervision);
- *facilitation of employment training*: this is an issue that seeks to deal with the problem of an ageing workforce, where an employer might have a number of people approaching retirement and be concerned about bringing in younger employees;
- *the particular training requirements of the post in question*: some jobs require a long training period and an employer might be reluctant to invest in such training for an older worker who has only a limited work-life expectancy;
- *encouraging and rewarding loyalty*: many pay and non-pay benefits that employees receive are linked to length of service (e.g. annual leave, incremental pay, trainee pay and long service awards). Most people consulted felt that these should be kept as a way of rewarding employees for their loyalty and service;
- *the need for a reasonable period of training before retirement*: an employer may feel that it does not wish to recruit a worker approaching retirement age for a job that requires a lengthy training provision.

Indirect discrimination (as has been shown in previous chapters) is said to arise when employers or others with obligations apply an apparently neutral provision equally to employees or prospective employees or

---

[24] SI 1998/1833.

others protected by the Directive and it puts people of a particular age at a disadvantage; and an individual can show that he or she has suffered a disadvantage. The Government plans to use the same approach as in new regulations on sexual orientation, religion or belief.

Professor Hepple (2001) argues that this should be confined to cases where it is possible to make a comparison between the persons of the claimant's age group and all other persons.

Harassment at work in relation to age will also become unlawful. Complainants will need to show that their dignity has been violated, or that they have been subject to an intimidating, hostile, degrading, humiliating or offensive environment.

Age rules in UK legislation

There are a number of potentially discriminatory rules contained in legislation. Some of these will need to be changed, but others are, according to the Government, justifiable. Two of these are as follows: first, the rules which entitle workers under the age of 21 years to a lower national minimum wage. This can be justified as a measure aimed at helping young people get into work and benefit from training. Secondly, there are specific rules contained in the Working Time Regulations 1998 which provide extra protection for young workers (up to the age of 18 years), e.g. in limiting the amount of night work that can be undertaken.

There is employment legislation that deprives employees who continue to work after normal retirement age, or the age of 65 years otherwise, of important employment protection rights. Section 156 of the Employment Rights Act 1996 (ERA 1996) states that a person loses any rights to a redundancy payment if they have attained normal retirement age for the organisation in which they work, or the age of 65 years in any other case. In *Secretary of State for Employment v Levy*[25] a female employee of 60 years of age challenged the decision not to make her a redundancy payment. The Employment Appeal Tribunal (EAT) stated: 'The logic of choosing pensionable ages for the purposes of disentitlement . . . must be that after retirement there can be no redundancy. The employee may cease to work, but the job may not cease to exist, and in any event there would be no dismissal caused by the redundancy . . .' The implication of this is that every employee who reaches normal or the state retirement age is deemed to have retired, regardless of whether they continue to work. Normal retirement age is, of course, actual rather than notional retirement age, so it is not possible for employers to invent retirement ages in order to further deprive their older employees of their rights.[26]

---

[25] [1989] IRLR 469.
[26] See *Waite v Government Communications Headquarters* [1983] ICR 653.

Section 109 of the ERA 1996 excludes those who have reached normal retirement age, or 65 years, from the right to protection against unfair dismissal. In *Secretary of State for Scotland v Taylor*[27] an employer, namely the Scottish Prison Service, embarked on a policy with regard to retirement of older employees in order to achieve a workforce generally of younger persons who could, as a consequence, be paid less. It is important to first note that the Scottish Prison Service is an executive agency and part of the Government's means of running its own prisons. The complainant claimed that the organisation's equal opportunity policy, which included age discrimination, had become incorporated into his contract of employment and, therefore, the change in retirement age to 55 years was in breach of that contractual term. The House of Lords eventually held that it was permissible to treat staff over the minimum retirement age differently from those under it in order to minimise or avoid redundancy. The contract of employment had to be taken as a whole and the equal opportunities policy statement said nothing about redundancy policy or about negating the conditions regarding retirement ages. Thus, according to the court, it was a contractual issue and the employees continued to lose any rights to claim unfair dismissal after their normal retirement age.

A different and, perhaps, more significant approach has been taken in *Rutherford v Towncircle Ltd.*[28] Mr Rutherford was told that he was to be dismissed on the grounds of redundancy. At the time he was 67 years old. He argued that the upper age limit in ss 109 and 156 of the ERA 1996 was indirectly discriminatory against men. The court considered all the factors, including the statistics, which showed that a greater proportion of men over 65 continued to work than the proportion of females who continued to do so. The conclusion was that the measures were, therefore, indirectly discriminatory against men. Having also concluded that the state failed to show objective justification for the measures, the court allowed Mr Rutherford to go ahead with his claims. This decision was subsequently reversed by the EAP using a different measure of comparator.[29]

The Age Discrimination Regulations will change this. A dismissal for reasons of retirement will be unfair unless it is at or past any agreed or default retirement age, i.e. if such an age is objectively justifiable under the Regulations, then it will be possible to dismiss someone for reasons of retirement age. Apart from this the maximum age barrier to be able to claim unfair dismissal will be removed.

There are some similar restrictions in eligibility for and entitlement to redundancy payments. According to s 156 of the ERA 1996, an employee loses the entitlement to claim redundancy payment after normal retirement age. Additionally, any entitlement is tapered off during the last year of work before retirement, so entitlement decreases by 1/12 every month

---

[27] [2000] IRLR 502.
[28] *Rutherford v Towncircle Ltd (t/a Harvest) and Secretary of State for Trade and Industry* [2002] IRLR 768.
[29] *Secretary of State v Rutherford (No 2)* [2003] IRLR 858.

in that year. Young workers have also been penalised in that there has been no entitlement to redundancy payments for any service before the age of 18 years. This is to be changed when the Regulations take effect, so that the discrimination against young and older workers will be removed. Unless there is a justified retirement age the entitlement to accrue service towards any redundancy period will continue while an employee is at work. The lower age limit is also to be removed.

Related to these two issues are the payments made for the basic award for unfair dismissal and redundancy payments. The current rules for such payments are: first, that there is a maximum of 20 years' service that can be taken into account; secondly, that the amount to be awarded is one-and-a-half week's pay for periods when the employee was aged 41 years and above, one week's pay for periods when the employee was aged between 22 years and 41 years, and half a week's pay for other periods of entitlement.

The Regulations will change this system so that, although the 20-year rule will stay, the amount paid will be the same regardless of the age of the employee. This clearly removes the payments related to age, although it still means that older (i.e. those with the longest service) employees will receive the greatest payment. This, however, is likely to be, under Article 6 of the Directive, objectively justified by reference to specific aims and is appropriate and necessary.

Mandatory retirement

It has been suggested that retirement is 'both the leading form of age discrimination and the driving force behind the wider development of ageism in modern societies'.[30] There is no national mandatory retirement age in the United Kingdom, but over one-half of men have a fixed retirement age in their contract of employment; three-quarters of these have the State Pension Age as their retirement age.

Traditional reasons for having a fixed retirement age are as follows:[31]

- occupational pensions have a normal retirement date
- correlation between state pension age and normal retirement date
- older workers make way for young ones
- younger workers have a higher level of productivity.

The Government had declined to consider this issue. In its consultation document prior to the 1999 Code of Practice it stated that the matter of

[30] See A Walker 'The Benefits of Old Age? Age Discrimination and Social Security', in E McEwen (ed) *Age – the unrecognised discrimination* (Age Concern, 1990).
[31] See P Meadows *Retirement ages in the UK: a review of the literature* (DTI Employment Relations Research Series No 18).

pensions was too complex and that retirement ages were a matter for collective agreement between employers and workers' representatives. As a result of the Equal Treatment in Employment Directive it has been required to change this approach.

There are perhaps three types of mandatory retirement age: the contractual retirement age; the pensionable retirement age; and the actual or normal retirement age. These may coincide and all take place at the same time, or they may occur at different times. Although all three clearly influence each other, it is important to consider them separately, however, in order to clarify precisely what is meant by a proposal to abolish the mandatory retirement age.

There is no law that requires an employer to set a mandatory retirement date in its contracts of employment, although there is an obligation to inform employees of any terms and conditions relating to pension schemes.[32] There are, however, legal consequences in terms of employment protection. Employees who continue in employment beyond the contractual retirement age (provided that this is the same as the normal retirement age) lose their right to protection against unfair dismissal[33] and their right to redundancy payments.[34] Normal retirement age may be different from the age set out in the contract. If employees regularly work beyond that contractual age they may establish a new norm that is the actual age at which individuals usually retire.[35] Indeed if, in practice, employees retire at a variety of ages, there may be no normal retirement age at all for the purposes of the Employment Rights Act 1996.

Pensionable retirement age

Pensionable retirement age is that established by the pension scheme to which an individual belongs. This may range, in future, from 55 years upwards, but may be lower for particular occupations. The state pension retirement age is being equalised so that, by 2020, it will be the same for men and for women. In order to eliminate the contractual retirement age, the link between it and the pensionable retirement age will need to be broken.

Many individuals do not retire at the contractual retirement age and many employers do, in some form or other, permit employees to work beyond normal retirement age. One DTI survey suggested that as many as one in four employers allowed this to happen, although it was less likely to occur in larger organisations.[36]

---

[32] ERA 1996, s 1(4)(d)(iii).
[33] Ibid, s 109.
[34] Ibid, s 156.
[35] See *Waite v Government Communications Headquarters* [1983] IRLR 168.
[36] Carried out for the DTI report on the Code of Practice on Age Diversity.

Table 9.5 School teacher retirements[37]

Year	Total	Age	Early	Health	Other
1998/99	10 901	5 266	2 917	2 718	–
1999/00	11 709	5 858	3 140	2 711	–
2000/01	13 107	6 084	3 139	3 023	861
2001/02	13 654	6 291	2 561	2 689	2 113

The effect of removing contractual retirement age may not in itself affect the age at which people retire. Pension scheme provisions can help make the contractual retirement age more flexible. Table 9.5 shows retirement levels amongst English and Welsh school teachers, as an example. The figures show overall a high rate of retirement for health reasons.

In the period 1998/99 to 2001/02, approximately 49% of teachers retired at their contractual retirement age. All the rest retired early, including about 23% of the total who retired for health reasons.

The more general evidence is that these figures are not unusual, both in the private as well as the public sector. Research suggests that about one-third of all those who begin to draw their pensions are aged 54 years or less and about two-thirds are aged 59 years or under.[38] A DTI survey showed that only 43% of the male respondents and 40% of the female ones expected to retire at the state pension age, although one in three would like to retire earlier.[39] According to the Government Green Paper on *Working and Saving for Retirement*,[40] the mean age for men retiring in the United Kingdom is 62.6 years and for women 61.1 years. Amongst those already retired and who had retired early, the survey found that 33% had retired because of illness or disability, 16% were made redundant and 17% had their workplace closed or changed. Perhaps not surprisingly, given these figures, some three-quarters of all firms have no employees over the age of 60 years.[41]

Article 6(2) of the Directive allows Member States to provide that the setting of age limits in occupational social security schemes, or setting ages for entitlement to retirement or invalidity benefits does not constitute age discrimination. Given the close relationship between pension and invalidity benefits and actual retirement ages, this does allow the process to be manipulated to achieve a later or earlier actual retirement practice, rather than some free-standing right to retire at any age. It is this relationship between state and pensionable benefits that is more likely

---

[37] Statistics and information from Teachers' Superannuation Working Party 2002.
[38] 'Early retirement schemes still the norm in final salary schemes' (2002) 160 *IDS Pensions Bulletin* 4.
[39] See DTI report on the Code of Practice.
[40] Department of Work and Pensions, 2003.
[41] P Grattan *Short guide to pensions, retirement and work* (Third Age Employment Network, October 2002).

to influence actual retirement ages than any straightforward abolition of the contractual retirement age.

The Government suggests that the concept of retirement needs to be challenged.[42] A traditional pattern of a lifelong job followed by retirement at the end of working life is an increasingly inaccurate description of the reality today. The reality, however, is that often the actual or normal retirement age is linked, where there is a choice, to the receipt of financial support from the state benefit system, the state retirement pension and any occupational pension scheme available. Merely abolishing the contractual retirement age is likely to achieve little on its own. It is the manipulation and availability of financial benefits, such as enhanced pension benefits on early retirement, that are likely to alter perceptions of when people should or could retire. Much also, however, depends upon how successful the Government is in changing attitudes of employers and employees to the justifiability of age discrimination, so that employers, for example, are not able to say that all persons of a certain age are too old to employ.

An example of employees' acceptance of age discrimination is cited in the DTI evaluation of the effectiveness of its Code of Practice. In relation to training opportunities, the report states

> . . . where training for new jobs was concentrated on younger employees, some older people believed this to be acceptable to ensure that they did not impede career progress of younger staff, especially if they believed they were close to retirement or beyond training.

The problem with discussing retirement and age discrimination is that it can be welcomed by those retiring. Certainly, the lack of pressure from members reported by trade unions and the sometimes apparent enthusiasm for retirement amongst career workers in occupational pension schemes might make it difficult to look at this as discrimination in the same way as abuse based upon racial or sexual grounds.

Objective justification

Article 6 of the Equal Treatment in Employment and Occupation Directive provides the opportunity for justification of differences of treatment on grounds of age. Such justification must be objectively and reasonably justified by a legitimate aim. This includes, in Article 6.1(c), for example, 'the fixing of a maximum age for recruitment which is based on the training requirements of the post in question or the need for a reasonable period of employment before retirement.' This might be difficult to turn

---

[42] *Winning the Generation Game.* Cabinet office report on improving opportunities for people aged 50–65 (April 2000); available on Cabinet Office website: www.cabinet-office.gov.uk.

into legislation because different occupations will clearly have different meanings applicable to the words 'reasonable period of employment'. One of the decisions the Government has to take is whether to have very specific legislation spelling out, as far as is possible, all the exceptions that should be regarded as justifiable, or whether to make a general statement and leave it to the courts to decide on specific circumstances.

One issue surrounding justification and retirement is whether it is possible to justify the setting of a mandatory retirement age as a policy that is objectively or reasonably justified by a legitimate aim. The alternative approach is to adopt the American model and justify excluding certain occupations or types of work from the provisions of the Directive. This is an important issue for the Government in its consultation process. Possible justifications in relation to a mandatory retirement age might be:[43]

- personnel planning – ensuring an age diverse workforce and providing promotion opportunities for younger employees;
- preserving the integrity of occupational pension schemes – ensuring that the occupational pension retirement age is the same as the contractual retirement age, so that the legitimate aim of encouraging the planning of retirement remuneration could be encouraged;
- preserving arrangements made contractually between employer and employee;
- to keep burdens on business at a proportionate weight – this might be relevant, according to the DTI paper, in determining whether a measure was proportionate.

Some of these are more arguable than others, but to try to justify excluding retirement ages from the provisions on age discrimination is to invite litigation and perhaps it will be left for the European Court of Justice to decide. To do this, however, would be to leave in place an obvious example of discrimination based upon chronological age and could only be an encouragement for other exceptions affecting older workers.

The question of justifiable exceptions to any rules allowing employees to continue working after current normal retirement ages is a difficult one, although the concerns amongst trade unions here was with physical work and the greater difficulties that might be experienced by older workers. Two examples given were, first, the teaching of young children, where there is a lot of physical bending and lifting that might take place, and, secondly, manual jobs such as refuse collectors. Most of the latter, it was claimed, would give up work at an age earlier than the state retirement age because of back problems.

---

[43] These are taken from a DTI consultation paper on *Implementing the Employment Directive: Mandatory Retirement Ages* (June 2002).

Conclusion

An individual's views as to what should be the nature of age discrimination regulations are likely to be strongly affected by that individual's starting point. There are a number of approaches which might suggest different starting points and, therefore, different conclusions about the correct content of such regulations. These approaches include:

(1) The human rights approach: this outlook suggests that it is wrong to discriminate on the basis of chronological age alone as such discrimination comes from unfounded stereotypical images of people of a certain age. All such discrimination is therefore absolutely wrong.

(2) The business approach: this outlook suggests that there are good business reasons for age discrimination legislation. This includes the process of demographic change which is reducing the supply of young people and increasing the numbers of older people in the workforce. It also includes concerns about the ability of fewer workers to support the pensions of an increasing number of retired people. It therefore makes good sense to make age discrimination unlawful.

Both of these approaches agree that age discrimination is wrong and can be made unlawful, but they will have a different outlook on the contents of the regulations. The first will argue for minimal exceptions, whilst the latter approach will argue that there can be some justifiable exceptions which make good business sense. An example of this might be in relation to training older workers: the first approach would allow all workers to receive training regardless of their age, whilst the second would place limits where a worker might be too old and not be able to spend long enough in a job after training to justify the cost, e.g. in the training of new medical doctors (which can be a long and expensive process – should a 50-year-old have the same opportunity as a 25-year-old?).

These are not easy questions to deal with, but if one really believes that age discrimination is wrong, the number of exceptions must be minimal.

Further reading

Department of Trade and Industry *Implementing the Employment Directive: Mandatory Retirement Ages* (June 2002)

Drury, E *Age Discrimination against Older Workers in the European Community* (Eurolink Age, 1993)

Fredman, S and Spencer, S (eds) *Age as an Equality Issue* (Hart Publishing, 2003)

Friedman, LM *Your time will come: the law of age discrimination and mandatory retirement* (Russel Sage Foundation, New York, 1984)

Gregory, RF *Age Discrimination in the American Workplace* (Rutgers University Press, New Brunswick, 2001)

Help the Aged *Age Discrimination in Public Policy* (2002)

McEwen, E (ed) *Age the unrecognised discrimination* (Age Concern, 1990)

Metcalf, H and Thompson, M *Older workers: Employers' attitudes and practices* (Institute of Manpower Studies, Report no 194, 1990)

Sargeant, M *Age Discrimination in Employment* (Institute of Employment Rights, 1999)

Taylor, P and Walker, A 'The ageing workforce: employers' attitudes towards older people' (1994) 8(4) *Work, Employment and Society* 569

Winning the Generation Game Cabinet office report on improving opportunities for people aged 50–65 (April 2000).

Chapter 10

Trade unions and discrimination

David Lewis

Introduction

This chapter will discuss discrimination by both employers and trade unions. In relation to the former, it will discuss unlawful refusal of employment, detrimental treatment and unfair dismissal on the grounds of trade union membership and activities. It will also examine union membership or recognition requirements in contracts for the supply of goods or services and outline the proposals contained in the Government's consultative document on blacklisting. As regards the obligations imposed on trade unions, it will mention their role as employers and describe the circumstances in which discrimination in relation to admissions, discipline and expulsions will be unlawful.

The strength of trade unions depends largely on their size, organisation and income. Historically, the law has always made it difficult for unions to flex their muscles. In the nineteenth century, the criminal law was used to inhibit their activities. For example, the Combination Act 1800 outlawed workers' agreements to campaign for the improvement of wages or the reduction of working hours. Although the Trade Union Act 1871[1] lifted the threat of workers' organisations being held to be illegal on the grounds that their rules were in restraint of trade, both legislation and the common law are still used to inhibit the ability of trade unions to engage in industrial action. Since the 1980s there has been more detailed regulation of the internal affairs of trade unions, for example, in relation to ballots, financial matters and political activities. The current statutory provisions on the right to associate and the rights of workers and trade unions in relation to each other are contained in the Trade Union and Labour Relations (Consolidation) Act 1992 (TULRCA).

It almost goes without saying that it is vital to the existence of trade unions that workers should have the right to associate and not suffer

[1] Section 2.

discrimination for doing so. Thus, freedom of association is now recognised internationally as a fundamental right. For example, Article 11 of the European Convention on Human Rights and Fundamental Freedoms states:

1. Everyone has the right to freedom of peaceful assembly and to freedom of association with others, including the right to form and join trade unions for the protection of his interests.
2. No restrictions shall be placed on the exercise of these rights other than such as are prescribed by law and are necessary in a democratic society for the prevention of disorder or crime, for the protection of health or morals or for the protection of the rights and freedom of others . . .

Of course, the extent of union membership does not depend solely on the type of legislation in place – much will depend on the state of the labour market. However, it is worth noting that since 1979, when Margaret Thatcher commenced her programme of union reforms, union membership has declined from 13.2 million to 7.75 million in 2003.

Definitions

A trade union is defined as an organisation, whether permanent or temporary, which consists either:

(a) wholly or mainly of workers whose principal purposes include the regulation of relations between workers and employers (or employer organisations), or
(b) wholly or mainly of constituent or affiliated organisations with those purposes, or representatives of such organisations whose principal purposes include the regulation of relations between workers and employers (or employers' associations) or include the regulation of relations between its constituent or affiliated organisations.[2]

This would cover not only individual and confederated unions and the Trades Union Congress, but also the union side of a joint negotiating committee.

The Certification Officer maintains a list of trade unions[3] and a listed union can apply for a certificate of independence. A trade union is independent if it is not under the domination or control of an employer (or group of employers) and is not liable to interference by an employer (or any such group) tending towards such control.[4] The Certification Officer

---

[2] TULRCA, s 1.
[3] Ibid, s 2. According to the Annual Report of the Certification Officer for 2002–03, 197 unions were listed at 31 March 2003.
[4] Ibid, s 5.

has to decide whether or not a union is independent[5] and a certificate constitutes conclusive evidence for all purposes that a union has this status.[6] The main advantage of being an independent trade union is that employees cannot have action taken against them on the grounds that they have sought to join, have joined or have taken part in the activities of such a union. Independent trade unions which are also recognised by an employer for the purposes of collective bargaining have additional rights:[7] e.g. to appoint representatives for the purposes of receiving information and consulting with an employer over redundancies, transfers of undertakings, and health and safety matters.

Refusal of employment on union membership grounds

It is unlawful for employers to refuse employment to applicants because:

(a) they are or are not members of a trade union, or
(b) they refuse to accept a requirement that they become a member or cease to be a member, or a requirement that they suffer deductions if they fail to join.[8]

References to being or not being a member 'are to being or not being a member of any trade union, of a particular trade union or one of a number of particular trade unions'.[9] Such references include being or not being a member of a particular branch or section of a trade union. However, for these purposes, the union does not have to be independent.

A striking feature of these provisions is that they do not expressly deal with discrimination on the grounds of union activities. However, in *Harrison v Kent County Council*[10] the Employment Appeal Tribunal ruled that the employment tribunal had erred in drawing a rigid distinction between union membership and taking part in activities. Thus, if applicants are refused employment for a reason related to their union activities, it is open to a tribunal to conclude they had been refused employment because they were union members. It is a question of fact in each case for the tribunal to determine the reason for refusal.

Applicants are deemed to have been refused employment if they seek work and the employer:

- refuses or deliberately omits to entertain and process the application or enquiry, or

---

[5] Ibid, s 6.
[6] Ibid, s 8.
[7] 'Recognition' is defined in ibid, s 178(3).
[8] Ibid, s 137(1).
[9] Ibid, s 143(3).
[10] [1995] ICR 434.

- causes the withdrawal or the cessation of the application or enquiry, or
- refuses or deliberately omits to offer employment, or
- makes a job offer on terms that no reasonable employer wishing to fill the post would offer (which is not accepted), or
- withdraws a job offer or causes the person not to accept it, or
- offers employment on terms which include a requirement within TULRCA, s 137(1) and the applicant declines the offer because of this requirement.[11]

Advertisements

Where an advertisement[12] indicates or might reasonably be understood as indicating that employment is open only to those who are or are not union members, or that there is a requirement applying to the post of the sort mentioned in section 137(1)(b) (see above), if those who do not meet the condition or requirement are refused employment it will be conclusively presumed to have been for that reason.[13] Similarly, if there is an arrangement or practice for jobs to be offered only to persons approved by a trade union, non-members who are refused employment are deemed to have been rejected because of their non-membership.[14] It would seem that both of these provisions apply even if the person lacks the essentials skills to perform the job!

Agencies

It is unlawful for an employment agency which finds jobs for workers, or supplies employers with workers, to refuse its services to people because they are or are not union members or are unwilling to accept a condition or requirement of the type mentioned in TULRCA, s 137(1)(b).[15] The provisions relating to advertisements also apply to employment agencies[16] but it is clear that a trade union is not to be regarded as such an agency 'by reason of services provided by it only for, or in relation to, its members'.[17]

Complaints

Complaints about the infringement of these provisions must normally be submitted to an employment tribunal within three months of the conduct complained about, or, if this is not reasonably practicable, 'within such

---

[11] TULRCA, s 137(5).
[12] Ibid, s 143 defines an advertisement as 'including every form of advertisement or notice, whether to the public or not'.
[13] Ibid, s 137(3).
[14] Ibid, s 137(4).
[15] Ibid, s 138. See above.
[16] An employment agency is defined in ibid, s 143(1).
[17] Ibid, s 143(2).

further period as the tribunal considers reasonable'.[18] The date of the conduct complained about will be:

- where there is an actual refusal, the date of refusal;
- where there is a deliberate omission to entertain and process an application or enquiry or to offer employment, the end of the period within which it was reasonable to expect the employer to act;
- where there is conduct causing the claimant to withdraw or cease to pursue an application or enquiry, the date of that conduct;
- where an offer is withdrawn, the date of withdrawal; and
- where an offer was made but not accepted, the date the offer was made.

Section 18 of the Employment Tribunals Act 1996 (ETA 1996) and TULRCA, s 288 provide respectively for conciliation and compromise agreements. Where a complaint is upheld, the tribunal will make a declaration to that effect.[19] It also has the discretion, if it thinks it just and equitable, to award either or both of the following remedies:

- an order to compensate;
- a recommendation that the respondent takes action within a specified period which the tribunal thinks is practicable to obviate or reduce the adverse effect on the claimant of the conduct to which the complaint relates.

If the respondent fails without reasonable justification to comply with a recommendation, the tribunal may award compensation or increase it. Compensation can include injury to feelings, although the amount of compensation cannot exceed £55,000 in 2004.[20]

Finally, a trade union may be joined as a defendant in tribunal proceedings if either party alleges that an employer or employment agency was induced to act in the manner complained of by union pressure exercised in the form of industrial action or a threat of it. Where compensation is awarded the union may be ordered to pay all or part of it.[21]

Detriment short of dismissal

Once a job has been secured, employees have the right not to be subjected to a detriment as an individual by any act, or deliberate failure to act, by an employer if the act or failure takes place for the purpose of:

(i) preventing or deterring them from being or seeking to become members of an independent trade union or penalising them for doing so,

---

[18] Ibid, s 139.
[19] Ibid, s 140.
[20] This figure is linked to the retail price index.
[21] TULRCA, s 142.

(ii) preventing or deterring them from taking part in the activities of an independent trade union at any appropriate time, or penalising them for doing so,

(iii) compelling them to become members of any trade union or of a particular trade union or of one of a number of particular trade unions,

(iv) enforcing a requirement that in the event of their failure to become, or their ceasing to remain, members of any trade union or a particular trade union or one of a number of particular trade unions, they must make one or more payments. For this purpose, any deduction from remuneration which is attributable to the employee's failure to become, or ceasing to be, a trade union member will be treated as a detriment.[22]

It was made clear in *Ridgway v National Coal Board*[23] that employees have a right to join an independent trade union of their choice. Thus, in *Carlson v Post Office*[24] the EAT ruled that the denial of a car park permit to a member of a non-recognised[25] independent trade union constituted an unlawful penalty within the meaning of TULRCA, s 146.

Penalising

As in other areas of discrimination law, 'penalising' means 'subjecting to a disadvantage'. In relation to the requirement that the action or omission must be directed at the employee as an individual, employers have argued that action has been taken against the union rather than individual members. In *Ridgway*'s case, where members of the National Union of Mineworkers were denied a pay increase, the Court of Appeal offered the following guidance: 'If an employee is selected for discrimination because of some characteristic which he shares with others, such as membership of a particular trade union, then the action is ... taken against him as an individual.'[26] Similarly, in *Farnsworth Ltd v McCoid*,[27] where the employer removed the employee's credentials as a shop steward, the Court of Appeal ruled that this constituted action taken against him as an individual.

The employer's purpose[28]

The words 'for the purpose of' connote an objective that the employer seeks to achieve and the purpose of an action must not be confused with

---

[22] The Employment Relations Bill 2003 proposes to give these rights to 'workers' and to protect them from suffering a detriment for using union services or refusing an inducement. TULRCA, s 146.
[23] [1987] IRLR 80. See below.
[24] [1981] IRLR 158.
[25] A trade union is recognised if it engages in collective bargaining: see TULRCA, s 178.
[26] [1987] IRLR 80 at 88.
[27] [1999] IRLR 626.
[28] The Employment Relations Bill 2003 proposes to replace the word 'purpose' by 'sole or main purpose'.

its effect. Two Court of Appeal decisions dealing with promotion are illustrative here. In *Gallacher v Department of Transport*,[29] the applicant was a union group assistant secretary who effectively spent all his working time on union duties. When he applied for promotion he was rejected because of doubts about his managerial ability. Since he could only demonstrate his management skills if he gave up his union post, Mr Gallagher considered that his employer had taken action against him for the purpose of deterring him from taking part in the activities of an independent trade union. Although the employment tribunal upheld his complaint, the Court of Appeal accepted that section 146 of TULRCA had not been infringed because the employer's purpose had been to ensure that only those with sufficient managerial experience were promoted.

By way of contrast, in *Southwark London Borough Council v Whillier*,[30] while the applicant was pursuing a grievance against her employer, she was elected branch secretary of her union. This position involved full-time release from the duties of her job. The grievance procedure resulted in the Council offering her promotion to a suitable post, with the increased salary being paid from the time she commenced her duties. The EAT upheld her claim that the employer's purpose in not paying the rate for the new job until she took up her duties was to deter her from engaging in union activities.

In this context, it should be noted that TULRCA, s 148(3) has introduced a serious anomaly. It states that, in deciding the purpose for which the employer acted or failed to act, 'where (a) there is evidence that the employer's purpose was to further a change in his relationship with all or any class of his employees, and (b) there is also evidence that his purpose was one falling within section 146', the tribunal must treat (a) as the employer's purpose 'unless it considers that no reasonable employer would act or fail to act in the way concerned'. Thus, unless the employer has behaved wholly unreasonably, purpose (b) is to be disregarded! However, s 17 of the Employment Relations Act 1999 now permits the Secretary of State to make regulations about cases where a worker is subject to detriment or dismissal on the grounds that the worker refuses to enter into a contract which includes terms which differ from an applicable collective agreement. No such regulations have been made to date.[31]

Activities of an independent trade union

As there is no statutory definition, tribunals have to determine what amounts to the 'activities of an independent trade union'. The following have been accepted as such: attempting to recruit new members or form a workplace union branch,[32] taking part in union meetings, and consulting

[29] [1994] IRLR 231.
[30] [2001] ICR 142.
[31] The Employment Relations Bill 2003 proposes to repeal this section.
[32] See *Lyon v St James Press Ltd* [1976] IRLR 215.

a union official.[33] Those claiming that they have been victimised because of their activities do not have to show that they were authorised union representatives. However, individual complaints or group meetings which have no union connection will not be protected.

Two cases are worth comparing here. In *Chant v Aquaboats Ltd*,[34] a union member who organised a petition about safety at work was held not to be taking part in union activities when he submitted it to the employer. Although a union official had approved the petition, Mr Chant was not a union representative and the majority of workers who signed it were not union members. By way of contrast, in *British Airways v Francis*,[35] the employer reprimanded a shop steward for making a statement to the press following a meeting of workers, which criticised the union for failing to achieve equal pay. According to the EAT, it was not conclusive that the employees did not get together at a committee or formal branch meeting. It would appear to be sufficient that union members have discussed matters with which an independent trade union is concerned. In *Therm-a-Stor v Atkins*,[36] a distinction was drawn between an employer's response to a trade union's activities and its reaction to an individual employee's activities in a trade union context. Here a union district secretary's letter requesting recognition led to the dismissal of ordinary members on the alleged grounds of redundancy. Although this reason was found to be spurious, it was held that the reason for dismissal had nothing to do with anything the employees concerned had personally done or proposed to do. According to the Court of Appeal, the expression 'activities of an independent trade union' refers to the activities of a specific trade union rather than the activities of unions generally. The complainants did not have the qualifying period of service needed to claim unfair dismissal, so the employment tribunal had no jurisdiction to hear their complaints. Given that the employer did not have a fair reason for dismissal, it seems clear that, if the complainants had had the requisite year's service, they would have obtained a finding of unfairness.[37]

In *Port of London Authority v Payne*,[38] it was held that the selection of shop stewards for redundancy because the employer believed that they would engage in disruption in the future amounted to dismissal on the grounds of trade union activities. The approach to be taken by employment tribunals in determining whether an employee was dismissed for union activities was set out in this case. According to the EAT, the tribunal must establish: the belief held by the employer upon which the decision to dismiss was taken; that such belief was genuinely held; and whether

---

[33] See *Speciality Care v Pachela* [1996] IRLR 248.
[34] [1978] ICR 643.
[35] [1981] IRLR 9.
[36] [1983] IRLR 78.
[37] It is important to observe that victimisation of individuals in the context of a claim for union recognition is now dealt with by Part VIII of Schedule A1 to TULRCA.
[38] [1992] IRLR 447.

the facts upon which that belief was based, judged objectively, fell within the phrase 'activities of an independent trade union'.

In *Rasool v Hepworth Pipe Ltd (No 2)*,[39] the EAT accepted that attendance at an unauthorised meeting to consider the views of employees in relation to impending wage negotiations was such an activity. Nevertheless, this type of action is not normally taken at the 'appropriate time' required by the statute because TULRCA, s 146(2) defines this as being outside the employee's working hours or within working hours 'in accordance with arrangements agreed with, or consent given by his employer'. Such consent might be express (e.g. by being mentioned in a collective agreement) or may be implied by the conduct of the parties. However, in *Marley Tiles v Shaw*,[40] the Court of Appeal ruled that consent could not be implied from the employer's silence when a shop steward unaccredited by management at the relevant time called a meeting of maintenance staff within working hours. In *Bass Taverns v Burgess*,[41] the same court accepted that the dismissal of a shop steward after he made disparaging remarks about the company at an induction course for trainee managers was for a reason relating to his trade union activities. It was not accepted that the employer's consent to the meeting being used as a recruitment forum was subject to an implied limitation that the recruiter would not undermine or criticise the company. Since it was not suggested that he had acted dishonestly or in bad faith, Mr Burgess' admission that he had 'gone over the top' did not justify a finding that during his speech he was not taking part in union activities.

If a person is sacked for engaging in deception at the time they were hired (e.g. concealing his or her identity as a known union activist),[42] the statutory protection will not apply (on the outlawing of prohibited lists, see below). However, this should be contrasted with the situation which arose in *Fitzpatrick v British Railways Board*.[43] When Ms Fitzpatrick obtained a job with British Railways Board she deliberately failed to provide full details of her employment record or to disclose her involvement in trade union activities. She subsequently joined the National Union of Railwaymen, took part in recruiting activities and intended to seek a position as a union official. When the employer learned of her previous union and political activities she was sacked. The Court of Appeal decided that, although the relevant union activities are those in the employment from which the individual has been dismissed, what happened in a previous job may form the reason for dismissal in subsequent employment. Thus, her dismissal because of union activities in a previous job was regarded as unfair because the only rational basis for it was the fear that those activities

---

[39] [1980] IRLR 135.
[40] [1980] IRLR 25.
[41] [1995] IRLR 596.
[42] See *City of Birmingham v Beyer* [1977] IRLR 211.
[43] [1991] IRLR 376.

would be repeated in the current employment. It was also held in this case that the statutory protection applies irrespective of whether the precise union activities can be identified.

Section 146(2) of TULRCA defines 'working hours' as any time when an employee is required to be at work. However, in order to protect union activities during paid tea breaks, the EAT in *Zucker v Astrid Jewels*[44] construed 'working hours' as the time when work is actually performed.

In *Wilson & National Union of Journalists v United Kingdom*,[45] claims were made by trade unionists that their right not to have action taken against them for the purpose of deterring them from being members had been infringed. Here the employers offered higher pay and benefits if the employees agreed to give up their right to union representation and denied them pay increases when they refused. The House of Lords held that the statutory protection was limited to union membership as such and did not extend to a right to make use of the union's services. Having failed to obtain a remedy under UK law, Wilson complained that his rights under Article 11 of the European Convention on Human Rights had been infringed (see above). The European Court of Human Rights (ECHR) held that there had been a violation of Article 11 in relation to both the applicant and his union. According to the ECHR, unions must be free to strive for the protection of their members' interests and individual members have a right to have their trade union heard. It is of the essence of the right to join that employees should be free to instruct or permit the union to make representations to their employer or to take action in support of their interests. Since it is the role of the state to ensure that members are not prevented or restrained from using their union to represent them in attempts to regulate their relations with their employers, it would seem that legislative changes will be needed.[46]

Making a claim

A claim that there has been detriment short of dismissal must normally be presented within three months of the date of the act or omission or, where the act or omission is part of a similar series, the last of them.[47] Where an act extends over a period, the date of the act is taken to be the last day of that period. An omission will be treated as occurring when it was decided on and, in the absence of evidence establishing the contrary, employers will be assumed to decide on a failure to act:

- when they perform an act inconsistent with doing the failed act, or
- when a period expires within which they might reasonably have been expected to perform the failed act.

[44] [1979] IRLR 385.
[45] [2002] IRLR 568.
[46] See Ewing (2003) 32(1) *Industrial Law Journal* 1.
[47] The Employment Relations Bill 2003 proposes to deal with inducements relating to union membership and activities and collective bargaining. TULRCA, s 147.

When section 32 of the Employment Act 2002 (EA 2002) comes into force, an employee wishing to complain under TULRCA, s 146 must first submit a statement of grievance to his or her employer.[48] Section 148 of TULRCA puts the burden on employers to show the purpose for which they acted or failed to act but, in deciding on this purpose, a tribunal may not take into account any pressure exerted on the employer by the threat or organisation of industrial action.

Provision is made for both conciliation and compromise agreements,[49] but where a tribunal finds that a complaint is well founded, it must make a declaration and may award compensation. This compensation will reflect what the tribunal believes to be 'just and equitable in all the circumstances having regard to the infringement complained of and to any loss sustained by the complainant which is attributable to the act or failure'. Such loss will include any expenses reasonably incurred in consequence of the act or omission and the loss of any benefit which might reasonably have been expected but for the act or failure complained of. There is no limit on how much can be awarded to employees, although compensation can be reduced if there is a failure to mitigate loss or the tribunal finds that the act or omission 'was to any extent caused or contributed to by action of the complainant'. When EA 2002, s 31 comes into force, compensation can be increased if the employer has failed to comply with a statutory procedure or reduced if the employee has failed to complete it.[50]

In *Brassington v Cauldon Wholesale Ltd*,[51] the EAT stated that the statutory provisions do not impose a quasi-fine, so compensation can be awarded only if the complainant can show that injury resulted. However, as is the case where other forms of unlawful discrimination occur, this injury is not restricted to pecuniary loss. For example, the stress engendered by the situation may have harmed the employee's health, or a sincere desire to join a union, with all the benefits that entails, might have been frustrated. Thus, in *Cleveland NHS Trust v Blane*,[52] a shop steward was awarded £1,000 for injury to feelings after his failure to be shortlisted for a management post on the grounds of his union activities. Similarly, in *London Borough of Hackney v Adams*,[53] £5,000 was awarded for distress and humiliation where discrimination on the same grounds resulted in the withdrawal of an offer of promotion. Nevertheless, it ought not to be assumed that injury to feelings flows from every act of discrimination.

Finally, it should be noted that a trade union may be joined as a defendant in tribunal proceedings if either the complainant or the employer alleges that the employer was induced to act in the manner complained

---

[48] See EA 2002, Sch 2, paras 6 and 9.
[49] ETA 1996, s 18 and TULRCA, s 288, respectively.
[50] See EA 2002, Sch 3.
[51] [1977] IRLR 479.
[52] [1997] IRLR 332.
[53] [2003] IRLR 402.

of by union pressure exercised in the form of industrial action or a threat of it.[54] Where compensation is awarded the union may be ordered to pay all or part of it.

Dismissal on trade union grounds

The law of unfair dismissal offers protection against termination of employment on union membership grounds. Thus, a dismissal is unfair if the reason or principal reason for it was that the employee:[55]

(a) was or proposed to become a member of an independent trade union, or
(b) had taken part or proposed to take part in the activities of an independent trade union at an appropriate time, or
(c) was not a member of any trade union or of a particular trade union, or had refused or proposed to refuse to become or remain a member.

Dismissals are treated as falling within (c) above if one of the reasons for them was that employees:

• refused or proposed to refuse to comply with a requirement that in the event of their not being a trade union member they must make some kind of payment, or
• objected or proposed to object to the operation of a provision under which their employer was entitled to deduct sums from their remuneration if they failed to be a member.

Additionally, if the reason or principal reason for dismissal was that the employee was redundant but the circumstances 'applied equally to one or more other employees in the same undertaking who held positions similar' who were not dismissed, and the reason or principal reason for selection was one of those specified in (a)–(c) above, the dismissal will be unfair.[56] Thus, in *Britool Ltd v Roberts*,[57] the EAT accepted that there had been a breach of TULRCA, s 153 when employees who had led a strike were selected for redundancy.

The meaning of 'activities of an independent trade union' and 'appropriate time' have already been discussed in relation to detrimental treatment. In *Crosville Motors Ltd v Ashfield*,[58] the ostensible reason for

---

[54] TULRCA, s 150.
[55] Ibid, s 152(1). The Employment Relations Bill 2003 proposes to protect employees from dismissal for using union services or refusing an inducement.
[56] Ibid, s 153.
[57] [1993] IRLR 481.
[58] [1986] IRLR 475.

Mr Ashfield's dismissal as a bus driver was a ticketing offence involving the sum of twenty pence. However, the dismissal took place against a background of disagreement between Ashfield and his union. At the time he was sacked Ashfield had made it plain that unless there were certain changes in union policy and organisation he would leave the union. The EAT confirmed that the true reason for dismissal was his proposal to leave the union. In doing so, it stated that a proposal to refuse to remain a member need not be unqualified but could cover a contingent event.

The usual qualifying period (currently a year) and the upper age limit (currently normal retiring age or 65) for claiming unfair dismissal do not apply if the reason or principal reason for dismissal, or selection for redundancy, falls within s 152(1) of TULRCA.[59] Provision is made for both conciliation and compromise agreements,[60] and, when s 32 of the EA 2002 comes into force, an employee wishing to complain of unfair dismissal must first submit a statement of grievance to his or her employer.[61] In *Maund v Penwith District Council*,[62] where the applicant alleged that redundancy was not the real reason for his dismissal, the burden of proof in such cases was explained. According to the Court of Appeal, employees who do not meet the service requirement have the onus of proving that they were dismissed for a reason within TULRCA, s 152(1). However, where the question of jurisdiction does not arise, once the employer has produced evidence that appears to show the reason for dismissal, the burden passes to the employee to demonstrate that there is a real issue as to whether that was the true reason. In the writer's opinion, one effect of the Human Rights Act 1998 should be that tribunals place the burden on the employer in all cases to show that a dismissal did not infringe Article 11 of the European Convention on Human Rights (see above).

If employees allege that their dismissals were unfair by virtue of TULRCA, s 152, there is provision for 'interim relief'.[63] This is available where employees present their claims within seven days of the effective date of termination[64] and, where TULRCA, s 152(1)(a) or (b) are relied on, they submit certificates signed by an authorised union official which state that there appears to be reasonable grounds for supposing that the reason for dismissal was the one alleged in the complaints. An employment tribunal must hear such an application as soon as practicable[65] and, if it thinks it 'likely' that the claimant will be found to be unfairly dismissed by virtue of TULRCA, s 152, it must ask whether the employer is willing to re-employ pending the determination of the complaint. If

---

[59] TULRCA, s 154.
[60] See note 47 above.
[61] See EA 2002, Sch 2, paras 6 and 9.
[62] [1984] IRLR 24.
[63] TULRCA, ss 161–166.
[64] This expression is defined in ERA 1996, s 97.
[65] TULRCA, s 162.

the employer is willing to reinstate or the employee is willing to accept re-engagement, the tribunal will make an order to that effect. Where the employer fails to attend the hearing or refuses to re-employ, the tribunal will order the continuation of the employee's contract. In practice, such an order will amount to suspension on full pay.[66] In *Taplin v Shippam Ltd,*[67] the EAT held that employment tribunals should ask themselves whether the applicant has a 'pretty good chance' of succeeding at a full hearing. It is not enough to show that there was a reasonable prospect of success.

Where employees are found to have been unfairly dismissed, tribunals must explain their powers to order reinstatement or re-engagement and ask claimants if they wish such an order to be made. Only if such a wish is expressed can an order be made and, if there is no order, the tribunal must turn to the question of compensation.[68] Compensation will usually consist of a basic and compensatory award. Currently the basic award will reflect the employee's age and length of continuous service and will be reduced by the amount of any redundancy payment received.[69] However, subject to any deduction on the grounds stated below, there is a minimum award of £3,600 in 2004.[70] The basic award can be reduced by such proportion as the tribunal thinks just and equitable on two grounds:

- the employee unreasonably refused an offer of reinstatement;
- any conduct of the claimant before the dismissal.[71]

The compensatory award will be of such amount as the tribunal 'considers just and equitable in all the circumstances having regard to the loss sustained by the complainant in consequence of the dismissal in so far as that loss is attributable to action taken by the employer'.[72] As with detrimental treatment, compensation can be reduced where the employee's action caused or contributed to the dismissal or there was a failure to mitigate loss. When the EA 2002, s 31 comes into force, compensation can be increased if the employer has failed to comply with a statutory procedure or reduced if the employee has failed to complete it.[73] The current maximum compensatory award is £55,000.

If there has been pressure to dismiss on the grounds of non-membership of a trade union, the person who applied the pressure can be joined as a party to the unfair dismissal proceedings.[74] A request that a person

---

[66] Ibid, s 164.
[67] [1978] IRLR 450.
[68] ERA 1996, s 112.
[69] Ibid, s 122(4).
[70] Ibid, s 120.
[71] Ibid, s 122.
[72] Ibid, s 123.
[73] See EA 2002, Sch 3.
[74] TULRCA, s 160.

be joined must be acceded to if it is made before the hearing but can be refused if it is made after that time. No such request can be entertained after a remedy has been awarded and the tribunal is empowered to apportion compensation in a just and equitable manner.

Union membership or recognition requirements in contracts for goods and services

Section 144 of TULRCA renders void any term or condition in a contract for the supply of goods or services which requires that the whole or part of the work to be done under the contract is performed only by trade unionists or members of a particular union, or only by non-members or non-members of a particular union. In addition, a refusal to deal with a supplier or prospective supplier on union membership grounds is prohibited.[75] For these purposes there is a refusal to deal where:

(a) a person is excluded from a list of approved suppliers;
(b) a person is not permitted to tender or enter into a contract;
(c) a contract for the supply of goods or services is terminated.

It is worth noting that a list of approved suppliers can take any form and might even be maintained by a trade union.

Any term or condition of a contract for the supply of goods or services is void insofar as it purports to require an employer to recognise one or more trade unions for negotiating purposes or to negotiate or consult with any trade union official.[76] Similarly, it is unlawful to refuse to deal[77] with a supplier or prospective supplier if one of the grounds for doing so is that the person against whom it is taken does not or is not likely to recognise, negotiate or consult as mentioned in s 186 of TULRCA.[78]

A person adversely affected by a failure to comply with ss 145 or 187 of TULRCA (e.g. an employer or employee denied work) can seek damages for breach of statutory duty from the employer concerned and can sue the union involved or its officials in tort. To establish a breach of statutory duty it will be sufficient to prove that one of the grounds for the refusal to deal was a union membership or recognition requirement prohibited by TULRCA, ss 145 and 187. Finally, there is no immunity from liability in tort for inducing or attempting to induce a person to contravene

---

[75] Ibid, s 145.
[76] Ibid, s 186.
[77] Defined in the same way as ibid, s 145 (see above).
[78] Ibid, s 187.

TULRCA, ss 145 and 187, or for boycotting the work or union or non-union members.[79] This is obviously intended to impact on trade unions who exert pressure on employers to enforce compulsory union membership (the closed shop).

Prohibition of blacklists

In some industries it has been the practice of employers to maintain and circulate lists of trade union members and activists. Those on the list are viewed as potential troublemakers and are therefore refused any jobs they apply for. It almost goes without saying that people placed on such lists might be unemployed for lengthy periods of time and suffer considerable hardship.

Section 3 of the Employment Relations Act 1999 enables the Secretary of State to introduce regulations prohibiting the compilation, dissemination and use of trade union blacklists. In February 2003 the Department of Trade and Industry published a consultative document containing draft regulations. However, the Government has stated that regulations will not be placed before Parliament 'until there is evidence that individuals or organisations are planning to draw up such lists, or if there is any evidence there is a demand from employers for them'. Although it seems unlikely that the legislation will be implemented in the near future, the draft regulations are outlined here because there are important principles about union discrimination at stake.

A prohibited list is one which:

(a) contains details of trade union members or people who have taken part in trade union activities, and
(b) is compiled with a view to being used by employers or employment agencies for the purpose of discrimination in relation to recruitment or the treatment of workers.[80]

It will be unlawful to compile or use such a list or to knowingly or recklessly sell or supply it. However, it will not be unlawful to compile or use a prohibited list for the purpose of employing or appointing to an office if it is reasonable to believe that significant trade union experience or knowledge is a necessary requirement for the job.[81] This would cover the positions of both trade union and industrial relations officers. Similarly, in order not to inhibit investigative journalism, it will not be unlawful to

---

[79] Ibid, ss 222(3) and 225.
[80] Draft reg 3(2).
[81] Draft reg 3(6).

compile, sell, supply or use a blacklist if a person can demonstrate that this was 'justified in the public interest because that person's sole or principal purpose was to expose a breach or potential breach in these regulations'.[82]

It will also be unlawful to refuse employment because a person's name is or is not on a prohibited list.[83] A person is deemed to be refused employment in the five circumstances outlined in s 137(5) of TULRCA (see pp 243–4 above). A refusal of employment will be unlawful if:

(a) there is reason to suppose that at the time of the rejection the potential employer had in his or her possession, or had seen, a prohibited list on which the name of the applicant appeared (or the applicant's name did not appear if it is alleged that the refusal was on the basis that the applicant's name was omitted), and
(b) the potential employer does not show that the reason or principal reason for refusal was unrelated to the use of the list.

Where there is an arrangement or practice under which a job is offered only to people on a prohibited list, those who do not appear on the list who are refused employment because of the arrangement or practice will be assumed to have been refused because their names were omitted.

Workers will have the right not to be subject to any detriment by any act or omission of their employer for a reason related to the fact that their names were or were not on a prohibited list.[84] Similarly, employees will be unfairly dismissed if the reason or principal reason for dismissal was on the same grounds.[85] It will be assumed that employers have unlawfully imposed a detriment or dismissed where:

(a) there is reason to suppose that at the relevant time the employer possessed or had seen a prohibited list on which the name of the individual appeared, and
(b) the employer failed to show that the reason or principal reason for the act or omission was unrelated to the use of the list.

Claims of unlawful refusal of employment must be submitted to an employment tribunal within three months of the date of the conduct complained about, or, if this is not reasonably practicable, 'within such further period as the tribunal considers reasonable'.[86] For these purposes the date of the conduct is established in the same way as under TULRCA, s 139 (see above). Conciliation will be made available.[87] However, where a complaint is upheld, the tribunal will be required to provide the remedies

---

[82] Draft reg 3(5).
[83] Draft reg 4.
[84] Draft reg 6.
[85] Draft reg 12.
[86] Draft reg 7.
[87] Under ETA 1996, s 18.

contained in TULRCA, s 140 (see unlawful refusal of employment above).[88] If detrimental treatment is alleged, the time limits provided by TULRCA, s 147 apply (see p 250 above). Similarly, where a complaint is well-founded,[89] the remedies contained in TULRCA, s 149 will apply.[90] It is also provided that dismissed workers who are not employees will have the same rights to compensation as employees (see below). Complaints of unfair dismissal can be submitted to the employment tribunal after notice of termination has been given and must normally be submitted within three months of the effective date of termination.[91] Where a complaint is upheld, the remedies available for infringing TULRCA, s 152 apply (see p 254 above).

Finally, where in a case brought under the draft regulations the complainant or respondent claims that a prohibited list was unlawfully compiled, sold or supplied by someone else, either party can ask the tribunal to order that the other person be joined as a party to the proceedings.[92]

Admission to and expulsion by a trade union

It will be gleaned from elsewhere in this book that the anti-discrimination legislation applies to trade unions in their dealings with both employees and members of the public. In addition, the Sex Discrimination Act 1975, the Race Relations Act 1976, the Disability Discrimination Act 1995, the Employment Equality (Sexual Orientation) Regulations 2003 and the Employment Equality (Religion or Belief) Regulations 2003 all make it unlawful for an organisation of workers to discriminate in the terms on which it is prepared to admit into membership, or on which it refuses or deliberately omits to accept an application for membership. It is also unlawful for an organisation of workers to discriminate on the prohibited grounds against a member in the way it affords access to benefits, facilities or services, or subjects him or her to any detriment, including deprivation of membership.[93]

In relation to positive action, s 48 of the Sex Discrimination Act 1975 and s 38 of the Race Relations Act 1976 allow organisations of workers

---

[88] Draft reg 9.
[89] Conciliation will be made available under ETA 1996, s 18.
[90] Draft reg 10.
[91] Conciliation will be made available under ETA 1996, s 18.
[92] Draft reg 13.
[93] See Sex Discrimination Act 1975, s 12, Race Relations Act 1976, s 11, Disability Discrimination Act 1975, s 13, Employment Equality (Sexual Orientation) Regulations 2003, SI 2003/ 1661, reg 15 (2003). See also the Equal Opportunities Commission, Code of Practice and the Employment Equality (Religion or Belief) Regulations 2003 s 1 2003/1660, reg 15, Part 3 of the Commission for Racial Equality's Code of Practice (1983) and the Code of Practice on the Duties of Trade Organisations to their Disabled Members and Applicants (1999). It is worth noting that the Race Relations Act and the Sexual Orientation and Religion or Belief Regulations all make specific mention of harassment.

to encourage persons of a particular sex or race to join or hold office if within the previous 12 months there has been significant under-representation within the organisation. Section 49 of the Sex Discrimination Act 1975 also permits a union to ensure that a minimum number of persons of one sex are members of an elected body 'where in the opinion of the organisation the provision is in the circumstances needed to secure a reasonable lower limit to the number of members of that sex serving on the body'. This does not affect a person's membership rights or the right to vote in an election.

In addition, union members will also have rights and obligations arising out of their contract of membership. However, TULRCA, s 82 provides that contribution to a union's political fund cannot be made a condition for admission nor can non-contributors to such a fund be disadvantaged compared with other members (except in relation to the control or management of the fund). Furthermore, Article 8 of EC Council Regulation on the freedom of movement for workers[94] provides that a national of a Member State who is employed in another Member State must 'enjoy equality of treatment as regards membership of trade unions and the exercise of rights attaching thereto, including the right to vote'.

In effect, TULRCA, s 174 gives individuals the right to join the trade union of their choice. It does so by providing that people can only be excluded or expelled from a union if:

(a) the person fails to satisfy an enforceable membership requirement in the union's rules. A requirement is 'enforceable' if it restricts membership solely by reference to one or more of the following criteria –
 – employment in a specified trade, industry or profession;
 – occupational description (including grade, level or category of appointment); and
 – possession of specified trade, industrial or professional qualifications or work experience;
(b) the person does not qualify for membership because the union operates only in particular parts of Great Britain;
(c) the union operates only in relation to one employer or a number of associated employers and the person is not employed by that employer or one of those employers;
(d) the exclusion is entirely attributable to the individual's conduct.[95] For these purposes, 'conduct' does not include being or ceasing to be any of the following – a member of another trade union; being employed by a particular employer or at a particular place; a member of a political party. Nor does it include any conduct for which an individual may not be disciplined by a trade union (see below).

---

[94] 1612/68/EEC.
[95] TULRCA, s 177 defines 'conduct' as including statements, acts and omissions.

A person excluded or expelled in contravention of these provisions can complain to an employment tribunal, except if, in relation to expulsion, they have successfully brought an action for unjustifiable discipline.[96] This must normally be done within six months of the date of exclusion or expulsion. However, if a tribunal finds that it was not reasonably practicable to comply with this time limit, the period may be extended by such amount as is considered reasonable.[97] If an application for membership is neither granted nor rejected before the end of the period within which it might reasonably have been expected to be granted, the individual is to be treated as having been excluded on the last day of that period. Similarly, an individual who ceases to be a member of the union on the happening of an event specified in the rules will be deemed to have been expelled from the union.[98]

Provision is made for both conciliation and compromise agreements[99] but, where a claim is upheld, the tribunal must make a declaration to that effect.[100] Complainants who are admitted or re-admitted to the union can apply to the employment tribunal for compensation after four weeks and must do so before six months have elapsed from the date of the declaration. If the union does not admit or re-admit, applications for compensation must be made to the Employment Appeal Tribunal. The employment tribunal and the EAT are both empowered to award such compensation as is considered 'just and equitable in all the circumstances'. However, provision is made for a reduction if the complainant's action caused or contributed to the exclusion or expulsion. The current maximum award is £63,100 and compensation fixed by the EAT must be at least £5,900.

In *NACODS v Gluchowski*,[101] the individual was suspended beyond the six-month period allowed for in the union's rules. The EAT held that the employment tribunal had been wrong to conclude that the word 'exclusion' in this context included exclusion from the benefits of membership. According to the Appeal Tribunal, 'exclusion' refers to a refusal to admit and not to suspension of the privileges of membership. In this case, Gluchowski had continued to pay his dues and, if he had complied with the union's conditions, he would have been restored automatically to all the benefits of membership without further application to become a member. In *McGhee v TGWU*,[102] the EAT indicated that there is no ground for construing the term 'unreasonably expelled' as including conduct on the part of the union which leaves the member with no reasonable alternative but to resign. Thus, it was held that there was no expulsion

---

[96] Ibid, s 177(4).
[97] Ibid, s 175.
[98] Ibid, s 177.
[99] See note 49 above.
[100] TULRCA, s 176.
[101] [1996] IRLR 252.
[102] [1985] IRLR 198.

when the member resigned as a consequence of being treated as in arrears because he had not paid a union-imposed fine. Two cases can be used to illustrate the circumstances in which reductions in compensation may be appropriate. In *Day v SOGAT*,[103] the EAT decided that the individual's failure to inform the union when he had been offered a job which might have led to the return of his union card had contributed to the situation. Similarly, in *Saunders v Bakers, Food and Allied Workers Union*,[104] the failure to attend an executive council meeting contributed to the union's refusal to re-admit her.

Discipline by a trade union

It is consistent with the provisions on unreasonable exclusion and expulsion, that members have the right not to be unjustifiably disciplined by the union.[105] For these purposes, an individual is to be treated as disciplined if a 'determination' is made under the rules of the union or by an official of the union that:

- the member should be expelled from the union or a branch or section of it;
- the member should pay a sum to the union or to any other person;
- sums tendered to the union by the member should be treated as unpaid;
- the member should be deprived to any extent of, or access to, any benefits, services or facilities which would otherwise be provided by virtue of union membership;
- another trade union should be encouraged or advised not to accept the individual into membership;
- the member should be subject to some other detriment.

In *TGWU v Webber*,[106] the EAT held that for a decision to constitute a determination for these purposes it must be one that disposes of the issue. Thus, the employment tribunal had erred in holding that a recommendation to the executive council that a member be expelled, which had to be affirmed and implemented, amounted to a determination. In *NALGO v Killorn*,[107] the EAT ruled that a member was subjected to a detriment when suspension deprived her of the benefits of membership and she was named as a strike-breaker in a branch circular with the intention of causing her embarrassment.

---

[103] [1986] ICR 640.
[104] [1986] IRLR 16.
[105] TULRCA, s 64.
[106] [1990] IRLR 462.
[107] [1990] IRLR 464.

Disciplinary action by a trade union is deemed to be unjustifiable for the following actual or supposed conduct:[108]

(a) failing to participate in industrial action or criticising such action. In *Knowles v Fire Brigades Union*,[109] the Court of Appeal ruled that what constitutes industrial action for these purposes is a mixed question of fact and law. Thus, it is necessary to look at all the circumstances, including the contracts of employment of those concerned and whether any breach or a departure from the terms is involved, the effect on the employer of what is done or omitted, and the object that the union or employees seek to achieve. In *Bradley v NALGO*,[110] nine members of the union were found to have been unjustifiably disciplined by being expelled for crossing picket line;

(b) alleging that the union or any of its officials[111] is acting or has acted unlawfully. This protects members who bring legal proceedings against the union;

(c) encouraging or assisting others to perform their contracts of employment (e.g. during industrial action) or encouraging others to make an allegation of the type mentioned in (b) above;

(d) refusing to agree to the deduction from wages of payments for union membership;

(e) resigning or proposing to resign from the union or another union, joining or proposing to join another union, refusing to join another union or being a member of another union;

(f) working with, or proposing to work with, individuals who are not members of the union or who are not members of another union;

(g) working for, or proposing to work for, an employer who employs or who has employed individuals who are not members of the union or who are not members of another union;

(h) requiring the union to perform an act which it is obliged to perform under TULRCA when requested to do so by a member;

(i) asking the Certification Officer for advice or assistance on any matter, or consulting another person about an allegation against the union or its officers that might fall within (b) above;

(j) refusing to comply with a requirement imposed by a trade union (e.g. during disciplinary proceedings), which infringes the above rights;

(k) proposing or preparing to engage in any conduct listed above.

However, this section does not apply to an act or omission comprised in the types of conduct listed above if it is shown that the act or omission is

---

[108] TULRCA, s 65.
[109] [1996] IRLR 617.
[110] [1991] IRLR 159.
[111] Defined by TULRCA, s 119.

one in respect of which individuals would be disciplined by the union anyway. Similarly, people are deemed not to be unjustifiably disciplined if it is shown that the reason (or one of the reasons) for the discipline was that they made a false assertion within (b) above and that it was made 'in the belief that it was false or otherwise in bad faith'.

Those wishing to complain about unjustifiable discipline can apply to an employment tribunal, and claims must normally be made within three months of the relevant union decision.[112] Section 288 of TULRCA ensures that individuals cannot be prevented from claiming by their union rule-book and any settlement will be binding only if ACAS has been involved or the conditions relating to compromise agreements are satisfied. If a tribunal upholds a complaint, it must make a declaration to that effect. Compensation is available where a separate application is lodged not earlier than four weeks and not later than six months from the date of the tribunal's declaration.[113] If the union has revoked its disciplinary action or taken all the steps necessary for securing its reversal, compensation will be asssessed by an employment tribunal; otherwise, individuals must apply to the EAT. In *NALGO v Courtney-Dunn*,[114] the EAT ruled that the word 'necessary' meant that the union was required to put the member back into the same position he was in before the unlawful expulsion. It was irrelevant that the member could have done this himself by request-ing the employer to deduct union dues from his salary.

Both the employment tribunal and the EAT are empowered to award such compensation as is just and equitable in the circumstances but the sum awarded can be reduced on the grounds of contributory fault or a failure to mitigate loss. As with exclusion or expulsion on impermissible grounds, the current maximum that can be awarded is £63,100 and com-pensation fixed by the EAT must be at least £5,900. However, the remedies for unjustifiable discipline are not available where the complainant has successfully brought an action for expulsion under s 174 of TULRCA.[115]

A member who claims that there has been a breach or threatened breach of the union rules in relation to discipline (including expulsion) can apply to the Certification Officer for a declaration.[116] However, the Certification Officer is entitled to refuse to accept an application if a complainant has not taken all reasonable steps to use the union's internal complaints procedure.[117] By way of contrast, it is worth noting that employ-ment tribunals cannot require claimants to invoke the union's internal complaints machinery. Nevertheless, individuals who unreasonably fail to do so might find that any compensation is reduced.

---

[112] Ibid, s 66.
[113] Ibid, s 67.
[114] [1992] IRLR 114.
[115] TULRCA, s 66(4). See above.
[116] Ibid, s 108A.
[117] Ibid, s 108B.

Conclusion

In the light of the above material, the reader might be tempted to conclude that the law provides greater protection against discrimination by trade unions than by employers. In relation to the latter, it is of concern that discrimination against union activists is not specifically dealt with at the point of hiring and it remains to be seen whether regulations prohibiting the use of union blacklists are ever introduced.

More positively, it would seem that the distinction drawn by the House of Lords between membership of a union and making use of its services can no longer be sustained as a result of the European Court of Human Rights' decision in *Wilson v United Kingdom*.[116] As a result of this case, the protection afforded to both unions and their members should be considerably enhanced. In relation to remedies, given that freedom of association is now regarded as a fundamental democratic right, reinstatement would seem to be the obvious form of redress for an unfair dismissal on union grounds.

Unfortunately, despite being the primary remedy identified by the legislation, tribunals rarely order reinstatement (or re-engagement) and employees can always be sacked if employers are prepared to pay compensation. Finally, we have noted that, in addition to the general anti-discrimination legislation, unions are severely restricted by the statutory provisions dealing with exclusions, discipline and expulsions. While detailed regulation can be justified where union membership is compulsory, arguably it is unnecessary to impose such a rigid regime today when membership is entirely voluntary.

Further reading

Annual Report of the Certification Officer available at www.certoffice.org
Barrow, C *Industrial Relations Law* (Butterworths, 2002)
Morris, G and Archer, T *Collective Labour Law* (Hart Publishing, 2000)
Smith, I and Thomas, G *Industrial Law* (Butterworths, 2003)
Wedderburn, Lord *The Worker and the Law* (Penguin, 1986)

---

[116] [2002] IRLR 568.

Useful web addresses

Age Positive	www.agepositive.gov.uk
BBC	www.bbc.co.uk
Confederation of British Industry	www.cbi.org.uk
Commission for Racial Equality	www.cre.gov.uk
Department of Trade and Industry	www.dti.gov.uk
Department for Work and Pensions	www.dwp.gov.uk
Disability	www.disability.gov.uk
Disability Rights Commission	www.drc-gb.org
Employers Forum on Age	www.efa.org.uk
Employers Forum on Disability	www.employers-forum.co.uk
Equal Opportunities Commission	www.eoc.org.uk
Equality Direct	www.equalitydirect.org.uk
European Court of Human Rights	www.echr.coe.int
European Court of Justice	www.curia.eu.int
European Industrial Relations Observatory	www.eiro.eurofound.ie
European Union	www.europa.eu.int
Government Legislation	www.legislation.hmso.gov.uk
Home Office	www.homeoffice.gov.uk
International Labour Organisation	www.ilo.org
Multifaithnet	www.multifaithnet.org
National Family and Parenting Institute	www.nfpi.org.uk
Parents at Work	www.workingfamilies.org.uk
Race for Racial Justice	www.racialjustice.org.uk
Stonewall	www.stonewall.org.uk
Third Age Employment Network	www.taen.org.uk
Trades Union Congress	www.tuc.org.uk
United Nations	www.un.org
United Nations Population Fund	www.unfpa.org
Women and Equality Unit	www.womenandequalityunit.gov.uk

Index